The Creation of an Ethnic Identity

The Creation of an Ethnic Identity

Being Swedish American in the Augustana Synod, 1860–1917

Dag Blanck

Southern Illinois University Press
Carbondale

Copyright © 2006 by the Board of Trustees,
Southern Illinois University
All rights reserved
Printed in the United States of America
09 08 07 06   4 3 2 1

Library of Congress Cataloging-in-Publication Data
Blanck, Dag.
　The creation of an ethnic identity : being Swedish
American in the Augustana Synod, 1860–1917 / Dag Blanck.
　　p. cm.
　Includes bibliographical references and index.
　1. Swedish Americans—Ethnic identity. 2. Swedish
Americans—Cultural assimilation. 3. Immigrants—Social
networks—United States. 4. Evangelical Lutheran
Augustana Synod of North America—History—19th
century. 5. Evangelical Lutheran Augustana Synod of North
America—History—20th century. 6. Augustana College
(Rock Island, Ill.)—History. I. Title.

E184.S23B544 2006
305.83'9707309034—dc22
ISBN 978-0-8093-2715-7 (alk. paper)
ISBN 0-8093-2715-5 (alk. paper)   2006008126

Printed on recycled paper. ♻

The paper used in this publication meets the minimum requirements of American National Standard for Information Sciences—Permanence of Paper for Printed Library Materials, ANSI Z39.48-1992. ∞

Contents

List of Illustrations vii
Acknowledgments ix

1. Setting the Stage: Ethnicity and Identity in Swedish America 1
2. Coming to America: The Establishment of the Augustana Synod 21
3. Schooling the Swedish Americans: Education in the Augustana Synod 45
4. A Swedish-American Tradition at Augustana College 70
5. Reading, Writing, and Identity Formation in Swedish America 106
6. The Augustana Book Concern as a Source for Swedish-American Identity 132
7. Putting the Past to Use: The Creation of a Swedish-American History 162
8. Epilogue: Being Swedish American in the Augustana Synod 188

Notes 205
Bibliography 229
Index 249

Illustrations

Plates following page 44
The Lutheran Augustana Book Concern in Rock Island, Illinois, ca. 1900
Gustav Andreen (1864–1940), ca. 1910.
Johan Alfred Enander (1842–1910)
Participants in the 1910 fiftieth anniversary celebrations in Rock island
The graduating college class at Augusta College, 1910
Jonas Olof Grafström, *Augustana College and the Mississippi River,* 1899
Student performance of *Fritiofs Saga* at Augustana College, 1905
Swedish Ladies Chorus, Augustana College, 1898

Tables
1. Augustana Synod Membership as Percentage of the Population of Swedish Extraction 32
2. Generations at Augustana College, 1871–1914 (percentages) 94
3. Social Background of Matriculating Augustana Students, 1871–1914 (percentages) 96
4. Social Background of Matriculating Augustana Students, 1871–99 and 1900–14 (percentages) 98

Acknowledgments

This study has been carried out on both sides of the Atlantic, and over the years I have incurred a number of debts to both individuals and institutions. In Sweden, I would like to recognize the unfailing support of Professors Hans Norman and Harald Runblom, both of Uppsala University, without which this study would never have been completed. I also thank my colleagues at the Centre for Multiethnic Research at Uppsala and with the Swedish-American literature project at the Department of Literature in Uppsala. I especially thank Professor Anna Williams from that group. Professor Torkel Jansson of Uppsala has also read and made important comments to my manuscript.

During my frequent stays in the United States, I have benefited greatly from my association with Augustana College in Rock Island, Illinois. It was during my student years at Augustana that I discovered Swedish America, and it has been as a staff member at the college that I have gotten to know America. In particular, Larry Scott, professor of Scandinavian, Thomas Tredway, president emeritus of the college, and Michael Nolan, associate dean, have been constant sources of discussions, support, and friendship. Michael Nolan and Larry Scott have also read and commented on the entire manuscript. At Augustana, I would also like to recognize my colleagues at the Swenson Swedish Immigration Research Center. Elsewhere in the United States, Professor H. Arnold Barton of Southern Illinois University generously shared his deep understanding of Swedish-American history with me for many years, Professor Rudolph Vecoli of the Immigration History Research Center at the University of Minnesota kindly received me on two prolonged occasions as a guest researcher, and Professor Philip Anderson of North Park University in Chicago helped guide my thinking about Swedish-American religion, among other things.

In addition, I would like to recognize the following persons who have provided support: Erik Åsard, Monica Blom, Tordis and Urban Dahllöf, Lars Furuland, John Rogers, and Henrik Williams, Uppsala; Daniel Culver,

Janina Erlich, Christina Johansson, Charles Mahaffey, and Harold Sundelius, Rock Island; Ingrid Edsman, Eva Tedenmyr, and Mattias Tydén, Stockholm; Bruce Karstadt, Mary and David Swanson, and Mariann Tiblin, Minneapolis; Jennifer Eastman Attebery, Pocatello; Ulf Jonas Björk, Indianapolis; Gunlög Fur, Växjö; Nils Hasselmo, Washington, D.C.; Eric Johannesson, Luleå; Byron Nordstrom, St. Peter; Nils William Olsson, Winter Park, Florida; Eva Österberg, Lund; Orm Øverland, Bergen; and Kate Tredway, Galena.

The following institutions have supported my work financially, which is gratefully acknowledged: American-Scandinavian Foundation, New York; Kungl. Gustav Adolfsakademien, Uppsala; and Knut och Alice Wallenbergs Stiftelse, Kungl. Vetenskapsakademien, and Lars Johan Hiertas Minnesfond, Stockholm. I also extend my recognition to the following archives and libraries in Sweden and the United States where I have received professional and courteous help: The Swedish Emigrant Institute, Växjö; the Royal Library, Stockholm; the Uppsala University Library; the Augsburg-Fortress Publishing House and the University of Minnesota Library, Minneapolis; the Augustana College Library and its Special Collections and the Swenson Swedish Immigration Research Center, Rock Island; the Minnesota Historical Society, St. Paul; and the Evangelical Lutheran Church in America, Chicago.

The present book is a revised version of my doctoral dissertation at Uppsala University, which appeared as *Becoming Swedish-American: The Construction of an Ethnic Identity, 1860–1917* (Uppsala: Acta Universitatis Upsaliensis, 1997). I thank Acta Universitatis Upsaliensis for the permission to reprint parts of the dissertation in this book.

A special recognition goes to my wife, Agneta Emanuelsson Blanck, whose help, comments, and insights have been of the greatest importance to me.

It should lastly be noted that throughout the text, "America" will be used interchangeably with "the United States."

The Creation of an Ethnic Identity

1

Setting the Stage: Ethnicity and Identity in Swedish America

Sometime around 1910, Swedish-American writer and editor E. W. Olson published a play called *Charley Washington. Studentkomedi* (Charley Washington. A Student Comedy). The play is set at Augustana College in Rock Island, Illinois, in the early part of the century and deals with the student Karl Törngren (also known as Charley Turngreen), who arrives on campus from his parent's farm in Wausa, Nebraska, to study at Augustana and, as he puts it, "become educated."[1] Augustana College was a leading institution of higher education in the Swedish-American Lutheran Augustana Synod and played a significant role within the Swedish-American ethnic and cultural community around the turn of the twentieth century. Charley appears on campus dressed in country style in a heavy wool coat and long scarf and speaking in heavy Swedish dialect, at times mixed up with some English.

He does not quite seem to know what he wants to study, just that he wants a good education at Augustana. He also decides that now that he is entering a new phase of his life, he needs a new name, "a student name."[2] The registrar, Professor Ultimus (who is obviously based on Augustana's professor of Swedish at the time, Jules Göthe Ultimus Mauritzson), suggests several names, ranging from the Swedish Oxenstjerna to the English Shakespeare, but Charley finally settles on Washington as a good name. (He objects to Shakespeare as he thinks that name sounds too much like a pitchfork.) Washington, Charley notes, not only indicates his allegiance to America but also identifies elements of both his hometown, Wausa, and the Swedish king (Gustav) Vasa.

Seven years later, in the third act of the play, we meet Charley again. By this time, he has completed his studies at Augustana, speaks eloquently in correct standard Swedish, and has rid himself of his uncouth country manners. As he calls on the house of young Miss Fifi Eklut, the daughter of a rather strict widow of an Augustana professor and also the young woman whom he proposes to marry, he quotes Bellman to Mrs. Eklut and bursts out in "Studentsången"—a traditional song among university students in Sweden. Charley has come a long way from his Nebraska farm and has indeed become an educated man.

Professor Ultimus also calls on the Ekluts to give Charley the good news that the college's faculty has just decided to offer him a position at the school to teach science and Swedish, something that finally convinces Mrs. Eklut that he is worthy of her daughter. She consents to the marriage, and as the curtain falls in the final scene of the play, the happy young couple is engaged to be married.

It is probably fair to say that *Charley Washington* never became a theatrical success, and it is uncertain whether it was ever staged. The play is instead more interesting because of its view of education: a young Swedish-American farmer's son leaves his home in rural Nebraska to travel several hundred miles east to Rock Island in order to receive a solid education at the leading Swedish-American institution of higher learning. The play illustrates two dimensions of the educational process at a school like Augustana College, namely how an uneducated young Swedish American confronts issues of identity and identity formation around the turn of the century and what role this Swedish-American educational institution played in this process.

"Charley Washington" and others like him were a part of the mass migration from Sweden to the United States, which sent some 1.3 million Swedes to North America between 1850 and 1930, primarily to the United States. This movement of Swedes across the Atlantic was a part of a general mass migration from Europe to the United States that came to include some 33 million persons between 1820 and 1930. In absolute numbers, the Swedes were one of the smaller groups among the European immigrants to America, dwarfed by other groups such as the Germans, the Italians, the Irish, and the British. If the number of emigrants is put in relationship to the size of the population of the sending country, however, the Swedes, together with the British, are in third place. Only Ireland and Norway sent more emigrants relative to the countries' population to North America.

Setting the Stage

The initial Swedish settlements were in the Midwest, and many became farmers. By the turn of the century, however, the majority of the Swedish immigrants lived and worked in the rapidly growing American urban areas, including substantial numbers on the East and West Coasts. By 1910, a Swedish-American middle class was also taking shape, consisting of teachers, lawyers, physicians, and other professional groups as well as merchants and shopkeepers. By this time, too, a significant group of American-born, second-generation Swedish Americans had come onto the scene.

Soon after the arrival of large numbers of Swedish immigrants, a Swedish-American community developed, helping the immigrants and their children to meet their various needs in the new country, to adjust to American society, and yet also to keep a sense of distinctiveness in the new multiethnic environment. By the turn of the century, the term "Swedish America" had been coined to describe this Swedish presence in the United States,[3] which consisted of many different groups, reflecting the social diversity of the community and addressing the community's varying needs.

Like other immigrants in the United States, Swedish Americans were confronted with the question of what it meant to be American and with the significance of ethnicity in their lives. One central issue facing the newcomers dealt with the question of their identity in the new land. Who were they? Were they Swedes or Americans? Or were they perhaps a combination of both? Was it possible to be Swedish in America, and if so, what did this mean? This book seeks to answer these questions and others of a similar nature. In particular, the construction of a Swedish-American ethnic identity will be discussed: the way in which this identity was established, what it consisted of, and why it came into being.

The answers to these questions will be provided by examining the Augustana Synod, a Lutheran denomination founded by a group of ministers from the Church of Sweden in 1860 that became the largest organization founded by Swedish immigrants in the United States. The Augustana Synod developed into an institution serving religious and other needs of Swedish immigrants and their children, and by the turn of the century it encompassed well over a thousand congregations across the entire North American continent, colleges, a seminary, academies, newspapers, magazines, a publishing house, bookstores, children's homes, hospitals, and old people's homes.

Although religion obviously was a fundamental aspect of the synod's life, concerns for a sense of Swedishness in America were also visible, and in 1901 one pastor declared that if the Augustana Synod had not existed, "Swedish culture and education [in America] would have been virtually dead,"[4] suggesting that the synod played an important role in maintaining a Swedish distinctiveness in America. Because Swedish America was such a diverse community, consisting of a great number of different—and at times competing—factions, it is possible to speak of a cultural struggle within the Swedish-American community, where Augustana's answer to the question of what it meant to be Swedish in America was one of many, albeit the dominant one.

Swedish immigrants in the United States were not alone in struggling with these kinds of questions. Nationalism and nation-building were important processes both throughout Europe and in the United States in the nineteenth century, and the construction of national and ethnic identities was thus of significance in both the country the emigrants left and the one in which they settled. The emergence of a Swedish-American identity should thus also be seen in this larger context, and by focusing on a fairly small and well-defined Swedish-American community, it will also be possible to contribute to the general discussion of the nature of both national and ethnic identities.

STARTING POINTS

As H. Arnold Barton has observed, the Swedes in North America have "one of the richest historical literatures that exists for any migrant group."[5] The first historical accounts of Swedish America were written by and for members of the Swedish-American community itself and were often highly celebratory with little critical perspective.[6] Many are the accounts of various Swedish settlements throughout the United States; histories of congregations, denominations, organizations, and clubs; and accounts of contributions by Swedish immigrants to American life, such as Eric Norelius's two-volume *De svenska lutherska församlingarnas och svenskarnes historia i Amerika* from 1891 and 1916, the two-volume work *History of the Swedes of Illinois* by Ernst Olson, Anders Schön, and Martin J. Engberg from 1908, and C. F. Peterson's 1898 book *Sverige i Amerika. Kulturhistoriska och biografiska teckningar*.[7] Today they are chiefly valuable as primary sources, and the term "filiopietistic" is often used to describe these works.[8]

The academic study of the Swedish migration to America began in earnest during the first decades of the twentieth century, and up until approximately 1960 a small group of scholars on both sides of the Atlantic were active in this field from disciplines such as history, geography, religion, and ethnology.[9] Noticeable contributions were made by George Stephenson, whose magisterial examination of the growth of the Swedish religious communities in the United States, *The Religious Aspects of Swedish Immigration* from 1932,[10] remains a landmark study in the field. Other contributions from this phase came from historians such as O. Fritiof Ander, Emory Lindquist, and Conrad Bergendoff and deal with the history of different Swedish-American individuals, institutions, and settlements.[11] The establishment of the Swedish Pioneer Historical Society in 1950 and its journal *Swedish Pioneer Historical Quarterly* (today *Swedish American Historical Quarterly*) were also important developments in the field in the United States.

The Swedish academic community was only marginally interested in the emigration and Swedish America during this early phase. Still, as official Sweden began to perceive the sustained emigration as a major societal problem by the beginning of the twentieth century, a Royal Commission of Inquiries (Emigrationsutredningen) under the leadership of statistician Gustav Sundbärg was established in 1907. Emigrationsutredningen was primarily concerned with the reasons behind the emigration, and the major part of its massive twenty-one-volume report included an exhaustive analysis of the economic conditions in Swedish society, especially those in the rural sector that, in the commission's opinion, had resulted in the mass emigration. A minor part of the report was also devoted to the conditions of the emigrants in America. Additional work was also done by church historian Gunnar Westin and geographer Helge Nelson, dealing with Swedish-American religious conditions and settlement patterns.[12]

With the heightened interest in social history after 1960, the volume of scholarship increased significantly. For the first time, Swedish historians entered the field in earnest, following Frank Thistlethwaite's 1960 challenge to European historians not to leave the history of the European transatlantic migration solely to American historians,[13] and there was a new, systematic interest in the homeland for the history of emigration. Much of the work was centered around the so-called Uppsala project that yielded a great number of studies, but work was also done elsewhere in Sweden, in the other Nordic countries, and in the United States. In accord with the general tendency of social history, much of the focus of this work was quantitative in nature. Questions that were studied included the demographic, economic, and social aspects of the migration process both in Sweden and the United States and the internal structure and development of the Swedish immigrant community. Issues such as who and how many emigrated, where they came from and why, where they settled, and social and economic circumstances in the New World stood out as particularly important. Some attention was also given to the patterns of return migration. The Uppsala project was summarized in Harald Runblom and Hans Norman's *From Sweden to America: A History of the Migration* (1976).[14]

A SWEDISH-AMERICAN IDENTITY

From the mid-1970s, emphasis has shifted toward more qualitative aspects of the history of the Swedish immigrant and ethnic group in the United States. The previous interest in quantification, social structure, and social mobility has now been replaced with a concern for such issues as cultural and linguistic persistence, organizational and religious life, literary and artistic activities, politically radical Swedes, and the role of women. Efforts have also been made to integrate the history of the Swedish ethnic group in the United States with that of general American ethnic history. Some comparative work has also been attempted, especially concerning the Swedish immigrant urban experience. In addition, the way in which Swedes and Swedish Americans viewed each other has been discussed. For the first time, for example, the creative and literary output among Swedish Americans has been systematically analyzed and placed in the context of literary and theatrical traditions, reading habits, and canon-building in different social spheres in Sweden and Swedish America during the late nineteenth century.[15]

In this context, the issue of a Swedish-American identity has also become important and has been addressed by several authors. It is one leading theme in several works by Barton,[16] and Ulf Beijbom has discussed different aspects of the content and development of what he calls the "Swedish Americanism" or "Swedish ethnicity."[17] Nils Hasselmo also raises the question of a Swedish-American identity in conjunction with his studies of the Swedish language in America,[18] and the Swedish-American identity has also been dealt with in the contexts of religion, political radicalism, education, and art in Swedish America.[19] Jennifer Eastman Attebery, Birgitta Svensson, and Anna Williams also explicitly deal with the formation and contents of a Swedish-American identity in their respective analyses of a Swedish-American culture.[20]

Many of these analyses of Swedish-American cultural life have shown how, while obviously being very much rooted in cultural traditions from Sweden, it was also shaped by the American context in which it existed.

Swedish-American cultural patterns thus exhibit a duality, and it is possible to speak of an identity drawing on cultural elements from both Sweden and the United States while at the same time maintaining a distance from both. They also show the immigrants and their descendants as active agents in shaping these cultural patterns and ethnic identities.

ETHNICITY, ETHNIC IDENTITY, AND ETHNIC GROUPS

All humans have multiple social identities. Each identity helps define who we are, varying both in different social contexts and in degree and significance. Ethnic identity is one of these. At one level, ethnic and other identities are deeply personal and a part of an individual's psyche. In the present study, however, the focus is on the collective level of the ethnic group. One general definition states that an ethnic group "is a segment of a larger society whose members are thought, by themselves or others, to have a common origin and to share important segments of a common culture, and who in addition, participate in shared activities in which the common culture and origin are significant ingredients."[21]

In the extensive discussion of ethnicity in America, some scholars have emphasized the primeval and enduring nature of ethnicity and ethnic identity, arguing that it is something so deeply rooted in human nature that it remains static and unchangeable. Others, however, have underscored its changing nature and content and have emphasized how ethnicity has been used in different ways, depending on the context, describing ethnic groups as "interest groups" mobilizing to achieve certain goals. One should not, however, exaggerate the dichotomy between the primordial and situational approaches. Some aspects of ethnic identity seem more difficult to shed than others and obviously are more important to an individual's conception of self.[22] For example, the maintenance of one's language seems to have been a more important component in the American ethnic identities than, say, the eating of certain foods. The primordial approach also seems to be more relevant for discussions of individual identities. But since the focus of this study is on collective representations, the situational perspective on ethnicity will form a basic starting point.

James McKay and Frank Lewins distinguish between ethnic categories and ethnic groups, a conceptualization that also points to how ethnicity can vary in significance. Ethnic categories are groups of people who share certain characteristics. Examples of such characteristics include religion, race, language, and national origin. According to these authors, these "ethnic characteristics" are but a few of—and no more meaningful than—many other cultural, social, and physical traits that group members exhibit. Instead, McKay and Lewins maintain that it is the degree of what they call ethnic identification that is significant for membership in the ethnic group. When a certain number of people "meaningfully interact" on the basis of shared ethnic characteristics, then a consciousness of kind and a sense of belonging develop, or, in the terminology of McKay and Lewins, an ethnic group develops.[23]

Anthony D. Smith also distinguishes between ethnic categories and communities. People who make up ethnic categories have only a "dim consciousness that they form a separate collectivity" because they lack "a myth of common origins, shared historical memories, a sense of solidarity or an association with a designated homeland." Ethnic communities, on the other hand, are characterized exactly by the presence of these attributes, even though these convictions may be held only by a segment of the population and even if some of the attributes "are more intense and salient than others at a given period."[24]

The strength of the ethnic community is related to the degree to which the population shares these attributes. The degree of ethnic identification that individuals exhibit can thus vary, from weak identifications to more fully developed ethnic identities, and although the strength of ethnicity in part depends on the criteria used, it is clear that a range of degrees of identification exists, all the way from a full to a minimal ethnic identity.[25]

It is important to underscore that this study focuses on the institutional rather than the individual level and is concerned with a collective self-representation, concentrating on one segment of a population associated with a particular organization—the Augustana Synod—and assuming some sense of ethnic identification among its members. We are thus dealing with what one could call an "ethnic institution" and its role for the creation of a Swedish-American ethnic identity. The part played by ethnic institutions in the establishment of ethnic communities was recognized early in American immigration history research and was strongly emphasized in one of the very first studies of ethnic life in the United States, William Thomas and Florian Znaniecki's *Polish Peasant in Europe and America* (1918–20).[26] This emphasis has continued ever since.[27]

The role of ethnic institutions for ethnic identity has also been discussed by Raymond Breton, who has advanced the concept of "institutional completeness."[28] He argues that there is a relationship between the degree of ethnic identity expressed and the number of institutions, both formal and informal, that exist within the ethnic community to serve the different needs of its members. The more "institutionally complete" the community is, Breton states, the stronger the sense of ethnic identity can be expected to be, and Edward Kantowicz has suggested that the Polish Americans in Chicago are one example of an institutionally complete American ethnic community.[29] A parallel situation can be found among Germans in Milwaukee, while the Irish in the same city did not create a sufficient number of institutions to develop an ethnic community and instead tended to identify themselves along class lines.[30]

Thus it can be said that the more needs that the Augustana Synod could fulfill for its members, the stronger the identification of Swedish Americans would be with the identity that Augustana represented. Becoming a member in one of the various congregations, attending an Augustana Synod school, or reading an Augustana Synod publication might be indicators of a high degree of identification with Augustana's ethnicity. Still, as the ethnic element was only one dimension of the activities of the Augustana Synod, it is difficult to determine exactly the degree to which Swedish Americans have identified with the Augustana version of what it meant to be Swedish in America. There may of course have been other reasons than Augustana's Swedish profile for joining one of its churches or attending one of its schools. This observation means that, although this study argues that the Augustana Swedishness was dominant in the struggle for defining a Swedish-American ethnic identity, it is the construction, contents, and maintenance of this ethnic identity that will be in focus, not the exact degree to and manner in which it was spread throughout and received in Swedish America.

The close link between religion and ethnicity has long been recognized, and several students of American immigrant and ethnic groups have shown the central role that religion has played for the development and shape of ethnicity in the United States. Church historian Martin E. Marty has even called religion "the skeleton of ethnicity in America."[31]

As will be shown, the maintenance of a particular form of Lutheranism was the paramount reason for the establishment of the Augustana Synod. Still, as the denomination's religious roots were found in Sweden, and as the vast majority of the membership were either Swedish-born or descendants of Swedish immigrants, ethnicity also shaped the synod's life in important ways. The relationship between religion and ethnicity varied over time, and it will be one of the questions that will be addressed in this study.

THE INVENTION OF ETHNICITY AND THE DUAL IDENTITIES

The nature of ethnic identities has been the subject of extensive scholarly discussion in American immigration history. Oscar Handlin's *The Uprooted* is the classic statement of a position that argues that the immigrants severed their cultural and social ties with the Old Country and that the new, often urban, American environment shaped the immigrants' lives and behavior in the United States.[32] The rise of the "new social history" and the "ethnic revival" in the 1960s saw a break with this view, and many studies concluded that instead of being uprooted, the immigrant groups experienced a cultural continuity in the United States. The first formulation of this view was Rudolph Vecoli's article "*Contadini* in Chicago: A Critique of *The Uprooted*," which showed how south Italian peasants in Chicago resisted assimilation and Americanization and instead maintained their traditional behavior and value systems.[33]

A further development of this discussion has suggested that the ethnic identities and cultures in America depended on a combination of both Old and New World contexts and that new cultural forms were created in the immigrant and ethnic communities in the United States specific to the groups' needs there. David A. Gerber has argued that the "immigrants' understanding of possessing a group identity comes as a result of existential fusing of its Old World cultural inheritance (language, religion, values, beliefs and expressive symbols) and New World experiences."[34] The ethnic identities had dual roots in and loyalties to both the old and the new countries and were, in Jon Gjerde's words, "complementary," where it was possible to express a simultaneous allegiance to the United States and to the ethnic institutions and traditions that were being forged in the new country.[35] Orm Øverland has argued in a similar vein in his analysis of how immigrants created "homemaking myths" through which they used "stories" of their ethnic pasts as a way to stake their claims for a place in American society, stories that thus "have contributed to an American rather than to an ethnic nationalism."[36] Ethnicity and ethnic identities are thus seen as invented or culturally constructed[37] and, as several immigration historians have concluded, developing in a continuous relationship with American society in "a process of construction or invention which incorporates, adapts, and amplifies preexisting communal solidarities, cultural attributes, and historical memories. That is, it is grounded in real life context and social experience."[38]

THE CREATION OF NATIONAL IDENTITIES

As noted earlier in this chapter, processes of nation-building were important in nineteenth-century Europe. Proceeding at different speeds and in greatly varying social, political, and cultural contexts, nations and national identities were being formed. There are parallels between ethnic and national identities, and a considerable "overlap" in their meaning and usage exists. National identities, like their ethnic counterparts, are also constructed, and already in 1983 Eric Hobsbawm advanced his now well-known term "invention of tradition," pointing to the novelty and creation of a number of traditions and customs of seemingly much older date. Hobsbawm also suggests that these inventions occur when rapid societal change "weakens or destroys the social patterns for which 'old' traditions had been designed."[39] Hobsbawm's concept of "invented traditions" shows great similarities to the ethnic identities of American immigrant groups, emerging when the old social patterns no longer were available and functioning as a unifying ideology for the group.

Nineteenth-century Sweden also experienced nation-building. As Torkel Jansson has suggested, the nature of the Swedish "nation" was discussed during the first half of the nineteenth century, often couched in the language of political liberalism and affecting only a small group of the population. Toward the end of the century, Swedish nationalism was expressed in conservative and patriotic terms, largely due to the increased strength of Swedish conservatives as a result of the breakup of the union with Norway.[40] The establishment of a compulsory elementary school was of great importance in this process, and, as Lars Furuland has shown, the reader *Läsebok för folkskolan*, which was widely used in Swedish elementary schools, was very significant in instilling a sense of national feeling among large strata of the Swedish population as a "patriotic canon of persons and events" was created.[41]

The 1890s are often seen as a high period for a conservative kind of nationalism, during which time a national romanticism was advanced, in which selected parts of the Swedish culture and past played an important role. Attention was, for example, given to Swedish folk and local culture, of which the establishment of the two ethnographic and folk life museums Nordiska Museet and Skansen in Stockholm are two examples.[42]

The question of to what degree the Swedish emigrants were affected by these attempts to create a Swedish national feeling is, of course, difficult to answer. The growth of Swedish national feeling in the nineteenth century was a complex phenomenon, affecting, for example, social strata of the Swedish population differently. Because the course of the emigration ran during a significant part of the nineteenth and early twentieth centuries, there is clearly a temporal dimension to be considered, suggesting that those emigrants who left after the turn of the century must have been much more exposed to Swedish national feeling than those who had left during the decades after the mid-nineteenth century.

Thus, it can be assumed that the sense of Swedish nationality was somewhat weakly developed among those Swedes who arrived in America, especially during the first several decades of emigration. The identity that these immigrants brought with them instead seems to have been much more regional or local in nature, and it was in the United States that a sense of national identity emerged, something that also was a general phenomenon among European immigrant groups in nineteenth- and early-twentieth-century America.[43] Two leading Swedish-American journalists and observers of Swedish America also made this point. In 1898, C. F. Peterson claimed in Sweden the immigrants had been more or less provincial, "an *östgöte, västgöte, smålänning* or *skåning* first, then a Swede," whereas in America, he continued, one becomes "first of all a Swede."[44] Twelve years later, Johan Person wrote that when most of his fellow Swedish Americans had left their homeland, it was hardly possible to speak of a "Sweden," except as a political and geographic entity,[45] as the country was divided in as many "nations" as its twenty-four provinces in the country. In America, however, these provincial loyalties had been overcome. "[D]uring the eight days of the Atlantic crossing," Person wrote, "the foundations were laid for the making of a Swedish-American people, which thus separates them from the Swedes in Sweden, who consist of at least twenty-four [nations]."[46]

The growth of a national identity in the United States proceeded from a different set of assumptions than in Sweden or Europe. It has been argued that the United States was the "first new nation,"[47] meaning that it was the first major European colony to successfully break away from colonial rule and establish itself as a "new nation." In the case of the United States, this new nation was founded on a set of abstract political and philosophical ideas, codified in such central documents as the Declaration of Independence and the Constitution. The United States was thus what Wilbur Zelinksy has called an "ideological construct," making it different from other "old" nations in that it lacked "strong historical or territorial traditions" or common "cultural bonds" such as a common religion or language.[48] Except for the vague sense of "the New World," America was not, as Sacvan Berovitch has put it, "a territorial definition" but "the symbol of ideological consensus."[49] Moreover, as Nathan Glazer has argued, there is an "avoidance" of "specific ethnic references" in the "founding documents" and in the debates on the American Revolution, as the framers of the Constitution "did not define their Americanness as an ethnic characteristic" but rather emphasized its universality.[50] To be sure, a sense of national identity also increased in the United States after 1776, replete with national symbols, heroes, and celebrations. This was a process that became especially marked during the half century or so following the Civil War, when, as John Higham has put it, there was an "intensification of nationalism," and many nationalist and patriotic practices and institutions came into being. Most of these ingredients were rooted in the political dimension of American nationality, which at times has also been referred to as American civic culture or civil religion.[51]

For immigrants coming to the United States, this "ideological quality" of American nationalism became very important. Becoming American did not require a particular national, linguistic, religious, or ethnic background but was a matter of committing to the abstract political ideals of liberty, equality, and republicanism. The universalist and ideological character of American nationalism meant, in Philip Gleason's words, "that it was open to anyone who willed to become an American."[52]

Still, the American nationality was not open to all groups, as some Americans, such as the African Americans, had been brought to the country as slaves or, in the case of the Native Americans, had been subdued by European settlers. Lawrence Fuchs makes this point in his discussion of the role of American nationality for the formation of ethnic identities in the United States in advancing the concept of "voluntary pluralism." According to Fuchs, as long as European immigrants, who had voluntarily migrated to the United States, embraced the political dimension of American nationalism, they could maintain and promote their own cultures and religion. They were, in Fuchs's words, "free . . . to choose to be ethnic" if they so wished, a choice that was "sanctioned and protected" by American "civic culture."[53] As Hasselmo and Gjerde also have argued, it was thus possible for European immigrant groups to maintain their own cultural traits; in fact, the persistence of ethnic identities was a central ingredient of American nationalism itself.⁵⁴ In this way, European immigrant groups were able to combine a pride in their separate antecedents while at the same time claiming a stake in the political American civil culture.

THE ROLE OF GENERATIONAL CHANGE AND THE SIGNIFICANCE OF HISTORY

The role of different generations has attracted much attention in the discussion of the changing nature of ethnic identity among American ethnic groups. One early and influential formulation is Marcus Lee Hansen's "third-generation hypothesis," which states that "what the sons wish to forget, the grandsons wish to remember." Hansen's thesis maintains that the American-born children of the immigrant generation showed little interest in maintaining an ethnic identity and that a concern for ethnic maintenance could instead be found in the third generation, the immigrants' grandchildren.⁵⁵ This thesis has been challenged and discussed throughout the years and, if taken literally, can be proven incorrect.⁵⁶

What is finally significant in Hansen's argument, however, is the notion of the dynamic nature of ethnicity, its capacity to wax and wane and assume different characteristics and serve different purposes at different points in time and in different historical contexts. This important point is also made by sociologists Joshua Fishman and Vladimir Nahirny, who point to the difference in the nature of ethnic identification among different generations of American ethnic groups. They suggest that to those members of the ethnic group who have no experience of the ancestral culture, the ethnic heritage becomes "a usable past" out of which a "transmuted" ethnic ideology emerges, based not on the immediate memories from the old country but embracing "the intangible values" of the ancestral past.⁵⁷ The historical authenticity of idealized versions of the ethnic pasts is not important; it is instead the way these elements of the past are used to construct the ethnic identity, or ethnic ideology as they also call it, that deserves attention. Fishman and Nahirny also underscore that the issue of in which generation this change occurs is not of central importance, pointing instead to the "elective affinity" that results in the "transmuted past."⁵⁸

The significance that Fishman and Nahirny and others attach to the role of history for the content of these ethnic identities is worth noting. Anthony Smith has maintained that one of the defining characteristics of an ethnic group is "the role of myths of descent and historical memories" and that "historical memories [are] essential to their continuance," and other scholars have also emphasized the role played by a sense of a common history and culture in the creation of national identities both in Europe and in the United States.[59]

Seen from this perspective, a sense of history is an active ingredient in the formation of an ethnic identity and is one that is used for specific purposes. In the introduction to a volume on history and ethnicity, a group of British social anthropologists also point to the way history is put to use by ethnic groups for their present needs by posing the question "How did the present create the past?" rather than the more traditional way of phrasing the problem, namely, "How did the past create the present?"[60] The parallel to Hobsbawm's discussion of "invented traditions" is worth noting, as he maintains that a prominent characteristic of "invented traditions" is that "as far as possible," history is used as a "legitimator of action and cement of group cohesion."[61]

The notion of ethnicity as invented or created acknowledges both the Old World heritage as well as the conditions under which the immigrants lived in the New World by analyzing how an ethnic identity based on the Old World culture was created in the New World. In the present study, I am thus talking of the construction of a specifically Swedish-American identity, a process in which American society set the boundaries and in which selected aspects of a Swedish cultural repertoire were used.

THE CULTURAL CONTENT OF ETHNICITY AND THE ROLE OF ETHNIC LEADERS

In 1969, anthropologist Fredrik Barth advanced the argument that ethnicity is a boundary construction process, delineating cultural lines between groups. This means that, in Barth's words, it is "the ethnic *boundary* that defines the group, not the cultural stuff that it encloses" (emphasis in original).[62] With regard to American conditions, Werner Sollors has commented that Barth's theory can "easily accommodate the observation that ethnic groups in the United States have relatively little cultural differentiation, that the cultural *content* of ethnicity (the stuff that Barth's boundaries enclose) is largely interchangeable and rarely historically authenticated" (emphasis in original).[63] Other scholars have also joined in this "relativization" of the significance of the "cultural stuff" for ethnic groups in the United States. Nathan Glazer and Daniel Patrick Moynihan point out that "the cultural content of each ethnic group, in the United States, seems to have become very similar to that of others, but that the emotional significance of attachments to the ethnic group seems to persist."[64]

Immigration historians have, however, been more interested in focusing scholarly attention on the "cultural stuff" and less on the boundaries. For example, Kathleen Neils Conzen has defended studying the "cultural stuff" of ethnic groups, maintaining that in past scholarship it has been the fact of "ethnic preservation" rather than the "actual contours of a particular culture" that has been studied and that the scholarly concern has been the "demarcation of ethnic boundaries, not defining the core."[65]

Conzen instead advocates a focus on ethnic cultures but with a different emphasis. In this context, "culture" is not viewed as baggage "to be unpacked or packed, uprooted or transplanted," but rather in "the Geertzian sense as the socially produced structures of meaning engendered by and expressed in public behaviors, language, images, institutions." If immigrant and ethnic cultures are seen as "the publicly constructed meanings in and through which that life is lived," she concludes, then the study of these cultures mean that we can "begin to explore directly how those meanings are constructed and constantly reconstructed over time."[66] This latter position, arguing that it is both possible and of scholarly interest to study the "cultural stuff" of immigrant cultures, forms an important starting point for analyzing the development of the Swedish-American ethnic identity among the Augustana Swedish Americans.

One consequence of viewing ethnicity from this perspective is that the ethnic leadership comes into focus. Ethnic leaders played an important role in the creation and invention of a "new" ethnicity that was specific and useful to the groups' experiences in the new land. In Higham's words, the American social structure was characterized by "pervasive mobility and . . . shifting, multiple allegiances," leaving the ethnic leaders with the task of "focus[ing] the consciousness of an ethnic group and in doing so mak[ing] its identity visible."[67] The ethnic leaders became what Victor Greene has called "agents of their groups' adjustment in America," assigning them the dual roles of preserving tradition through their efforts to maintain the old country heritage and promoting their people's participation in American life.[68] It also means that there were struggles for cultural hegemony within ethnic groups as different factions of the groups tried to establish control over the contents of ethnicity and that, in Breton's words, the "symbolic order"

Setting the Stage

created within an ethnic community is best seen as an "outcome of struggles and accommodations among contradictory cultural-symbolic interests."[69]

For the present study, the role of the ethnic leadership means that attention will be focused on the sometimes self-styled group of Swedish-American intellectuals, authors, journalists, educators, and ministers. They constituted the elite within Swedish America that helped formulate the competing versions of Swedishness that emerged around the turn of the century. This was a small group of persons, and few of them could make a living from their cultural work alone. In her study of Swedish-American journalist and author Jakob Bonggren, Williams uses the term "literary leader" to describe his role in the Swedish-American community, and Greene has also called attention to the significance of T. N. Hasselquist and Johan Enander, leading persons within the Augustana Synod.[70] Attempts to identify the Swedish-American canon of writers by the writers themselves is another interesting example of the fact that a self-awareness of belonging to a particular stratum existed among Swedish-American intellectuals.[71] Their work was often unrewarding, and they were frequently met with little understanding among their fellow Swedish Americans.

For example, two of the most ambitious cultural undertakings by the Augustana Synod—the literary calendar *Prärieblomman* (The Prairie Flower) and the journal *Ungdomsvännen* (The Friend of Youth)—included many of these cultural leaders as contributors and editors. Both publications eventually had to be discontinued due to lack of interest among the audience, and their influence on rank-and-file Swedish Americans is thus hard to determine exactly. Still, Conzen's observation with regard to a similar group of German-American cultural activists—that the discussion that took place in "German-American books and journals of opinion" hardly was representative of the mass of German Americans, the "ethnic rank and file," but that the group was nevertheless influenced by these discussions—seems relevant for the Swedish Americans as well. Moreover, as Conzen concludes, those German Americans who rejected these formulations by the ethnic leadership "rejected the only formal ethnic identity Germans in America ever achieved," a statement that seems equally valid for the Swedish Americans.[72]

A CONTINUUM OF ETHNIC IDENTITIES

Ethnic identities in America have operated on different levels. Gerber points to two, at times overlapping, levels, where the first is the ways in which "the foundations of the inherited culture of daily life" are maintained and the second is the "formalistic group activities" through which different institutions seek to establish the group's identity. In a similar vein, Breton has called attention to ethnic identities both as "spontaneous creations from below" and as "consciously created from above."[73] In a discussion of the variety of Swedish-American cultural expressions, Hasselmo distinguishes between the "little" and "great" cultural traditions, the former dealing with the culture of daily life and the latter concerned with an elite culture, which Hasselmo also calls an "ideology."[74] Beijbom also makes a similar distinction in his discussion of "Swedish Americanism," in which he contrasts the attempts by a Swedish-American cultural leadership to create an elite culture with the everyday ethnicity of the rank-and-file Swedish Americans.[75]

Thus, it is possible to speak of a continuum of ethnic identities, stretching from what can be called an "everyday" level to a "higher," more elite level. The everyday ethnicity from below can be said to include aspects that shape the way people live their daily lives, such expressions as food habits, folk traditions, holiday celebrations, residence patterns, marriage preferences, the friends one keeps and associates with, and so on. These dimensions of ethnicity and ethnic identities are often rooted in the ethnic neighborhoods, with their informal networks providing immigrants with an opportunity to meet their own.

At the other end of the continuum is the actively constructed or invented ethnic identity, which to a large degree was formed by, in this case, a Swedish-American cultural leadership, including various opinion shapers, such as pastors, educators, writers, and cultural activists. This ethnicity was intended to be national, transcending the neighborhoods and regionalism of Swedish America. As opposed to the "everyday ethnicity," this Swedish Americanism or Swedish-American identity, as both contemporary leaders and later scholars have called it, emphasized "high culture," focusing on such things as literature, history, and the arts, and was promulgated in America through the Swedish-American schools, books, newspapers, and journals and through public manifestations such as jubilees and celebrations.

It is thus within the tension between these extremes on the continuum that various versions of what it meant to be Swedish in America were created and recreated. This study will deal with one end of the continuum of ethnic identities: exploring how a "high culture" Swedish-American identity was shaped within the Augustana Synod and focusing on the qualitative expressions of this ethnic institution.

The nineteenth century was a period of nation-building and nationalism in both Europe and the United States. The construction of an ethnic identity in the Augustana Synod can be seen in the light of this general process, and the ethnic experiences of the Augustana Synod will provide an example of how one well-defined part of an ethnic community of European origin in the United States dealt with the issue of its identity.

The study covers the period from 1860 to 1917, with a special emphasis on the decades around the turn of the century. The Augustana Synod was established in 1860, and the entry of the United States in World War I in 1917 radically changed circumstances for American ethnic groups. A variety of primary sources will be used, including official records from the Augustana Synod, Augustana College, and the Augustana Book Concern. In addition, college and book catalogs, historical accounts, speeches, newspapers and periodicals, and Swedish-language books of different kinds published in America will be used. Archival material from organizations and private letters from significant individuals will supplement the printed materials.

Based on the discussion on the nature of ethnicity and ethnic identities above, the starting points of this study include a view of a Swedish-American ethnic identity as a cultural construct and how this "Swedish Americanism," as it was often called, was invented or shaped by an ethnic leadership. This also means that the cultural contents of ethnicity will be central to the analysis and that the focus will be on the Augustana Synod as an ethnic institution, especially its deliberately formulated elite-level ethnicity. The malleable nature of the ethnic identity will be emphasized, with special attention paid to the role of the passing of time and change in generations. The duality of the Swedish-American identity will also be underscored, and particular attention will be given to how the new American context shaped the way in which Augustana's ethnic identity was configured and to the process through which selected Swedish cultural elements were transplanted to America and given new meaning in their new circumstances.

Chapter 2 provides a general overview of the Swedish-American community and places the Augustana Synod in this context. In chapters 3 and 4, the way in which a Swedish-American identity emerged and what it consisted of at Augustana College, the oldest and largest of the synod's colleges, will be examined. As the synod's leading educational institution, the college played a central role in educating the members of the Augustana Synod, and special attention will be devoted to the role and content of Swedish in the college's academic curriculum and on a number of Swedish-related activities outside of the curriculum, such as student organizations and festivities. The student body at the college will also be analyzed, with focus on who the students at Augustana were and on what role they played in the Swedish-American community.

Chapters 5 and 6 are devoted to an analysis of the Swedish-language publishing and literary endeavors of the Augustana Synod and of the role they played for the synod's ethnic identity. As will be shown, a considerable body of Swedish-language reading matter was published in and imported to Swedish America. The chapters will discuss what was read and published both in Swedish America in general and in the Augustana Synod in particular. Schoolbooks and a few publications that specifically addressed the cultural identity of the Swedish Americans will be of special interest in an analysis of how Augustana's publishing activities also contributed to the group's ethnic identity.

The role of history for ethnic identities has already been underscored. In chapter 7, the forging and use of a Swedish-American history will be discussed. What did Augustana's view of history consist of? What historical persons and symbols were important? Special emphasis will also be given to how a Swedish-American history was formulated by leading persons in the Augustana Synod. Chapter 8, finally, is a conclusion where the results of the study are discussed and placed in a larger perspective.

2

Coming to America: The Establishment of the Augustana Synod

The Augustana Synod was the largest Swedish-American organization and played a significant role in the Swedish-American community, so much so that well-known Swedish-American journalist and author Vilhelm Berger asked rhetorically in 1933 if it was "possible to imagine a Swedish America without the Augustana Synod?"[1] In this chapter, the Augustana Synod and its role in Swedish America will be addressed in greater detail. The chapter will also attempt to define the Augustana Synod in relationship to other parts of the Swedish-American community and to Sweden. As a background, the course of Swedish immigration to the United States and the organizational complexity of Swedish America will be discussed.

SWEDISH IMMIGRATION TO THE UNITED STATES

The Swedish mass-migration to the United States in the nineteenth and early twentieth centuries was a part of the economic and social transformation that affected both Europe and North America from about 1800. Sharp population growth and the rise of an industrial and capitalist economic system were important factors behind the European overseas migration, which between 1850 and 1950 saw 50 million Europeans settle in non-European areas, the majority in the United States.

As Hans Norman and Harald Runblom have shown in *From Sweden to America: A History of the Migration* and in *Transatlantic Connections: Nordic Migration to the New World after 1800*, the mass exodus of some 1.3 million Swedes, often young and healthy men and women, during the nineteenth and early twentieth centuries was fundamentally due to the limited outlook and economic opportunity available in Sweden. A combination of so-called push and pull factors on either side of the Atlantic as well as the establishment of migratory links were other important factors that more precisely determined the scope and course of the migration patterns. The transatlantic mass exodus must also be considered one of the major events of Swedish history during the last two centuries, with important and long-lasting consequences.

Swedish mass-migration to the United States began in earnest in the mid-1840s, when a number of pioneers, often migrating as groups, established an emigration tradition between certain sending areas in Sweden and particular receiving locales in the United States. Examples of colonies founded by these group migrants include settlements in western Illinois, Iowa, central Texas, southern Minnesota, and western Wisconsin.

When the American Civil War broke out, ending the pioneer period of Swedish immigration, the federal census recorded some 18,000 Swedish-born persons in the United States.[2] Ten years later, following the first heavy peaks of Swedish immigration in 1868–69, largely due to crop failures in Sweden, the figure was almost five times higher, or 97,332. The rapid increase of Swedish immigration continued. By 1880, the figure had more than doubled to 194,337, and in 1890, following the single decade of the largest Swedish immigration, 478,041 Swedes were living in the United States. During the 1880s alone, some 330,000 persons left Sweden for the United States, the peak year being 1887 with over 46,000 registered emigrants.

The pace of immigration remained high after 1890. Well over 200,000 Swedes landed in the United States during both the 1890s and the first decade of the twentieth century. By 1910, the U.S. census recorded over 665,000 Swedish-born persons in the United States. Just as the Civil War had restricted the number of foreigners who could enter the country, World War I curtailed the number of immigrants during the second decade of the century. A little fewer than 100,000 Swedes arrived in the United States during that decade, and by 1920 the number of Swedish-born in America declined for the first time, standing at 625,000. The peak year of 1923, when over 26,000 Swedes left for the United States, represents the end of some eight decades of sustained mass migration from Sweden to America.

As the decades of Swedish immigration to the United States progressed, a second generation of Swedish Americans entered the scene. For the purposes of this study and partly due to the way the federal census is organized, the

Coming to America

second generation is defined as persons born in the United States to at least one Swedish-born parent. The second generation was first recorded by the census in 1890, and in that year some 250,000 persons in the United States were classified as second-generation Swedish Americans. During the next decades, this figure increased quickly. In 1900, the second generation stood at 500,000, and by 1910, the second generation had passed the first and numbered 700,000. In 1920, the figure was 824,000.

The rural and agricultural profile of Swedish immigration of the first decades gradually changed; by the turn of the century, a majority of Swedish Americans were urbanites and a part of the rapidly growing American industrial economy. This also reflected a development from a migration of families during the first decades of emigration to a movement dominated by single young men and women after the turn of the century.

Return migration was also a part of the Swedish migratory patterns, and approximately one-fifth of the emigrants returned to their homeland. Re-migration was especially strong toward the end of the emigration era and was more common among men, urbanites, and persons active in the American industrial sector.

Settlements in America

As the result of immigration, the population group in the United States of Swedish extraction was thus well over 1 million during the first decades of the twentieth century. However, as Helge Nelson's *The Swedes and the Swedish Settlements in North America* so clearly shows, this number was not evenly distributed throughout the country. The early phase of Swedish immigration established the midwestern states as a prime receiving area. The agricultural areas in western Illinois, Iowa, Minnesota, and western Wisconsin formed the nucleus of the first Swedish settlements. As Hans Norman and Robert Ostergren have underscored, migration chains were quickly established between many places in the Midwest and in Sweden, encouraging and sustaining further movement across the Atlantic.[3] After the Civil War, the Swedish settlements spread farther west to Kansas and Nebraska, and in 1870 almost 75 percent of the Swedish immigrants in the United States were found in Illinois, Minnesota, Kansas, Wisconsin, and Nebraska. Ten years later, 74 percent of the Swedish immigrants still resided in the Midwest.[4]

By 1910, the U.S. census revealed that the position of the Midwest as a place of residence for the Swedish immigrants and their children was still strong but had weakened. Now 54 percent of the Swedish immigrants and their children lived in these states, with Minnesota and Illinois dominating, while 15 percent lived in the East, where the immigrants were drawn to industrial areas in New England. New York City and Worcester, Massachusetts, were two leading destinations. A sizable Swedish-American community had also been established on the West Coast, and in 1910 almost 10 percent of all Swedish Americans lived there; the states of Washington and California had the largest Swedish-American communities. In Washington, a heavy concentration of Swedish Americans grew up in the Seattle-Tacoma area.

Minnesota became the most Swedish of all states, with the Swedish Americans constituting more than 12 percent of Minnesota's population in 1910. In some areas, such as Chisago or Isanti counties on the Minnesota countryside north and northwest of Minneapolis, Swedish Americans made up close to 70 percent of the population. If Minnesota became the most Swedish state in the union, Chicago was the Swedish-American capital. In 1910, more than 100,000 Swedish Americans resided in Chicago, which meant that about 10 percent of all Swedish Americans lived there. At the turn of the century, Chicago was also the second-largest Swedish city in the world; only Stockholm counted more Swedish inhabitants than Chicago.[5]

Swedish-American Community

The preceding discussion has provided figures from the U.S. censuses about the size of the Swedish immigrant group in the United States. However, it does not necessarily follow that the figures also measured the magnitude of the Swedish-American community. The mere fact that a person was born in Sweden or to parents of Swedish descent does not necessarily mean that he or she was a member of the Swedish-American ethnic group. It is clear that many Swedish immigrants as well as their children and grandchildren did not associate with or become a part of the Swedish-American community, which, as Sture Lindmark has pointed out, was "a collective description of the cultural and religious heritage which the Swedish immigrants brought with them and perpetuated in America,"[6] primarily through institutions such as churches, organizations, associations, and clubs that served the varied needs of its members.

One of this study's contentions is that ethnicity and expressions of ethnic sentiments vary in different historical contexts. Thus, as has already been discussed in chapter 1, different individuals can express their ethnicity in different degrees. The census figures recorded the genealogical characteristics of individuals, figures that did not necessarily translate into feelings of either ethnic awareness or consciousness. The different organizations formed by Swedish immigrants from the middle of the nineteenth century on will instead be used to gauge the size of the community. By focusing on organizations and their members, we can establish a clearer element of identification with a Swedish-American ethnic organization and interaction with other members on the part of the individual. This in turn can be seen as an identification with the ethnic group and its ethnic identity and will provide an alternative to the census measurements of the Swedish-American community.

Swedish-American Organizations

Swedish immigrants and their descendants founded a great number of organizations, such as churches, associations, clubs, and cultural societies of different kinds in the United States, and together they formed an intricate pattern of institutions that by the turn of the century spanned the entire American continent. It is difficult to establish how many organizations have existed, and various estimates have been offered. In 1898, journalist C. F. Peterson believed that about 1,000 secular organizations existed in that year, a figure Ernst Skarstedt, a keen observer of the Swedish-American scene, concurred with in 1917.[7] In 1938, it was estimated that about 2,000 religious Swedish-American organizations had existed up until that time.[8]

The largest organizations were the various religious denominations founded by Swedish immigrants in the United States. These churches had their roots in the religious experiences both of the homeland and of the United States: the Augustana Synod was founded by ministers from the Church of Sweden, the Swedish Evangelical Mission Covenant Church had its Swedish parallel in Svenska Missionsförbundet, and the Evangelical Free Church developed from the Covenant Church. Other "American" denominations also attracted Swedish immigrants as members. In some cases, as with the Baptists, Methodists, Adventists, and Salvation Army, separate Swedish-language conferences were organized as part of the American mother institution, whereas still others, such as the Congregationalists, Mormons, and Presbyterians, organized Swedish-language services in the American congregations with some regularity.[9]

As already noted, the Augustana Synod was by far the single largest Swedish-American organization. In the second decade of the twentieth century, it was almost nine times as large as the Mission Covenant Church, which came in second place. In 1915, the Augustana Synod had 274,000 members and the Mission Covenant Church about 30,000. The Methodists counted 20,000, and the other denominations all fell below that figure.[10] The total membership in the Swedish-American denominations has been estimated at 365,000 at the end of the immigration era,[11] which means that roughly a quarter of the Swedish Americans of the first and second generations were members of a Swedish-American church at that time. The larger Swedish-American denominations not only served the religious needs of their members but also founded educational and benevolent institutions, such as colleges, academies, hospitals, orphanages, old people's homes, and the like.

The secular organizations attracted fewer members. The statistics are not as easily available as for the churches, but the largest organizations included the mutual-aid societies, which began to be established toward the end of the nineteenth century. The largest of them in the 1920s were the Vasa Order (approximately 50,000 members), the Svithiod Order (approximately 15,000 members), the Viking Order (approximately 15,000 members), and the Scandinavian Fraternity of America (approximately 40,000 members), all of which became national organizations with substantial financial resources. In addition, there were numerous smaller organizations and clubs scattered throughout Swedish America, with a wide array of undertakings. Some examples include organizations for individuals from a particular province in Sweden, whereas others focused on musical, theatrical, educational, or political activities.[12] A small but vocal Swedish-American labor movement also developed, mainly in the urban areas.[13] Ulf Beijbom has estimated that at the close of Swedish mass-immigration in the mid-1920s, the total membership in the secular organizations, both mutual-aid societies and social clubs, stood at 115,000, which represented not quite 10 percent of the first- and second-generation Swedish Americans.[14]

A very important dimension of the Swedish-American community was the Swedish-language press.[15] The beginnings of a Swedish-American press had already been laid in the 1850s, and it has been estimated that between 600 and 1,000 Swedish language newspapers were published. The Swedish-American press was the second largest foreign-language press in the United States. In 1910, the German-language press dominated greatly, with an estimated 3 million–plus copies of German-language newspapers and periodicals published, but in second place came the Swedes, with a total of over 650,000 copies.

It can thus be estimated that the Swedish-American organizations counted close to half a million Swedish Americans among their membership ranks in the 1920s, or about a third of all Swedish Americans recorded in the census. Allowing for individuals with membership in several organizations, the actual figure might be somewhat lower. This figure constitutes a much more narrow definition of the Swedish-American community than the census figures provide, but it gives us an indication of how many Swedish Americans showed a high enough degree of ethnic identification to join a Swedish-American organization. Using the circulation figures for the Swedish-American press in 1910, we find that the circulation statistics correspond to close to half of the first- and second-generation Swedish Americans in that year. Following the reasoning of McKay and Lewins from chapter 1, this does not necessarily mean that the ethnic identification was higher, since reading a Swedish-language newspaper suggests a lower degree of interaction with other Swedish Americans than did belonging to a Swedish-American organization.

The different organizations catered to the different needs of their membership—religion, sick insurance, or the affection for a particular province in Sweden, for example. However, they also eventually transcended these specific functions and came to serve as places where one could meet fellow country-persons, speak the Swedish language, and partake in the various social activities that were connected with the organization. This was particularly true with the churches and mutual-aid societies. They allowed the Swedish-American community to develop toward institutional completeness and can thus be said to have been the bearers of a Swedish-American ethnicity.

THE AUGUSTANA SYNOD

The Augustana Synod was founded in June 1860, but as G. Everett Arden, Hugo Söderström, and George Stephenson have shown in their respective studies, it traced its origin back to the beginnings of Swedish immigration during the previous decade.[16] In 1849, Swedish minister Lars Paul Esbjörn led a group of immigrants to the prairies of western Illinois, where they established a Lutheran congregation in Andover in 1850. During the following years, Esbjörn was followed by several other Swedish ministers, including Erland Carlsson, Tuve Nilsson Hasselquist, Eric Norelius (who received his theological training in the United States), and Jonas Swensson, all of whom also brought groups of emigrants with them to the New World and founded congregations where they settled in America. During the 1850s, emigration from Sweden continued, and more congregations sprang up. When the

Augustana Synod was formed in 1860, it included thirty-six Swedish and thirteen Norwegian Lutheran congregations with some 4,900 communicant members.[17]

Prior to the establishment of the Augustana Synod, the Swedish Lutherans maintained different kinds of relationships with other American denominations, both Lutheran and non-Lutheran. Both Esbjörn and Hasselquist were supported in their work among the Swedish immigrants by the American Home Missionary Society, a Congregationalist association, and were employed as missionaries among their fellow Swedes in Illinois during the 1850s. In addition, the Swedish Missionary Society, an interconfessional mission group, had given Esbjörn some travel support.[18] The Swedish Lutheran congregations were from 1851 also affiliated with the Synod of Northern Illinois, which was a district synod of the General Synod, a larger American Lutheran body organized in 1820.[19]

Several reasons for the organization of the Augustana Synod have been advanced, including confessional differences, personality problems, and issues of nationality.[20] The most prominent of these seems to have been the confessional differences between the Swedes and a group of Norwegians, and the rest of the Synod of Northern Illinois, which came to the fore toward the end of the 1850s. The discussion centered on, among other things, the interpretation of the Augsburg Confession, from whose Latin form, *Confessio Augustana,* the name Augustana was chosen. Hugo Söderström has also argued that in addition to the confessional differences, the issue of nationality was an important factor for the establishment of the Augustana Synod.[21] Although the early leadership of the synod downplayed the issue of nationalism and expressed hopes that Americans with the correct confessional viewpoint would join the synod as well,[22] this did not come to pass, and the synod did remain a distinct ethnic institution.

The cooperation with the Norwegians lasted until 1870, when the latter withdrew to form their own denomination. Arden argues that the reasons for the separation had to do with the much more divided and competitive religious scene among the Norwegians in America, as well as with the fact that the Norwegian congregations remained a minority within the synod.[23] Still, issues of nationality also played a role, and in 1869 August Wenaas, Norwegian professor in the Augustana seminary, wrote in *Den Norske Lutheraner* that the Swedes "cannot fully understand our peculiar Norwegian character and our ecclesiastical and national traditions."[24] The withdrawal of the Norwegians from the Augustana Synod seems to conform with a general pattern of interaction between the Scandinavian groups in America. Although little systematic work has been done on the issue, it is clear that pan-Scandinavian cooperation, such as joint organizations, were not uncommon during the early phases of Scandinavian immigration to the United States. Eventually, however, many of these organizations were dissolved and reorganized on purely national grounds.[25] One reason for this, Runblom has argued, was the different development and character of nationalism in the Scandinavian countries themselves, which also affected the Scandinavian groups in America. For example, Norwegian immigrants to the United States in the mid- to late nineteenth century had been exposed to the growth of the Norwegian nationalism of the period prior to leaving Norway, a nationalism that was much stronger and far-reaching than that which their fellow Swedish immigrants had experienced.[26]

The early leadership in the Augustana Synod was a part of the low-church revival movement that affected Sweden in the mid-nineteenth century and that was one dimension of a realignment of Swedish society in general and religion in particular during the nineteenth century.[27] Complex in its nature, this movement represented a Swedish religious dissent, which emphasized the role of the individual as opposed to church hierarchy and which was critical of both the Church of Sweden and its status as a state church. The movement was, in the words of Hanne Sanders, a way of questioning the established society, of "breaking the church's monopoly of interpretation . . . and of creating its own alternatives."[28] During the nineteenth century, several new religious bodies were also established in Sweden, both inside and outside the Church of Sweden. Evangeliska Fosterlandsstiftelsen (The National Evangelic Foundation), founded in 1856 and with which the Augustana Synod shared many traits, worked to create a revivalistically inspired institution within the Church of Sweden.[29] The establishment of Svenska Missionsförbundet in 1878 is an example of how the low-church revival resulted in the creation of a denomination outside the Church of Sweden.

This Swedish religious background shaped the way the Augustana Synod developed. The suspicion of central ecclesiastical authority in the Swedish revival can be seen as one of the reasons for the relatively strong position of individual congregations in the Augustana Synod. Another reason was the refusal of the synod to establish the office of bishop, as well as the fact that the head of the denomination was always called president.[30] Moreover, the religious heterogeneity that characterized the American scene as a whole left the Augustana Synod in a much more vulnerable situation than was the case for the Swedish state church, which benefited from compulsory membership. After less than three years in America, Esbjörn expressed concerns over American religious pluralism in a report to Svenska Missionssällskapet, a Swedish mission group from which he had received financial support prior to his emigration. There were many religious groups competing for the souls of the Swedish immigrants, and he warned those in Sweden who advocated religious freedom there.[31]

The Augustana Synod grew very rapidly during its first four decades. The membership increased from some 3,700 in 1860 to nearly ten times that number, 33,000, a decade later. During the following two decades, the membership doubled twice to 75,000 in 1880 and 146,000 in 1890. Although the synod kept growing during the following decades as well, the pace was somewhat slower. In 1900 there were 210,000 members, in 1910 261,000, and in 1920 the synod counted 291,000 members.[32] The number of congregations grew equally fast, from 37 in 1860 to 1,250 in 1920, and various congregations were organized into conferences. The synod also expanded geographically beyond its midwestern origins; in 1870 the New York Conference was established for the East Coast congregations, and in the 1890s two new West Coast conferences were established.[33]

The nucleus of the Augustana Synod was the individual congregations, which were present throughout both rural and urban Swedish America in the form of the church building and its spire. Typically, a congregation would be founded in an area with a large Swedish population, and after some time the congregation would decide to apply for membership in the Augustana Synod. Especially during the first several decades, the individual congregations retained a great deal of independence from both the conferences and the synod as a whole. In this way, it is possible to see parallels between the synod during its first several decades and the Swedish low-church revival. For example, Svenska Missionsförbundet had no bishops and had a strong emphasis on congregational independence, something that Stephenson has called the "decentralizing tendencies" present in the synod until 1894.[34] In that year, a new constitution was adopted, balancing the relationship between the congregations, the conferences, and the synod. It strengthened the position of central authority held by the synod while still granting considerable independence to the congregations. This arrangement represented what one historian of the Augustana Synod called "a Lutheran middle way between an ecclesiastical hierarchy on the one hand and congregationalism on the other."[35] The lack of synodical authority also meant that control over individual congregations became much more difficult than in Sweden, as is seen, for example, during the schism with the Mission Covenant Church in the 1870s and 1880s.

In addition to the local congregations, a number of other institutions were formed, which all contributed to the growth of the Augustana Synod. The synod and its conferences operated over a dozen educational institutions—colleges, academies, and a theological seminary. Of these, Augustana College was in many ways the central institution, as it was the oldest of the colleges and also owned by the synod as a whole, unlike the other schools, which were operated by one of the eleven regional conferences into which the Augustana Synod was divided. Moreover, the synod's only seminary was located at Augustana, which meant that all the ordained ministers in the Augustana Synod had to attend school in Rock Island.

Apart from educational institutions, the synod operated a great number of what were officially called "benevolent institutions," including orphanages, hospitals, deaconess institutes, and homes for the aged. With the exception of the Immanuel Deaconess Institute in Omaha, Nebraska, these institutions were regional in character and support and were owned and controlled by the different conferences. In 1917, the synod's annual report included twenty-eight benevolent institutions, including nine orphanages, five hospitals, two deaconess institutes, eight homes for the aged, two immigrant homes, one home for invalids, and one home for women.[36]

The Augustana Synod also had an extensive publishing program.[37] One of the largest and most influential Swedish-American newspapers, *Hemlandet,* was started by Augustana Synod president Hasselquist in 1854, and although it was sold in 1872, it remained closely associated with the synod. Over the years, the Augustana Synod also published at least twenty other magazines, newspapers, and journals of religious and cultural-literary character, including the synod's official organ, *Augustana,* as well as such literary and cultural publications as the annual calendar *Prärieblomman* and the monthly magazine *Ungdomsvännen.* A great number of books were also published by the synod's publishing house, the Augustana Book Concern. Between 1891 and 1920, 643 Swedish-language titles were published by the Augustana Book Concern, and between 1911 and 1915 alone, a total of 840,000 copies appeared of the Swedish-language imprints. It was not until after World War I that the English-language editions overshadowed the Swedish at the Augustana Book Concern.

Augustana in Swedish America

It is difficult to measure exactly the Augustana Synod's influence in Swedish America, but table 1 shows the relationship between the size of the synod and the persons of Swedish extraction living in the United States between 1860 and 1920. The synod statistics do not state the ethnic background of its members, but it can be safely assumed that the vast majority of the Augustana members, until at least 1920, were of Swedish background, and the figures can thus be seen as one indication of the synod's relative position in the Swedish-American community. For the period 1860–80, the percentage is calculated on Swedish-born individuals, and between 1890 and 1920, the figure includes those born in Sweden and those born in the United States of at least one Swedish parent. As can be seen in table 1, the synod's dominance was probably greatest during the decades prior to the turn of the century, particularly during the 1870s and 1880s, when the synod's membership corresponded to more than a third of the Swedish-born population. The inclusion of the American-born Swedish Americans lowers the share to about a fifth, but this is still much higher than for any other Swedish-American group.

TABLE 1. AUGUSTANA SYNOD MEMBERSHIP AS PERCENTAGE OF THE POPULATION OF SWEDISH EXTRACTION.

1860	1870	1880	1890	1900	1910	1920
20.1	34.2	38.4	19.9	19.4	19.6	20.1

Sources: U.S. Censuses, Augustana Synod Statistic

It should, however, also be noted that Augustana's influence in Swedish America cannot be measured only through its membership figures. A fairly large number of Swedish Americans who did not belong to the denomination still used its services at different times and can thus be said to have been included in the synod's field of influence, although to a lesser extent than were the actual members. It was quite common for nonmembers to be married, buried, or have their children baptized in an Augustana congregation, a tradition that many of the immigrants most likely brought with them from Sweden. The sources are at best uneven in their information about these activities, but in 1920 there were roughly as many nonmembers as members who sought out Augustana congregations for these ceremonies.[38] No information is available for how many nonmembers might have been affected by other Augustana Synod activities, but the figures do suggest that the Augustana influence probably extended beyond the limits of its membership. Conrad

Bergendoff has in fact suggested that the synod reached as many as half of the Swedish immigrants.[39]

Another way of measuring the synod's relative importance in Swedish America is to compare its membership figures with those of other Swedish-American organizations. As noted above, not quite 40 percent of all persons of Swedish extraction in the United States in 1920 belonged to one of the many Swedish-American organizations at that time. Of that group of close to half a million individuals, the Augustana Synod membership was made up of close to 300,000 persons, or 60 percent. Allowing for the fact that some persons may have belonged to other Swedish-American groups in addition to the Augustana Synod, the figure still clearly illustrates the dominance of the synod among those Swedish Americans who chose to identify with one of the many Swedish-American organizations.

The position of the Augustana Synod in Swedish America varied in urban and rural areas. The synod had many strongholds in rural Swedish America, where large parts of heavily Swedish-American communities belonged to the Augustana Synod. In an analysis of a rural Swedish settlement in Frankfort Township, Montgomery County, in southwestern Iowa, Ann Legreid shows that in 1895, 83 percent of the Swedish-born heads of household were members of the local Augustana congregation, whereas 14 percent belonged to the local Covenant congregation.[40] Almost the entire Swedish population in the area thus professed membership in a Swedish-American denomination in this area, with a clear preference for the Augustana congregation. Similarly, Ostergren has shown that in the heavily Swedish-settled Cambridge West Township in rural Isanti County, Minnesota, some 70 percent of the households claimed membership in the (Augustana) Cambridge Lutheran Church.[41]

The situation was much different in the urban areas, where a smaller fraction of Swedish Americans tended to belong to a church of any denomination and where the Augustana Synod thus had a much weaker position. Anita Ruth Olson's analysis of religious patterns among Swedish Americans in the largest Swedish-American urban settlement, Chicago, shows that in 1900, some 11 percent of the Swedish-born population in that city were members of an Augustana congregation and that roughly a quarter of the Chicago Swedes belonged to any Swedish-American denomination, thus leaving two-thirds of the group outside of organized Swedish-American religious life.[42] It should, however, be noted that these figures do not include nonmembers who still chose to get married or baptize their children in a Swedish-American church, which was, as noted above, a sizable number.

It is also evident that the synod had a geographic profile rooted in the Midwest. In 1910, six midwestern states (Minnesota, Illinois, Iowa, Michigan, Nebraska, and Kansas) represented 67 percent of the Augustana Synod membership, while the same six states encompassed only 53 percent of the first- and second-generation Swedish Americans recorded in the U.S. census that year.[43] Minnesota and Illinois alone made up close to half of the 1910 Augustana membership (47 percent), while 37 percent of all Swedish Americans lived in these two states. Augustana's position on the East and West Coasts was weaker: 12 percent of all Swedish Americans lived in the two major East Coast states of New York and Massachusetts in 1910, but only 7 percent of the Augustana Synod members lived there, and while 8 percent of the Swedish Americans lived in California and Washington, only 3 percent of the Augustana membership was found in those western states.

The geographic profile of the Augustana Synod can at least partly be explained in generational terms. Those states with the largest share of Augustana Synod members were also those states that had experienced early Swedish immigration. Illinois, Minnesota, Iowa, Kansas, and Nebraska belonged to a core group of early Swedish settlements from the 1850s on. In 1880, for example, the Illinois, Minnesota, and Iowa conferences of the synod made up 80 percent of its membership.[44] Although Swedish immigration to these midwestern core areas continued all throughout the immigration era—especially to urban areas such as Chicago and Minneapolis–St. Paul—a gradually larger part of the immigration after the turn of the century went to urban destinations on the East and West Coasts, where the Augustana Synod was weaker.

Its relative weakness in those areas was to a large extent a result of the synod's inability to attract newer immigrants as members. The post-1900 Swedish immigrants were different from their compatriots of the early decades of Swedish immigration, as the Sweden they left in the first decades of the twentieth century was also quite different in terms of social and economic development from the Sweden of half a century earlier. The newer immigrants were often younger, single, more urban and industrial in their Swedish background, and more urban-oriented in their choice of American destination than those who had arrived before 1900.[45] Apparently, these immigrants were less likely to be attracted to the Augustana Synod, and Bergendoff notes that the synod began having problems in attracting Swedish immigrants arriving in the 1880s and 1890s, characterizing many groups that came after World War I as openly hostile to the synod. To Bergendoff, the "height of the Synod's activities among Swedish immigrants was reached around 1910."[46]

The synod leadership was also aware of this problem, and it was discussed frequently after the turn of the century. In March 1902, the dilemma was addressed in the official synod organ *Augustana* in an article with the appropriate title "The Mission of Our Church with Regard to the Scores of Country-Men, Especially in the Larger Cities, Who Remain Outside Her." The author points out that the immigrants of recent times came from a Sweden in which many people showed indifference to religion and therefore chose to remain outside the church. The article states that this was a radically different situation from the early years of the Augustana Synod, when the immigrants influenced by the pietism associated with the revival were "true Lutherans" and actively sought out the Lutheran church.[47] A year later, Pastor C. W. Andeer addressed the same question when he encouraged the synod to try to attract as many of the 45,000 new Swedish immigrants as possible that year. However, he realized that this would be a difficult task, since "they have another mindset than those who founded Swedish America," affected as they were by political, social, and religious struggles in Sweden and "contaminated" by socialism.[48] In 1912, *Augustana* attributed the problem to religious indifference. A couple of decades earlier, the paper noted, the immigrants had "deep religious needs" and founded churches in America, whereas at the present time the Swedish immigrant was indifferent or even hostile toward religion.[49] A comment from 1914 also emphasized the difference between rural and urban areas; most Swedes were settling in urban areas at the time, and as these Swedes were of "a completely different mind-set," they were also the most difficult to recruit as synod members.[50]

As a consequence of this shift, by the turn of the century the Augustana Synod seems to have been on its way to becoming an institution dominated by an immigrant generation from the early decades of the immigration era and their children. It is difficult to make a generational analysis of the synod membership, since the synod statistics provide no such information. However, those states with the highest membership shares in the synod were also those states where the second generation (American-born) of Swedish Americans dominated. In 1910, the second generation made up 55 percent of all Swedish Americans in the Midwest, the source of strength for the synod. On both the East and West Coasts, the first generation dominated (55 and 57 percent, respectively).[51] The picture is even clearer when one examines the data for individual states. In such strong Augustana states as Iowa,

Nebraska, and Kansas, the second generation dominated, making up over 60 percent of the Swedish Americans, while the situation was reversed in states dominated by first-generation immigrants such as Massachusetts, New York, Washington, and California, where the synod was weak.

To summarize, the Augustana Synod was the largest and most dominant of the organizations in Swedish America. The synod based its membership on a group of core states in the Midwest, where the original Augustana congregations and other institutions were established during the decades after 1850. It continued to draw its strength from these areas, even when the first generation was fading from the scene and being replaced by the second generation of Swedish Americans and was less successful in attracting members from later waves of Swedish immigrants.

Augustana and Swedish America

In discussing the various facets of the Swedish-American community, Arnold Barton has pointed to four major components in organized Swedish America: four groups that represented different social categories of Swedish Americans as well as differences in their attitudes about the nature and identity of the Swedish-American group. According to Barton, the Augustana Synod was the leading of these, and from it emerged Swedish America's "dominant ethnic ideology." The second group consisted of other Swedish-American religious groups, notably the Swedish Evangelical Mission Covenant Church, but also Swedish Methodists, Baptists, Adventists, and Mormons. Secular groups, or "freethinkers" as Barton also calls them, made up the third segment. Included here were, for example, several newspapers and other, often urban-based, organizations, such as the Swedish-American orders and lodges. Although very small numerically, the politically radical Swedish-American groups, often Socialist in nature, made up the fourth part of Swedish-American opinion. These groups competed for influence within the Swedish-American community and were frequently in conflict with each other. The strong dichotomy that existed especially between the religious and secular organizations has often been underscored.[52]

It should, however, also be noted that the strife within Swedish-American religion could also be keen. For the Augustana Synod, the relationship with the Mission Covenant Church became especially important. The Mission Covenant Church was formally established in 1885, although several organizations had preceded it from the late 1860s. Like the Augustana Synod, the Mission Covenant Church had its roots in the nineteenth-century Swedish religious revival movement and maintained a close relationship with Svenska Missionsförbundet, established in 1878, and it seems likely that many members of the Mission Covenant Church had been associated with Svenska Missionsförbundet prior to their emigration. In Sweden, the early Augustana leaders had maintained close contact with persons connected with what would become Svenska Missionsförbundet, and its leader, Paul Peter Waldenström, had even been offered a professorship at the Augustana seminary in 1862.[53]

Still, when controversy broke out in Sweden over Waldenström's teaching on the atonement in 1872, a parallel conflict developed in America between the sympathizers with Waldenström and the Augustana Synod.[54] In 1874, the synod minutes mentioned the "firestorm" that the teachings of the Covenant movement had set off among the Augustana Lutherans,[55] and an Augustana pastor from Jamestown, New York, spoke of the Mission Covenant sympathizers as "worse than the grasshoppers in Minnesota and Kansas" as they "buzz, bite, eat, and gnaw wherever they advance."[56] Thus, Augustana and the Covenant grew apart; Philip J. Anderson speaks of their conflict as a religious "schism," and Arden talks about "the theological crisis."[57]

Like certain high church groups in Sweden, the Augustana Synod also showed hostility to many of the secular societies, or "secret societies" as they were called, which seem to have included a variety of groups, ranging from the Freemasons to temperance organizations. Hugo Söderström has suggested that no fewer than 258 members were excommunicated in 1890 for being members of "secret societies,"[58] and in 1892 synod president A. A. Swärd complained about the great number of associations that existed in the cities, which had become an "anti-church movement" and hindered the synod's work.[59] In addition, as will be shown in chapter 3, the synod objected to many cultural expressions associated with the secular groups, such as dancing and theater, throughout the period of investigation. The small Socialist groups also seem to have maintained a distance from not only the religious community but also other secular groups.[60]

The Augustana Synod clearly sought to establish itself as the dominant Swedish-American organization. In 1910, synod president Norelius reflected on the first half century of the synod's life. Although he noted the existence of other Swedish-American denominations, Norelius underscored the great significance of the Augustana Synod in Swedish America, claiming that it better than any other denomination had succeeded in establishing educational and benevolent institutions and a publishing house. The schools, for example, had been especially important for the creation of a Swedish literary culture in America, and the synod as a whole, Norelius claimed, was thus "the only force among Swedish immigrants in America which has preserved the faith of our fathers [and] the Swedish culture and language which has sprung from it."[61]

The distance between the Augustana Synod and other groups in Swedish America was clearly expressed during the celebrations of the fiftieth anniversary of both the synod and of Augustana College and Theological Seminary in 1910. During the weeklong celebrations, many greetings were received from both Sweden and the United States.[62] The American greetings came from other colleges and academies in the Augustana Synod, several colleges and universities in Illinois and elsewhere in the Midwest, other American Lutheran seminaries, several other American Lutheran denominations (including three Norwegian-American synods and the Finnish-American Suomi Synod), as well as a number of individuals, such as President Taft. It is striking that, with the exception of the Covenant North Park College in Chicago, no other Swedish-American institutions or organizations were among those sending congratulatory messages. Thus, to the Augustana Synod, contacts with other Lutheran institutions, including other Scandinavian-American groups and other American institutions of higher learning, played a more important role than did contacts with other Swedish-American organizations outside the Augustana Synod.

The cultural differences between the various factions in the Swedish-American community have not yet been systematically studied, but some examples will illustrate these variations. Swedish-American cultural expressions, as they were formulated by David Nyvall of the Mission Covenant Church, have been discussed by Scott E. Erickson, and analyses by Beijbom and Anna Williams of the often acrimonious newspaper debates in Chicago and by Janet Nyberg in Minnesota over such crucial issues as assimilation, language retention, and political preferences further point to the strong diversity of opinion within the community, especially between religious and secular groups. Lars Wendelius's study of cultural life among Swedish Americans in Rockford, Illinois, also shows the differences in cultural outlook between the religious groups on the one hand and the temperance and radical organizations in the city on the other. Finally, the special nature of the cultural expressions among Swedish-American radicals in Chicago and their connections to similar secular and culturally radical patterns in the labor movement in Sweden has been analyzed by Per Nordahl.[63] As will be shown in chapter 4, a specific cultural and literary profile also emerged within the Augustana Synod that at times was quite distinct from other factions of the Swedish-American community.

One should also, however, recognize the commonality of interests among the various factions in the Swedish-American community. At times, and especially after the turn of the century, opposing sides of the community could come together for joint manifestations when there was opportunity to show their strength to the surrounding American society. Two such Swedish-American examples were the celebrations of the 250th anniversary of the New Sweden colony in Minneapolis in 1888 and the "Swedish Day" during the Columbian Exposition in Chicago in 1893. Williams has also pointed to a convergence of opinions within Swedish America after the turn of the century, concluding that the "antagonism" between the religious and secular groups of the 1870s and 1880s had been overcome. Instead, the earlier antagonists (excepting the Socialists) could now unite behind an ethnic identity, in which the Augustana Synod and its "ideology" played a leading role. There are also parallels between Erickson's description of Nyvall's views of what it meant to be Swedish American, with its focus on the development of a distinct Swedish-American identity, based on a dual Swedish and American heritage,[64] and what we shall see developed within the Augustana Synod.

Augustana and Sweden

The relationship between the Augustana Synod and Sweden varied over time. During the early phase of the emigration era, some homeland Swedes often looked with skepticism at the growing Swedish-American community on the other side of the Atlantic, portraying the emigrants, in Barton's words, "as vain seekers after purely material advantages, gullible dreamers, 'deserters,' and even violators of God's Sixth Commandment." This was a sentiment especially noticeable in conservative intellectual and religious circles in the country.[65] Following this general pattern, contacts between the Augustana Synod and the Church of Sweden were not particularly close up until around 1890, and the Church of Sweden seems to have regarded the synod with some suspicion. This attitude can be traced as far back as the emigration of Esbjörn, when Archbishop af Wingård expressed his "displeasure" with the migration of Esbjörn and his group.[66] The Church of Sweden had also at times suggested that the Episcopal church in the United States would be the logical church for the Swedish emigrants to belong to, a judgment that of course resulted in negative reactions in the Augustana Synod.[67]

By the turn of the century, however, this relationship was improving. For example, in the early 1890s, when the faculty of the Augustana Theological Seminary wrote to the Swedish bishops to ascertain how they viewed the Augustana Synod, six wrote back saying that they saw the synod as the "daughter church" in America of the Church of Sweden.[68]

Moreover, in 1893, the 300th anniversary of the Uppsala meeting of 1593 at which the Swedish Reformation was codified, Knut Henning Gezelius von Schéele, professor of theology at Uppsala University from 1879 and Bishop of Visby from 1885, became the first Swedish bishop to come to Swedish America in general and to the Augustana Synod in particular, a visit that can be seen as a turning point in the relationship between at least the Augustana Synod and official Sweden.[69] Von Schéele participated in a major celebration in Rock Island in June 1893 as the official representative of the Church of Sweden, where such leading figures in the Augustana Synod as Norelius and P. J. Swärd welcomed him and noted with great pleasure that his visit marked the first recognition from the Church of Sweden that the Augustana Synod had received since its beginning in 1860.[70] It is "quite remarkable" to greet a Swedish bishop as an official visitor, wrote *Augustana*, given the fact that the Church of Sweden has paid "very little attention" to the synod and its important work among the Swedes in America,[71] and at the jubilee celebrations in Rock Island, synod president Norelius said that the synod thought "it took very long" before "the mother church turned her eyes upon the daughter church."[72]

Von Schéele returned to America twice: in 1901, when he visited several of the Swedish-American colleges and was greeted as an old friend by the Augustana Synod, and in 1910, when the Augustana Synod and Augustana College celebrated their fiftieth anniversary on a grand scale in Rock Island. *Augustana* commented that his visit in 1901 showed that the Swedes in America were better appreciated in Sweden now than they had been during the past five decades, attributing a major role to von Schéele for this.[73]

Von Schéele was obviously impressed by the intellectual and religious life he found during his visits to Swedish America. For example, in his account of his journey in 1893, he gave high praise to the Augustana Synod as the church that was preserving the old Swedish faith in America.[74] He noted that the graduating class at Augustana College in 1893 was of the same academic standard as those at comparable schools in Sweden and was especially pleased by the fact that many students in Gotland (his home province) would have a hard time measuring up to the level of expertise exhibited at Augustana

College in Swedish language and literature "by boys and girls born and raised in America."[75] Von Schéele's positive assessment of Augustana was also shown by his interest in admitting many returning Augustana pastors to the Diocese of Visby, more than any other contemporary Swedish bishop.[76] In total, six pastors were admitted to Visby diocese, which Sten Carlsson calls "remarkable" since not one out of the fifty-eight returning Augustana pastors identified by Carlsson was born on Gotland.[77]

Following von Schéele's first visit to America, official Sweden began to bestow orders and medals to prominent Swedish Americans. Up until 1910, about a dozen medals were bestowed, and the recipients were almost exclusively connected with the Augustana Synod. It is also clear that Bishop von Schéele played an important role in proposing the candidates for the medals to the Swedish government.[78]

Contacts between the Augustana Synod in general and Augustana College in particular became substantially strengthened after the turn of the century. One illustration of this was a campaign to raise money for Augustana in Sweden in which the fourth (and first American-born) president of Augustana College, Gustav Andreen, played an important role. Andreen was born in Baileytown, Indiana, in 1864, the son of Swedish-born Andreas Andreen, one of the first ministers in the Augustana Synod.[79] It was only natural that Gustav would attend Augustana College, and he graduated in 1881.[80] Following his graduation, he taught for two years at Augustana and later, between 1886 and 1893, at Bethany College in Lindsborg, Kansas. In 1893, he attended Yale University, earning a bachelor's degree in 1894 and a PhD in Germanic languages in 1898. An offer of a position as instructor in Scandinavian languages at Yale required that Andreen spend two years in Scandinavia,[81] and in the summer of 1898 the Andreen family sailed for Sweden. Andreen spent two years in Scandinavia, mainly at Uppsala University but also at Christiania and Copenhagen. At Uppsala he spent most of his time studying in the Department of Scandinavian Languages with Professor Adolf Noreen and was an active member of Noreen's seminar in Nordic languages. In a letter to Noreen, Andreen speaks fondly of the seminar and the pleasant informal get-togethers after the seminar.[82] It was also during Andreen's time at Uppsala University that he presented a lecture about the Swedish language in America, which was also published in Sweden in 1900.[83]

During his years in Sweden, Andreen managed to establish a number of important contacts for Augustana College, as he met several prominent

Swedes, primarily in the universities. He also conceived of a plan to raise money for Augustana College in Sweden, and the so-called Augustana Plan was launched with his Swedish academic contacts playing important roles in enlisting support in the Swedish academic, cultural, and political establishment for the plan.[84] The plan was officially announced in 1901 in a "petition to the Swedish public," and a campaign was launched in Sweden to raise 100,000 Swedish crowns.[85] The money would be used for a professorship at Augustana College, which, the petition claimed, had an "immeasurable influence on the Swedish-American people" and was said to be the "main center for the preservation of Swedishness" in America. It was signed by a number of leading Swedish academics, authors, church people, and politicians, including Professors Harald Hjärne and Adolf Noreen, authors Selma Lagerlöf and Verner von Heidenstam, Bishop von Schéele, Archbishop J. A. Ekman, and Prime Minister Erik Gustaf Boström.

The campaign went on for several years, and Andreen returned to Sweden in 1903 to lecture about Augustana and further promote the plan, at which time he was also received by King Oscar II, who agreed to lend his name to the professorship.[86] The campaign eventually raised 100,000 crowns in Sweden, a sum matched by funds from the United States, so that by the fiftieth anniversary of the college in 1910, it was announced that a total of more than $250,000 had been collected.[87]

It is thus possible during the years after the turn of the century to discern a new interest in and understanding for Swedish America in general and Augustana in particular in circles of Swedish society, which until then had had little contact with the emigrants and their descendants in the United States. Augustana's professor of Swedish from 1901, Jules Mauritzson, followed in Andreen's footsteps at Uppsala University in 1902, studying both literature and Scandinavian languages. He observed that there was a great interest in what the Swedish Americans were doing culturally and that some of the Uppsala academics were pleasantly surprised to learn about the academic life at Augustana College.[88] As mentioned above, the fiftieth anniversary celebration of the synod, the college, and the seminary also attracted numerous Swedish visitors and congratulatory messages. The Swedish delegation included Bishop von Schéele, now on his third visit to Swedish America, as well as Henrik Schück, professor of literature and *rector magnificus* of Uppsala University. Greetings were conveyed from various quarters in Swedish society, including religious, governmental, and educational institutions, as well as from individuals such as Lagerlöf and Noreen.[89] Both von Schéele and Schück spoke in very positive terms of the Augustana Synod and of the college and seminary, Schück calling the college "that place where Sweden and America join together, Augustana Conciliatrix, a patriotic institution of higher learning of both the homelands of the Swedish Americans: that large, new, and energetic country which has become his, and that old home where his forefathers rest, but over which the sun of memories always will shine."[90]

Finally, a definite shift in attitude from the Church of Sweden toward the Augustana Synod can also be noted at this time. In 1912, a brochure was published by the Reverend Per Pehrsson from Göteborg called *Råd och anvisningar till utvandrare* (Advice and Instructions to Emigrants).[91] Prospective emigrants were here actively encouraged to seek out and join an Augustana congregation upon arrival in America, and the brochure included a listing of addresses to Augustana churches throughout America.

The Augustana Synod was by far the single largest Swedish-American organization in the United States. Organized in 1860 in the Midwest, the synod was by the turn of the century made up of individual congregations that spanned the entire North American continent. In addition, a number of other institutions were connected with Augustana, such as schools, benevolent organizations, and a publishing house. Throughout the period of my investigation, the Augustana Synod seems to have attracted at least 20 percent of the entire Swedish-American population and at least half of those Swedish Americans who were a part of the Swedish-American ethnic institutions. The synod played a major part in building the institutional completeness of the Swedish-American community through its varied and extensive activities. There were other Swedish-American organizations as well, meaning that a number of Swedish-American ethnic institutions existed that both competed with and complemented each other, but the Augustana Synod was the most developed of these organizations and became the dominant ethnic institution in Swedish America.

During the years prior to World War I, when the Swedish-American community in different respects stood at its apex, the Augustana sphere was well developed with established institutions and a substantial population. However, it was also unquestionably rooted in the early phase of the Swedish immigration to America, and the institution remained shaped by this heritage, geographically, generationally, and socially.[92] This "traditional" character of the synod is not least illustrated by the fact that Augustana seems to have had difficulties attracting the large number of Swedish immigrants who landed in the United States after the turn of the century and who clearly had a greater urban-industrial background than had their compatriots of the previous decades.[93] It is against the background of this nature and character of the Augustana Synod that the analysis of the ethnic consciousness that developed within the synod has to be made.

The years around the turn of the century seem to have been of great importance for the synod, with a number of changes. The new constitution of 1894 curbed the earlier decentralizing tendencies, giving more authority to the synod's central leadership. Moreover, because the synod had difficulty in attracting recent Swedish immigrants as members, it was thus becoming dominated by American-born Swedish Americans. By this time, there was also a change in the relationship between Sweden and the Augustana Synod, beginning with Bishop von Schéele's visit to Rock Island in 1891, and in many ways both the synod and the college received almost an official sanction from Sweden as the Swedish cultural and religious outpost in America. The history of the Augustana Synod between 1860 and 1917 can thus be divided into two phases, the first extending from 1860 to around 1890 and the second from around 1890 to 1917. Further support for this periodization will be given in the following chapters.

An "Augustana sphere" thus existed within Swedish America, in which a particular form of a Swedish-American identity was created. Other versions of a Swedish-American identity emerged within other sections of the diverse Swedish-American community, which at times was quite intense. It is, however, clear that the Augustana Synod represented the leading cultural force in the community, and, as we will see in the following chapters, in its struggle for cultural hegemony in Swedish America, the synod sought to establish its version of a Swedish-American identity as the predominant one.

The Lutheran Augustana Book Concern in Rock Island, Illinois, ca. 1900.
Courtesy of Swenson Center, Augustana College, Rock Island, Illinois.

Gustav Andreen (1864–1940), fourth president of Augustana College and Theological Seminary, ca. 1910. Note the combination of the Swedish, American, and religious symbols—the Swedish Vasa Order, the American academic cap and gown, and the clerical collar. Courtesy of Special Collections, Augustana College, Rock Island, Illinois.

Johan Alfred Enander (1842–1910), a leading Swedish-American writer, newspaper editor, and public opinion maker. Frontispiece in *Valda Skrifter* (1892) by Joh. A. Enander.

The graduating college class at Augustana College, 1910. Courtesy of Special Collections, Augustana College, Rock Island, Illinois.

Participants in the 1910 fiftieth anniversary celebrations in Rock Island, including Bishop von Schéele from Sweden (#1), Governor Eberhart from Minnesota (#2), and Eric Norelius (#3), president of the Augustana Synod. Courtesy of Special Collections, Augustana College, Rock Island, Illinois.

Jonas Olof Grafström (Swedish American 1855–1933); *Augustana College and the Mississippi River*; 1899; oil on canvas; 92.1 x 137.2 cm.; 36¼ x 54. The painting depicts the campus when the college had been located in Rock Island for almost twenty-five years. Courtesy of the Augustana College Art Museum. Gift of Edward, Helen and Mia Thorson, 1950, Augustana College Art Collection, reproduced from the book *Härute—Out Here: Swedish Immigrant Artists in Midwest America*, edited by Mary Em Kirn and Sherry Case Maurer (Rock Island, 1984).

Student performance of *Fritiofs Saga* at Augustana College, 1905.
Courtesy of Special Collections, Augustana College, Rock Island, Illinois.

Swedish Ladies Chorus, Augustana College, 1898.
Courtesy of Special Collections, Augustana College, Rock Island, Illinois.

3

Schooling the Swedish Americans: Education in the Augustana Synod

Education was of great importance to many immigrant groups in the United States. Although many immigrants embraced the American system of public education, there were notable exceptions, with some that sought to provide their own educational opportunities for their children. As M. Mark Stolarik has underscored, education in the United States has never been uniform in its practice, and "private, parochial, and public schools have existed side-by-side since the early nineteenth century and have all vied for support from different constituencies."[1] Even so, the majority of the scholarly work in American educational history has focused on public education, and relatively little attention has been devoted to schools that provided an alternative to American public education.[2]

The immigrants' need to maintain and affirm religious traditions was one of the most important reasons for the creation of private schools, as the separation between state and church excluded religious instruction from the curricula of American public schools. This was particularly true for Catholic immigrant groups; thus a system of Catholic elementary, secondary, and postsecondary education was established in the United States. Similar tendencies can also be found among Lutheran groups, in particular among German Lutherans, as well as among Swedes, Norwegians, and Danes. Separate schools also existed among different Orthodox groups and the Jews.[3]

Another reason identified by several scholars for the ethnic schools was the maintenance of ethnic traditions in the new land. Often, these ethnic traditions were linked to a religious heritage, but preserving the language and more general ancestral patterns was also important to ethnic educators.[4] In some cases, these schools became important foci for attempts to provide answers to the question of how the immigrants and their children could best combine their ethnic backgrounds with the demands of the new land, as we have seen in the case of the education of Charley Washington in the student play referred to in chapter 1. Educational historian Timothy Smith has pointed to the role these schools played in the search for a definition of "national identity" that was able to combine "a sense of duty to their homeland . . . and still not contradict their new allegiance to America."[5]

This chapter focuses on the role of Augustana College—the leading school in the Augustana Synod—in creating a Swedish-American identity. The major issues that will be addressed include how the college and its curriculum developed from 1860 and what its role was in the creation of a Swedish-American identity. The first part of the chapter will trace the institutional developments at Augustana College. Following this brief history, we will look at the general educational development at the college by examining how the curriculum at Augustana developed and what was taught at the school. Furthermore, the question of how the Augustana Synod viewed education will be addressed. What was the purpose of the school? To what extent was it influenced by Swedish and American educational ideas? Given the fact that the school was operated by a denomination, the role of religion will also be examined. To what degree did religion shape the Augustana curriculum? Finally, the role of the subject of Swedish in the Augustana curriculum will be analyzed.

EDUCATION IN THE AUGUSTANA SYNOD

Fourteen colleges and academies were established in the Augustana Synod.[6] The first was Augustana College and Theological Seminary, created simultaneously with the synod in 1860, followed by Gustavus Adolphus College in Minnesota, which can trace its history to 1862. These two schools remained alone on the scene for about two decades; then, beginning in the 1880s, a period of what one historian of Swedish America has called "college mania" set in.[7] During the two following decades, no fewer than seven academies or colleges were started. What became Bethany College in Lindsborg, Kansas, Luther College in Wahoo, Nebraska, and Upsala College, eventually located in East Orange, New Jersey, all survived well into the twentieth century. (In 1962, Luther College merged with Midland Lutheran College in Fremont, Nebraska, and Upsala College closed its doors in 1995.) Other schools fared less well. Lund Academy in Melby, Minnesota, and Martin Luther College in Chicago lasted only two to three years, whereas the two Minnesota academies, Hope in Moorhead and Emanuel in Minneapolis, were in operation for half a decade. During the first decade of the twentieth century, five more schools connected with the Augustana Synod were started, three in Minnesota, one in Texas, and one in Idaho. But by the mid-1930s, all of these had closed. Of the total of fourteen schools supported by the Augustana Synod, only five lasted beyond the Depression.

Of all these schools, only four—Augustana, Gustavus Adolphus, Bethany, and Upsala—developed into full four-year colleges, granting baccalaureate degrees. The others were academies granting secondary school degrees, mainly serving as feeder schools to the four colleges or to non–Swedish-American institutions of higher learning. In 1910, it was estimated that over 22,000 persons had matriculated in an Augustana Synod school and that over 5,000 had been graduated from one of them, with three dominating: Augustana, Gustavus Adolphus, and Bethany. However, one must remember that these figures include all divisions of the schools, including both the more strictly academic programs as well as the very popular commercial departments teaching stenography and other secretarial skills primarily to students in the immediate vicinity of the colleges. For example, in 1910, official statistics listed more than 5,000 students as having been enrolled in the collegiate departments in the three largest colleges, whereas only 900 students were noted as having a collegiate degree.[8] These figures should be used with care, as they were sometimes exaggerated.

In addition to the academies and colleges, attempts were made to create a system of parochial schools that would supplement the subjects taught in the elementary public schools with instruction in Swedish and religion.[9] Still, a full Swedish Lutheran parochial school system never really developed, and by and large Augustana Swedes were supporters of the American public school system. As early as 1873, the Augustana Synod approved of sending students to the public schools, as long as they were characterized by "Christian morality" and proper instruction in Christianity was given either in the homes or through the church.[10] This meant that after 1890 or so, a system of so-called Swede Schools emerged, which were conducted for several weeks in the summers by individual congregations and in which students from the Augustana seminary or one of the colleges would teach religion and Swedish language and literature. The enrollment figures for these schools ranged from 12,000 in 1889 to 22,000 in 1903 but was down to

10,000 in 1918.[11] It is interesting to note that even when attempts were made in the late 1880s to restrict the foreign language schools in several states in the Midwest,[12] the synod still expressed support of the public schools, though it vigorously argued that the U.S. Constitution did not ban religious instruction in private schools.[13]

Thus in the Augustana Synod, most of the efforts were directed toward the establishment of institutions of higher learning, such as colleges, academies, and seminaries, although some not very successful attempts were made to create a Lutheran parochial school system. Obviously the religious element played an important role in these schools—indeed the training of ministers was one of the main reasons behind the establishment of what became Augustana College and Theological Seminary. A system of academies and colleges developed soon, however, that not only prepared the prospective seminarians for their theological studies but also, especially after the turn of the century, provided students with a basic academic training that would enable them to pursue other careers.

In addition to providing the theological and general academic training for Swedish Americans, the institutions of higher learning in the Augustana Synod were also important in maintaining what was perceived as a sense of Swedish distinctiveness in America. As we shall see, this dimension was also an important part of the educational program in the Augustana Synod, and chapter 4 will be devoted to an examination of how a sense of Swedish-American ethnic identity emerged at the central institution of higher learning in the Augustana Synod, Augustana College.

AUGUSTANA COLLEGE AND THEOLOGICAL SEMINARY

When the Augustana Synod was formed in 1860, one of the first items on the agenda in the newly founded denomination was establishing its own educational institution to train ministers and teachers. During their affiliation with the Synod of Northern Illinois, the Swedish Lutheran immigrants had attended that synod's school, Illinois State University in Springfield, where Lars Paul Esbjörn had served as professor for a group of both Swedish and Norwegian students. Following the break with the Synod of Northern Illinois and the establishment of the Augustana Synod, a new solution to the synod's educational needs had to be found, and thus "the Augustana Seminary," as it was originally known, was established, consisting of a theological and preparatory department.[14]

The new school struggled during its first years.[15] The initial location was the basement of the Immanuel Lutheran Church on Chicago's Near North Side, a setting that was considered temporary from the beginning. Following a search for a more suitable site, synod and college officials accepted an offer for land by the Illinois Central Railroad, and in 1863 the school was relocated to Paxton, Illinois, a small rural community a hundred miles south of Chicago.

The location in Paxton never proved a success, primarily because it was too far away from the streams of Swedish immigrants in the 1860s and 1870s, who tended to settle farther west in Illinois and Iowa and farther north in Minnesota. Thus, a search for a new location was conducted, and eventually the school bought a plot of land in Rock Island in western Illinois, close to such early Swedish settlements as Andover, Moline, and Galesburg, all dating back to the 1840s and 1850s. On September 22, 1875, the school opened its doors in Rock Island, which has been the permanent location for the institution ever since.

Following the move to Rock Island in 1875, the college grew. In 1877, the first collegiate class was graduated, and during the next decade, the curriculum for students in the college included a growing number of courses in the humanities and the natural sciences. The completion of a new main building in 1889—then known as Memorial Hall, now as Old Main—and of Denkmann Hall in 1911 symbolized the physical growth of an expanding institution.

Student enrollments stood between 15 and 20 during the pioneer years in Chicago and between 50 and 70 in Paxton. Following the move to Rock Island, growth quickened; in 1880, there were 136 students at the institution, and in 1890, 286. In 1900, the figure stood at 602; ten years later, somewhat lower at 555; and in 1920, at 944.[16]

The institution was incorporated in the State of Illinois in 1863, from that time consisting of a college and seminary.[17] In 1870, a new constitution was adopted for the school.[18] It now became formally known as "Augustana College and Theological Seminary," and its constitution identified three departments: preparatory, collegiate, and theological.[19] The preparatory department—or the academy, as it was called after 1898—was to be of "a practical nature," preparing students for "various branches of business" as well as for collegiate study; in the 1883–84 catalog, it was described as "corresponding to a common American academy or high school."[20]

Schooling the Swedish Americans

The collegiate department was organized into four classes, "corresponding to four years and similar to the course of the American Colleges generally," which led to the degree of bachelor of arts. The theological department's goal was to prepare students for the ministry in the Augustana Synod, initially requiring two years of study; over the years, the requirement was expanded to three.[21]

These three units made up the institution until the late 1880s, when a number of other programs were added to the curriculum, often in the form of separate "schools." In 1887, the school's board of directors reported to the synod that courses in music and bookkeeping had been introduced at Augustana, as a need for them existed, and the synod decided that a "conservatory of music" and a "commercial department" should be started.[22] The conservatory and the commercial departments got underway in 1888,[23] and especially the latter attracted numerous students, many from the local area and of non-Swedish background. A normal department was also started in 1891, which trained teachers for parochial and public schools.[24] A school of art was established in 1895,[25] which eventually became an art department within the college. Some of these programs became quite successful in terms of enrollments. In 1910, 688 persons had graduated from the Augustana commercial department compared to 468 from the college itself. The situation was similar at Gustavus Adolphus College and Bethany College.[26]

Development of the Curriculum

What kinds of courses were offered at the school, and how did various tracks of study develop? How strongly influenced was the school by educational traditions in Sweden, and what role did American educational practices play? An examination of the significance of Swedish and of its position in the school's curriculum will also be important, as it will provide a basis for an answer to the question of the role that ethnicity played at the college.

The 1860 constitution stated that the purpose of the institution was to train ministers, especially for the Augustana Synod, and to educate schoolteachers.[27] Article III had established two parts of the school: a preparatory department (which developed into the college) in which languages, history, geography, mathematics, and the natural sciences would be taught, and a theological department, including both theoretical and practical courses. A standard of "[t]hree or more professors, of which one should be Swedish, one Norwegian, and one English"[28] was also established, suggesting that different subjects were taught in different languages and that one teacher had to teach in more than one field.

The instruction during the early years included languages (the Scandinavian languages, English, German, Latin, and some Greek and Hebrew), history, geography, mathematics, and natural sciences but seems to have varied somewhat.[29] In 1863, chemistry and physics were mentioned as new additions.[30] In 1865, President Hasselquist reported that fifteen students were enrolled, studying Latin, Greek, English, German, Swedish, world history, geography, philosophy, arithmetic, and algebra, as well as a number of theological subjects. The medium of instruction was one of the Scandinavian languages in seven of these subjects and English in six.[31]

As noted above, the new constitution from 1870 established a more coherent structure for the institution with the three distinct elements: the preparatory department, the college, and the seminary. Except for a general course in Christianity required of all students, the theological education offered at Augustana was concentrated at the seminary, while the general, more advanced academic schooling was located in the college. The following analysis of the academic developments at Augustana and the role Swedish played will thus concern the college.

From an examination of the curricular developments in the college, one notices that, from the very beginning, a distinction was made between two tracks of study, the classical and the scientific. The 1875–76 catalog from the school's first year in Rock Island speaks of the classical course as the most extensive one, with special emphasis on Greek and Latin. However, the catalog noted that the scientific course *(realvetenskapliga kursen)* had recently been growing in strength and was placing special emphasis on mathematics and the natural sciences. The former course was said to be of special importance to ministers and scholars with a need for classical training, while the latter was suited for persons seeking positions in public life, the law, the military, and industry.[32]

This duality in the curriculum can be followed over the years. The 1883–84 catalog noted two courses of study, a classical and a scientific, leading to bachelor of arts and bachelor of science degrees. In both courses, all students studied Christianity, languages (Swedish, English, German, Latin), history, mathematics, natural sciences, and philosophy. The classical track added Greek and more Latin, whereas the scientific track included more mathematics and natural sciences.[33] The following year, the catalog also noted that it was possible to graduate from the classical course without studying Swedish and that this arrangement would be made more permanent in the coming years.[34]

At the synod meeting in 1889, the faculty of the college and seminary reported to the synod that these changes had been achieved as there were now three tracks of study in the college: a classical course including Swedish, a classical course without Swedish, and a scientific course with both Swedish and English,[35] a system first mentioned in the college catalog in 1890–91. Most of the courses in the three tracks were similar, including a number of core subjects such as languages, Christianity, and scientific subjects that were required in all three tracks. In the English classical track, Swedish was substituted for more scientific subjects such as physiology, and more mathematics was included than in the Swedish-classical track. The scientific track included even more scientific subjects, such as chemistry and botany, omitting some Greek and Latin.[36]

The curricular discussions continued, resulting in the continuance of two basic tracks of study in 1895, one classical and one scientific, with the choice between Swedish and English in each. Both tracks included subjects such as Christianity, languages, philosophy, history, political economy, mathematics, and physics. The classical tracks put greater emphasis on Latin and Greek, while the scientific track included more mathematics and subjects like natural history, chemistry, botany, and German. In addition, a number of elective subjects were introduced in both tracks, for example, French and more advanced mathematics.[37] In 1900–1901, a further distinction was made, and the catalog mentioned two classical tracks, one scientific and one mathematical-language track, in which Swedish was a required subject of study in one of the classical tracks.[38]

Beginning in 1902–03, the courses of instruction in the college were arranged in several "groups," which were intended to be "equally difficult . . . and designed to promote specialization . . . of the student's own choice." In addition to these groups, students also had a number of elective courses to choose from. In that year, six groups of study were listed: the classical, the modern language, the Latin-scientific, the general science, the pre-medical, and the mathematical.[39] The classical group was subdivided into two, the second one called "the classical group with Swedish."[40]

Although the Augustana curriculum thus became even more diversified, there were still a number of core subjects required of all students, as the school, according to the catalog, insisted "upon certain fundamental disciplines with which it is believed that every educated man of the present day should be familiar."[41] These subjects included Christianity, English, German, history, mathematics, physics, and logic.

This curricular model with groups of subjects, elective courses, and required courses continued at Augustana College throughout the two first decades of the twentieth century. In 1916–17, the number of groups was changed to ten while the Swedish-classical group disappeared from the curriculum.[42]

The Augustana view of education was rooted in the Swedish experience out of which its early leadership came but was obviously also shaped by the new American context in which the school functioned. In Sweden, the church played an important role in all levels of education, and when compulsory elementary education became law in 1842, for example, the educational system was outlined by the state but was by and large controlled and conducted by the church.[43] The connection between church and education was thus a natural one for the school's founders and became an integral part of the lives of the Augustana Synod schools. The American separation between church and state and the subsequent ban of religious instruction in public schools made this connection even more important for the Augustana Swedes.

In assessing the development of the Augustana curriculum, one can distinguish influences from both Swedish and American educational traditions. The Swedish influence seems to have come mainly from the secondary schools, the *läroverk*—the word used when Augustana and other colleges were referred to in Swedish. The significance of the Swedish schools was also noted by O. Fritiof Ander, who wrote that up until 1890, developments at Augustana were more influenced by European practices than by American and that the methods of instruction "were similar to those employed in the Swedish and German *Gymnasia*."[44]

The division of the curriculum in two basic tracks—the classical and scientific—also showed an influence from a Swedish practice. In Sweden, much of the discussion on secondary education during the nineteenth century revolved around the relationship between the "classical" and what was called "practical" subjects, which, for example, included the modern languages and the natural sciences.[45] The changing needs of a society that was undergoing major economic and social transformations also required a different kind of education. Christina Florin and Ulla Johansson have shown how the emphasis in the secondary school education gradually shifted from an older ideal of training civil servants to educating students who would make and execute decisions, where the more "practical" subjects, such as modern languages, natural sciences, and the like, were introduced as complements and alternatives. This development can be traced in several ordinances from 1849, 1856, and 1859. The 1859 ordinance established two tracks of study *(linjer)*, a classical and a scientific (*klassisk* and *real*), terms also used in the Augustana collegiate curriculum.

It is also clear that Augustana was not conceived of as a university in the Swedish sense, although there were hopes that the college would eventually develop into such. It was, for example, possible to receive a master's degree from 1888, but relatively few degrees were ever awarded.[46] At the fiftieth anniversary in 1910, the visiting rector of Uppsala University, Henrik Schück, also expressed his hope that the school would develop into a university, noting that this had not happened yet.[47]

American patterns of higher education can also be discerned. Already in 1870, the new constitution of the school claimed that Augustana College was to be comparable to American colleges in general, the degree granted was an American bachelor of arts, and the American practice of organizing the students into the four classes (freshman, sophomore, junior, and senior) was also adopted. The role the American context played for Augustana is clearly evidenced in the curricular reform of 1902. The division of the curriculum into a classical and scientific track of study was replaced with an elective system, where students could choose between several groups of subjects, an approach that was gaining prominence among American colleges and universities toward the end of the nineteenth century.[48] The college catalog from 1902 also clearly stated that its curriculum was "patterned after the most modern and approved models" and that the institution sought to be "in the very front rank of American institutions of learning."[49]

Role of Religion

As noted in chapter 1, religion was a powerful factor in many nineteenth-century American immigrant communities. This was also the case at Augustana College. One of the main reasons behind the founding of the institution was to educate a clergy for the Augustana Synod. In 1865, Esbjörn reported on the conditions in the Augustana Synod to the ministerium of the archdiocese in Uppsala. He emphasized the necessity for the synod to establish its own educational institution by reminding his listeners of the history of the Swedish congregations in the New Sweden colony from the seventeenth century, "which little by little were absorbed by the Episcopal

Church precisely because they lacked facilities for the training of their own ministers."[50] T. N. Hasselquist, Esbjörn's successor as president of the college and seminary, made a similar point in a letter to Peter Wieselgren in 1867 when he underscored that the synod needed ministers trained in America, not in Sweden, so that they would be familiar with conditions in the New World.[51]

The theological training needed for the ministry in the synod was provided by the Augustana Seminary, where the curriculum during the final decades of the nineteenth century gradually became longer and more comprehensive.[52] By the end of the century, the admission requirements for the seminary had also developed to the point where an adequate academic preparation was obligatory, and this was most often interpreted to mean an undergraduate collegiate training of the nature provided by Augustana College or one of the other collegiate institutions in the synod.[53]

The religious dimension at Augustana was, however, not limited to the seminary. From the very beginning, religion played an important role in the collegiate curriculum as well. The synod minutes from 1872 speak of the need for a Christian education,[54] something that was reiterated throughout the years. In 1891, Edward Nelander, a minister in the synod and president of Bethany College from 1883 to 1889, maintained that the Swedish Americans needed an education rooted in the Lutheran religion and that it was the mission of Augustana College to provide a "true, Christian education."[55] The third constitution of the college and seminary, adopted in 1893 following several years of discussion, stated in its first article that "the object of the institution" was to "impart a general classical and scientific education under Christian influences" as well as to provide theological training for the ministry.[56]

Many other examples of this attitude can be given. During the search for a new president in 1901, an editorial in *Augustana* emphasized that it was necessary to safeguard the "Christian and confessional nature" of the college.[57] In 1903, the synod president spoke of the schools in the Augustana Synod as a place for both learning and promotion of a Christian, Evangelical Lutheran worldview,[58] and in 1914 the synod president identified two dimensions of the work of the denomination's colleges, namely the inculcation of knowledge and the development of a Christian character, maintaining that only a college based on Christian principles would be able to provide both these elements.[59] These sentiments were also echoed in the general description of the institution that appeared in the college catalogs, which in

1902–03 stated that although not "sectarian," the school was still a "denominational institution" open to all "who desire a liberal education based upon the Christian religion and permeated by the Christian spirit."[60] Not even the commercial department was excluded from this, as it was considered to offer "a thorough business training under Christian influences."[61]

These religious considerations at the school established a set of boundaries of behavior in many spheres at the school. For example, activities such as drinking alcohol or dancing were not permitted, and the 1893 constitution stated that students at the institution were not allowed to "visit billiard rooms, dances, theatres, or similar places" to drink or gamble or to organize or belong to "any secret society."[62] These attitudes remained strong well into the twentieth century. In 1911, the synod protested against the "introduction of dancing and theatrical performances" in the public schools, and in the same year and in 1912 *Augustana* warned of the negative influences of dancing and theater. In 1913, the paper maintained that there was no possibility that the church would be able to accept the theater, as the love of the Lord diminished as the interest in theater increased.[63]

Other examples of the religious dimension at the school included the twenty-minute daily religious services at the school's chapel as well as longer Sunday services, both of which all students were expected to attend.[64] The Augustana Foreign Missionary Society, established in 1886 to attract support for the synod's foreign missions,[65] was also an important element of the religious presence on campus, which by the turn of the century counted half the college student body as well many faculty and others in its membership.[66]

From the more strictly educational or curricular view, the religious dimension meant that the study of Christianity was required of students at all levels and in all programs offered at the school in Rock Island and at other Augustana Synod schools as well.[67] As noted above, the study of Christianity was required of all students from 1870, when the institution started distinguishing between the seminary, college, and preparatory departments. Throughout the curricular reforms at Augustana during the following decades, with the introduction of various elective courses, Christianity remained a subject that all students were required to study, regardless of their other curricular choices.

While an Augustana education certainly emphasized the religious dimension, the schools founded by the synod were not merely preacher schools. Although there was a great need to educate ministers, the schools also sought to provide Swedish Americans with an education for other professions, and from the very beginning, the curriculum included languages, history, geography, mathematics, and the natural sciences, as well as Christianity.[68] As Oscar N. Olson put it in a retrospective article at the seventy-fifth anniversary of the Augustana Synod in 1935, the synod wanted a well-educated ministry.[69]

The most common profession for an Augustana graduate was a ministerial career in the Augustana Synod. However, a growing number also pursued professional careers, especially after the turn of the century and among the American-born generation. Of all students enrolled in the college in the 1880s, for example, some 47 percent were ordained in the Augustana Synod, while only 20 percent of the college attendees between 1910 and 1914 followed the same career pattern. Of those students who completed four years of study and graduated from the college, 54 percent of the graduates in the 1880s went into the ministry, while 36 percent of the seniors from 1910 to 1914 became Augustana ministers.[70]

This fact has also been noted by Walter H. Beck, a historian of Lutheran educational endeavors in America, who wrote in 1939 that the Swedish-American schools were not solely intended for "ministerial preparation" (which was much more the case among, for example, German-American Lutherans), meaning that a denomination like the Augustana Synod provided its members with educational training that prepared them for "secular" careers in American society.[71] One illustration of this attitude comes from the dedication ceremony of the new main building at Augustana College in Rock Island in 1875, when college president Hasselquist stated that "religion and theology must not be isolated from the rest of human knowledge and experience, but must inform and be informed by it, and education must be the hand-maiden of this cross-fertilization."[72]

When Hasselquist's successor as president, Olof Olsson, spoke to the incoming students in 1892, he insisted that it was their mission to "bind together all Swedes in America in a Swedish-American Lutheran church." Olsson asserted that the college played a central role in this process, as it trained ministers but also educated persons for secular life. In this way, a common education on a Christian basis would be provided to all students who then would be able to go out in all walks of life and thus tie together all Swedish Americans.[73] In the same way, *Augustana* argued in favor of keeping the "commercial school" as a part of the college's curriculum. A commercial school, the paper wrote, did not necessarily mean that the synod would engage in adoration of Mammon. Instead, since earthly matters had to be taken care of, it was better if they were done on a Christian foundation and not left to "institutions that are irreligious or hostile to Christianity."[74]

At the installation of Gustav Andreen as president in 1901, M. C. Ranseen made a similar point, referring to Augustana as the most significant Swedish-American college, which initially had been mainly a theological institution. Now, however, the institution prepared students for "many other professions" as well, at the same time realizing that "true education" must rest on a Christian foundation. Ranseen also expressed the hope that the college eventually would develop into a university.[75] Andreen himself echoed these sentiments by saying that demands in recent years for the inclusion of more natural sciences as well as modern languages in the curriculum had been heard and that he saw it as an important task to build a coherent curriculum, incorporating these subjects with the previous emphasis on the humanities.[76]

The teaching of natural sciences was of course a potentially explosive issue for church-related schools. At the Augustana Synod schools, however, this does not seem to have been a major problem. At Augustana College in Rock Island, a strong program in the natural sciences was established by Joshua Lindahl, with a PhD from Lund University, who taught at the school between 1878 and 1881 and who was followed by the geologist J. A. Udden.[77] The significance attached to the natural sciences at Augustana schools was also expressed by President Olsson in 1898 when he talked about the many excellent courses in the natural sciences at the college, which he thought provided students who were not going into the ministry with a more useful preparation than the classic curriculum. "We have enough of . . . literary people, but we often lack practical persons," Olsson concluded.[78] In the 1920s, school officials also supported the Darwinian biology taught at the college that had come under criticism from certain parts of the synod.[79]

It is instructive to compare the view of education in the Augustana Synod with other Swedish-American denominations that had a much more difficult time dealing with the issue of both formal education as well as instruction in nonreligious subjects. Within the Mission Covenant Church, for example, the establishment of schools and the acceptance of formal education did not come as easily as in the Augustana Synod. C. A. Björk, the denomination's president when it was founded in 1885, claimed that practical experience could give as much training and necessary preparation as formal education.[80] In this he was echoing P. P. Waldenström, the leader of Svenska Missionsförbundet, who had scorned university training in his *Brukspatron*

Adamsson (Squire Adamsson), where the fountain of wisdom is an unlearned woman named Mother Simple who counsels the main character to get his schooling not from Theology College, which has enrolled Strong, Cock-Sure and Wise-in-His-Own-Conceits, but from Father Experience in the Misery Class.[81]

This attitude made it much more difficult to gain support for the Covenant North Park College in Chicago, where its president, David Nyvall, struggled to establish not just a preachers' school but "a solid academy and college as the underpinning for the seminary."[82] This fact was also noted in the Augustana Synod seventy-fifth anniversary publication from 1935, which stated that the leadership in the Augustana Synod did not see "culture and learning as hindrances to spirituality, which was the case in some other religions."[83]

Position of Swedish in the Curriculum

During the first several decades of Augustana's history, learning English and becoming American were strongly emphasized. The early leadership in the synod and at the school believed that the Swedish language would disappear within a few decades and that the synod needed to be ready for the day when English would be the dominant language.[84] When Esbjörn organized his first Sunday schools in Andover, Illinois, he used English as the language of instruction for the younger children, and in his report to the American Home Missionary Society of 1852, he stated his intention to start preaching in English to make his countrymen "more acquainted with the English language."[85] Eric Norelius, one of the most influential Augustana leaders, wrote in 1860 that "[w]e are not and will never be shut up within our own nationality" and that we "become more and more Americanized every day."[86] Years later, Erland Carlsson also told Gustav Andreen that he believed "that the Swedish language would be dead in America in twenty years, and therefore I prepared myself for the change and studied the English language."[87]

When the original constitution for the Augustana seminary was drawn up in 1860, one of the three professorships was designated to be filled by an English-speaker. However, it proved difficult to find teachers for the institution in general, and in his annual reports to the synod, President Hasselquist at times mentioned the fact that English-speaking teachers were needed if the school was to become successful.[88] This attitude was also reflected in the curricular developments that made Swedish an elective subject by the mid-1880s.

In 1867, the synod minutes also spoke of the institution as a school in which Swedish immigrants would be shaped by their own religious confession and where they could get the necessary education in the English language. The following year, the synod declared that no student should be allowed to leave the school without sufficient knowledge of English or Swedish.[89]

In his study of Hasselquist, the dominant figure in the synod and president at Augustana College and Theological Seminary from 1863 until his death in 1891, Ander also notes the tendency to emphasize English. He writes that Hasselquist "became a 'good' American in nearly every respect" and was an advocate for "Americanization"—even calling opposition to it "sinful." In Hasselquist's view, it was inevitable that the Swedish language in America would disappear, and Ander concludes that he sought to prepare the synod, "through its educational institution, for the day when the Swedish language no longer could be used."[90]

These attitudes were also reflected in the role of Swedish in the Augustana curriculum. Although Swedish was used as a language of instruction during the early years, the college catalogs show that beginning in the 1880s, the number of hours and subjects taught in Swedish declined. In 1884–85, almost half of the hours in the classical track were taught in Swedish, whereas the share in the scientific track was about a third.[91] The language was primarily used in Christianity classes, as well as in the Swedish, German, Latin, and Greek courses. One example of the cause of its decline was the September 1884 recommendation by the professor of Greek that English be used as the means of instruction in Greek throughout the four years of collegiate study.[92]

During the following years, the college catalogs give little specific information about the number of hours taught in the different languages. Still, the selection of textbooks for different subjects suggests that English was becoming the dominant language. Aside from the subject of Swedish, Swedish-language textbooks were partly used in Greek, Latin, and Christianity throughout the 1880s,[93] but by 1893–94, Swedish-language books were used only in Christianity and Swedish.[94] After the turn of the century, the use of Swedish disappeared in the Christianity courses as well. In 1902–03, one of the three college-level courses in Christianity was taught in Swedish; three years later, the catalog stated that the course was "at present" given in Swedish; and by 1908–09, no mention was made of any Swedish-language requirements in Christianity.[95]

As Swedish declined as the language of instruction in the college, the different curricular reforms also meant that its relative position in the curriculum receded. As shown above, from the mid-1880s it became possible to graduate from Augustana without having studied Swedish, when the classical track without Swedish was introduced. As the curriculum became even more diversified, this deemphasis continued. It seems likely that part of the reason for establishing non-Swedish courses of study, at least in the 1880s, had to do with an increasing interest from students of non-Swedish background from the local area to study at Augustana.

The college made efforts to accommodate those students who did not wish to study Swedish. The non-Swedish track was announced in 1884–85 and made even more permanent in 1890–91. After 1895, the college catalogs did not include any information on the track of study of individual students. The general tendency in the college toward a predominance of American-born students of both Swedish and non-Swedish background during the decade before the turn of the century suggests that after 1900, the possibility of graduating without Swedish was not only due to the enrollment of "American" students but also a reflection of the fact that many American-born students of Swedish parentage who did not speak or wish to learn Swedish may have attended the school.

This seeming deemphasis on Swedish at Augustana did not go unnoticed in Swedish America. Concerns were voiced that the disappearance of Swedish was changing the nature of the school. During the early spring of 1890, a discussion took place in the pages of *Hemlandet* regarding the position of Swedish at Augustana College. A writer using the pseudonym "Skolvän" (A Friend of the School) noted that the number of hours taught in Swedish was declining and suggested that this might constitute a threat to "Swedish-American education" *(svensk-amerikansk bildning)*,[96] whereas "En läroverkets vän" (A Friend of the College) wrote that recent curricular changes might lead to the suspicion that the school was changing to "a solely English institution of education . . . without interest for the real needs and national feelings of our people."[97] *Hemlandet* commented that the Swedish-American colleges should pay equally large attention to teaching both English and Swedish, and a knowledge of the latter was particularly important for those students who would work "among and for the Swedish-American nationality."[98]

At the synod meeting in 1890, the president of the board of directors commented on this discussion, suggesting that it was rooted in misconceptions in newspapers about the situation of Swedish at the school and the question of plans to move the college to Chicago. Now that these misunderstandings had been cleared up, it should be possible for the entire synod to financially support the college and seminary even more.[99]

The role of Swedish was discussed again in 1892, when *Augustana* noted that some critics maintained that English played too large a role at Augustana, that Swedish was left behind, and that the college "will become solely an English institution of learning." The paper took issue with this opinion, responding that even though all instruction, except in the Swedish language and literature, was conducted in English, Swedish still remained a popular subject in the college, and anyone who attended one of the Swedish classes would understand that at Augustana it was "of the greatest importance" to educate persons who "in writing and speaking are able to use the English and Swedish languages fluently."[100]

Another sign of the decreasing use of Swedish among at least parts of the Augustana student body was the decision to conduct the daily morning prayers at the college in English. In its decision from December 1898, the board of directors based its reasoning on the fact that the school "has a large number of students who understand only the English language," so the prayers at the required morning devotions should be conducted in English.[101]

This decision also generated discussion. According to George Stephenson, the 1899 synod convention approved it after "a lengthy discussion," which included critical voices.[102] In the monthly journal *Ungdomsvännen*, which had recently been started by a group of Augustana pastors in Minnesota, pastor C. A. Hultkrans commented that not much could be done about the matter but that the goal of making Augustana "American" as fast as possible had been reached, something that he deplored.[103] In an article in December 1899, President Olsson responded to these critics who, he stated, "had caused the present administration of the college such bitter sorrow, through the harsh attacks of some of our papers." In the article, Olsson asked, "How did it go with morning prayers at Augustana College and Theological Seminary?" and answered, "It went well, very well," continuing that "[f]aculty and students to a man" had been in attendance at the devotions. To Olsson, the prime concern was not the language issue, as it "was already settled." Instead, it was of the highest importance that the "love of our people to our common school" be maintained, which he hoped would not be "quenched" by what he termed "the Swedish-enthusiasts."[104]

There is also evidence from the decade after the turn of the century that some students at the college had difficulty understanding Swedish. In the fall of 1908, Marcus Skarstedt reported in his diary that, at a meeting celebrating the centennial of Esbjörn's birth, seminary professor C. E. Lindberg introduced the speaker Eric Norelius, saying that as Norelius would be speaking in Swedish, "some of you may not be able to understand him."[105] Skarstedt also noted that the classes on the subject of the Swedish language were "rather difficult" for most students, which resulted in many humorous linguistic mistakes in the classroom.[106]

It is thus possible to see the developments sketched above as a process through which the position of Swedish and the school's "Swedishness" gradually declined at Augustana College from the 1880s on, a development that would be in line with the sentiments of early leaders such as Norelius and Hasselquist quoted earlier. The historian of Augustana College, Conrad Bergendoff, has also noted that "[t]hese were the years of transition" and that "English was replacing Swedish."[107]

Certainly, the nature of the institution was changing. More and more American-born students enrolled and the curriculum became more diversified, gradually leaving the model of the Swedish *läroverk* behind and approaching that of an American college. In addition to the developments in the college noted above, other educational needs were also met, as special units for music, commerce, and art were established. In his annual report to the synod in 1896, President Olsson also noted the changing times, observing that "our times of Americanization, which is now over us in full force, bring certain difficulties in our school life," something he thought should be kept in mind by "our mild and harsh friends."[108]

Still, although the language may not have been spoken on a daily basis as much as before and it was no longer a compulsory subject of study, an examination of the enrollment figures in the Swedish courses suggests that, at least during the years before and after 1900, the subject held its own, attracting large numbers of students.

The Swedish language's continued importance at Augustana can be seen in the number of students who studied Swedish voluntarily. Between 1888–89 and 1894–95, the college catalogs noted the track of study in which individual students were enrolled. During these years, a relatively small part of the Augustana student body chose a track of study without Swedish.[109] During the 1888–89 and 1989–90 school years, under the new curriculum, only two students enrolled in the English-classical track. In the 1890–91 academic year, three students were noted in the English-classical track, whereas the figure for the two Swedish tracks was forty-eight. This relationship remained stable for the next several years: in 1892–93 there were eight students in the track without Swedish and sixty-nine in the two others; in 1893–94 the ratio was thirteen to seventy-seven; and in 1894–95, the final year with statistics of this nature, it stood at nine to seventy-five students.[110] Thus, no more than 15 percent (and often fewer) of the students noted in the catalogs during the early 1890s were enrolled in a non-Swedish track.

Although information is lacking for the following years, it seems plausible to assume that the low interest in the track without Swedish continued during the next several years. No freshmen were enrolled in the English-classical track in 1894–95.[111] Moreover, the figures for the enrollment in the English-classical track in the preparatory department in 1894–95 were also low, with only one in each of the three classes. Although the Augustana freshmen were not exclusively recruited from the preparatory department, many were—from the third class in 1894–95, nineteen of the forty-one students became Augustana freshmen the following year. The low figures for the English-classical track in both the freshman class and the preparatory department in 1894–95 suggest a limited recruitment pool for and interest in the non-Swedish tracks in the college during the years after 1895–96. Thus, although the possibility of graduating from Augustana without studying Swedish existed, a fairly small portion of the student body availed itself of the opportunity in the 1890s. Looked at from this perspective, the creation of the non-Swedish track of study in the college should not necessarily be interpreted as a sign of erosion for Swedish at Augustana.

Instead, although the emphasis on English among the Augustana leadership from the college's first decades did mean that English would eventually become the dominant language at Augustana, both in the curriculum and most likely also in the everyday life of the institution, the interest in Swedish at Augustana did not disappear. There is some evidence of interest in Swedish at the college in the 1870s. Looking back at his student years at Augustana, 1873–76, Carl A. Swensson recalled an upsurge of interest in things Swedish. Swensson and his fellow students spoke and wrote Swedish, sang Swedish songs, and were, in the author's words, "consumed, almost beyond measure, by our Swedish patriotism."[112]

If Swensson found an interest in "Swedish patriotism" at Augustana in the 1870s, the evidence suggests that this attitude was even more prevalent during the decades around the turn of the century. With regard to the interest in studying Swedish, in January 1902 *Augustana* reported that the interest in Swedish courses was increasing at the college and that in those tracks of study in which Swedish was an elective subject in the college and academy, 60 percent of the students had chosen Swedish.[113] Later the same year, the newspaper noted that close to 100 students were enrolled in the Swedish language courses and commented that "the Swedish language lives a healthy life" in Rock Island.[114] The following year, *Augustana* wrote that the college classes in Swedish were even larger than in the previous year, something that was credited to the skills of the teachers.[115]

According to an article in *Augustana* from 1905, the Swedish language had a "peculiar situation" at Augustana. To most students it was a foreign language, rarely used in conversations outside the classroom. Still, students were expected to be able to use the language with the same ability with which they spoke their native language, English, after a few years at the school. Swedish was thus a very important subject and was to be practiced as much as possible, even outside the classroom. The author also encouraged Augustana students to join one of the several organizations that promoted the study of Swedish on campus.[116]

After the curriculum reform in 1902–03 establishing the six main groups of subjects, the significance of Swedish in the curriculum was underscored, as the classical group included a separate Swedish-classical track until 1916–17. Moreover, in Andreen's second report to the synod as college president in 1903 in which he detailed the organization of the new curriculum, he added that "it is also our serious desire and goal that each student of Swedish background thoroughly shall study the language of his ancestors."[117]

The commitment to the study of Swedish was also reflected in every college catalog from 1902 through 1930–31, in which a separate statement about the role of Swedish in the curriculum was included. All students "of Swedish parentage" were urged to "devote as much time as possible to the study of the beautiful language of their forefathers," not only for "sentimental" reasons but also, the catalog claimed, since the "practical advantages of such study to the minister, the teacher, the physician, the lawyer, the business man, the cultured man in any walk of life, are too obvious to require special mention."[118]

Moreover, Augustana's role in the development of a specific Swedish-American identity was also emphasized at the school. In 1891, one of the topics for the final examination in the Swedish language was "Swedish Americanism as a factor in our country's cultural development," and from 1903–04 until 1929–30, the Augustana College catalogs also described one of the purposes and "future missions" of the school to be an "exponent of

Swedish-American culture."[119] Similar ideas were also expressed by President Andreen in a speech in Stockholm in March 1903 on Swedish America and its cultural work, raising the question of whether something called a "Swedish-American culture" existed. Andreen answered in the affirmative, claiming that it was indeed possible to be a Swede and an American at the same time, something one did not need to be ashamed of in either country.[120] This notion seems to have been fully developed by the fiftieth anniversary in 1910, when one of the official addresses discussed how the Swedish immigrants in the United States had "coalesced into a Swedish-American people," the identity of which had been maintained by the Augustana Synod through its educational and cultural endeavors.[121]

The special position of Swedish in the Augustana curriculum was also articulated in several ways during the years around the turn of the century. In March 1891, Lindberg, who had just assumed his duties as professor in the seminary that academic year,[122] wrote in *Augustana* that all who loved the "Swedish name, Nordic literature and our Lutheran faith" must also love Augustana. He saw the purpose of the school as a Lutheran alternative to many of the negative and secularizing influences of American society in general but also underscored that it provided its students with a general education and "useful knowledge of English and Swedish." Were it not for the training offered by college and the seminary, Lindberg argued, the Swedish language would no longer be alive in America, and the influence of the "Swedish nation" in the United States would be far less than it is now.[123]

Similar sentiments were echoed in conjunction with the 1901 visit to Rock Island by Bishop von Schéele, who, as noted in chapter 2, was the first Swedish bishop to visit the Augustana Synod in 1893 and who returned several more times. In discussing the bishop's visit, *Augustana* commented on the contemporary state of the college's Swedishness. The paper noted that the founders of the synod had sought to abandon their Swedishness, promoting a rapid Americanization. This had not occurred, however, and at the time "the Swedishness among the Swedish Americans is stronger and its value more widely recognized than ever before." The Augustana Swedish Americans had learned, the paper observed, to combine Swedish culture with an American education and that "it is not impossible to be both a Swede and an American at the same time."[124] During the same visit, Augustana geology professor Udden addressed the audience on the topic of Augustana College as "the center for Swedish-American culture."[125] The same year, a report in *Augustana* noted that the seniors in the college had sent for Swedish student caps *(studentmössor)*, which they and the seminary students had begun to wear. In this respect, "things look very Swedish at Augustana College," the paper commented.[126]

Augustana's role in the preservation of Swedishness in America was also noted and appreciated by persons outside the synod. In 1898, liberal journalist C. F. Peterson published *Sverige i Amerika* (Sweden in America), which in the words of Arnold Barton was "the most objective and penetrating discussion of the Swedish Americans offered by one of their number during the crucial decade of the 1890s."[127] In it Peterson argued that to date, the Augustana Synod had been of crucial importance for the maintenance of a Swedish identity in America. "Without this ark," he wrote, "our nationality would soon have lost its distinct Swedish characteristic in the cosmopolitan whirl."[128]

An example of the combination of the Christian dimension with an emphasis on Swedishness comes from 1903. Alfred Bergin, author and longtime minister in Lindsborg, Kansas, commented that the Augustana Synod schools did not seek to compete directly with the public schools but instead were "hearths" of Christian education and that it was "Lutheran Christianity and Swedishness that provide the rationale for our schools." The Augustana Synod schools, he continued, "are quite necessary for our own existence as a Swedish people and [for] a Lutheran Augustana Synod."[129] Similarly, a 1906 editorial in *Augustana* spoke of the synod colleges as excellent educational institutions providing the Swedish-American youth with a general American education without forgoing "our Christian belief" and all "the noble and beautiful" things that the Swedish Americans "possessed as an inheritance from old mother Svea."[130]

A further illustration of the discussion of the nature of the institution can be found in the *Augustana Observer,* the English-language student newspaper, which also highlights the combination of ethnicity and religion. In August 1903, the newspaper addressed the question of "what Augustana is" and gave several main characteristics.[131] The articles emphasized that Augustana was a Christian institution, which set it apart from public schools; a denominational school, supported by the Augustana Synod; and of a co-educational nature. More important, the article also called Augustana an "American" school, with English as the language of instruction, preparing students for work in American society. But, Augustana was also a Swedish-American institution, with "one of its main objects to be an exponent of a distinctly Swedish-American culture," an emphasis that accounted for its Swedish curriculum. Similar sentiments were expressed by a newly matriculated student at the college in that same year. K. G. William Dahl, who after graduation became a minister in the Augustana Synod and an author within the Augustana sphere in Swedish America, wrote in a letter back to his parents in Sweden in very positive terms about Augustana College, concluding that "I am happy to be Swedish, but I am happier to be Swedish American, as those people have accomplished marvelous things."[132]

The role of Swedish at Augustana College thus changed during the latter part of the nineteenth century. The early leadership emphasized the need to learn English and to "Americanize." Swedish also declined as a language of instruction, morning prayers began to be held in English, and it became possible to graduate from Augustana without studying Swedish. At least two reasons for this attitude can be given. Although there was a sustained large Swedish immigration to the United States during the first decades of the synod's history, it was, of course, at this early time impossible to predict how large the Swedish-American community would eventually become and thus to what degree it would be realistic to maintain the Swedish language or Swedish cultural traditions in general. Moreover, a sense of cultural nationalism was weakly developed in mid-nineteenth century Sweden. Religion was a more important source of identity, especially to those Swedish immigrants who became members of the Augustana Synod, many of whom, as shown in chapter 2, had their roots in the low-church revival movement and to whom the preservation of a religious identity was more important than the maintaining a sense of Swedish ethnicity. This was also true at Augustana College, where religion played a central role in the curriculum and the college's life in general. As discussed in chapter 2, it was also during the 1860s and 1870s that the religious rift between the Augustana Synod and what became the Mission Covenant Church developed, which further emphasized the synod's religious identity.

However, Swedish was always a part of the Augustana curriculum. The language was taught at the school from its beginning, and although no longer obligatory from the mid-1880s, the Swedish classes still attracted students, and the subject was given a special position in both the curriculum and in official pronouncements by college officials. Beginning around the turn of the century, voices were heard arguing for the importance of maintaining the Swedish language and Swedish cultural traditions in general. In addition to emphasizing Augustana's Christian character, the college's role in maintaining a Swedish heritage was now also frequently mentioned. Often these two elements, the religious and the ethnic, were conflated into one, suggesting that the maintenance of the one depended on the maintenance of the other. Instead of the earlier gloomy predictions of the quick demise in America of the Swedish language and culture, leading Augustana figures now spoke about the possibilities of the Swedish language surviving for decades to come.[133] This renewed emphasis on Swedish took place during a time when a generational shift had begun at the college, so that by the turn of the century the majority of the students were second-generation Swedish Americans, that is, American-born but of Swedish background.

In looking at the role of Swedish at Augustana College during the institution's first half-century, one must distinguish between, on the one hand, what can be called a Swedish tradition at the college—that is, a concern for the contents and meaning of Augustana's Swedishness—and, on the other, the use of the Swedish language as a means of instruction or measured by the number of hours of Swedish required of Augustana students in various tracks of study. The decline in the use of the Swedish language did not mean that the Swedish tradition disappeared at Augustana. On the contrary, especially from the 1890s on, we find the college leadership discussing and attaching significance to Augustana's "Swedishness" *(svenskheten)*, which in many cases transcended the issue of the language per se, and instead the Swedish element at the school was now conceptualized more culturally. As we have seen, this ethnic tradition was also frequently linked to or even a part of the religious dimension of Augustana College.

Moreover, the renewed interest in Swedish expressed around the turn of the century was not limited to the study of Swedish language and culture. Clearly, an awareness had developed of Augustana College as a Swedish-American institution and of the development of a Swedish-American identity, which was seen as different from that in Sweden. The Swedish ethnic tradition at Augustana was thus also becoming a Swedish-American tradition, and one of the missions of Augustana College was, as the college catalogs phrased it, to be "an exponent" of this culture. In the following chapter, the specific nature and contents of this Swedish-American ethnic tradition at Augustana College will be analyzed.

4

A Swedish-American Tradition at Augustana College

The analysis of Augustana's Swedish-American tradition will be based on an examination of the subject of Swedish in the college as well as on the many extracurricular Swedish-related activities at the college. The development of the teaching of the discipline at Augustana will be explored by looking at both the organization and the content of the subject. Who were the teachers? What was taught in the Swedish courses at Augustana? Which authors were studied, and what aspects of the Swedish cultural heritage were presented to the students at Rock Island? Because much of the Swedish-American tradition at Augustana was played out outside of the classroom, we will also examine in some detail the many extracurricular Swedish activities on campus, especially two of the student literary societies. What picture of Sweden and Swedish America was portrayed in them? How did the visitors from Sweden play a role in the college's Swedish-American tradition?

THE TEACHING OF THE SWEDISH LANGUAGE AND LITERATURE

As already mentioned, the Swedish language, literature, and to some degree history were taught at Augustana from the school's very beginning. Due to the scarcity of staff, a few teachers had to do instruction in several subjects at a time during the first several decades. In 1875–76, Pastor C. O. Granere had the main responsibility for teaching Swedish in the college. In addition, he taught several other subjects: Latin and Greek in the college and church history in the seminary. In 1876–77, Granere combined his instruction in Swedish with Latin as well as some Greek. During most of these years, assistant teachers in Swedish were also hired, seemingly on a yearly basis.[1]

In October 1882, the board of directors extended a call to C. M. E. Esbjörn to become professor of Christianity and Swedish in the college, and Esbjörn accepted.[2] The son of Augustana's first president, Esbjörn was a graduate of Augustana's first class in 1877 and had after his graduation prepared himself to return and teach at the college. He belonged to a group of early graduates who, with the assistance of the synod, attended universities in both Sweden and the United States further before joining the faculty.[3]

By the academic year 1883–84, Esbjörn had taken up his position as "professor of Christian Science and of the Swedish language and literature," a post he would hold until 1890. In that year, he announced his resignation because he felt that "several recent actions" at the college had "adversely affected" the position of his two subjects in the curriculum. If the school wished Esbjörn to stay on, it would have to meet a number of his demands, including that the number of hours previously taught in Christianity and Swedish be restored and that Swedish "once again" be made a subject of instruction at all levels in the college and preparatory department. The board of directors did not meet these requests, which led to Esbjörn's resignation.[4] The "recent actions" he referred to were most likely the introduction of the English-classical track of study, which, as mentioned earlier, did not require all Augustana students to study Swedish and which had generated protests from other quarters as well.

Still, the board of directors of the college and seminary showed its continued support for instruction in Swedish, and at the synod meeting in 1890 it was reported that Swedish and Christianity were subjects of "such fundamental importance" that it was necessary to split the previous joint position in the two subjects and create one professorship of Swedish and one of Christianity, a proposal that won the approval of the synod meeting.[5]

The first person to be called as professor of Swedish was J. S. Carlson at Gustavus Adolphus College in Minnesota. When Carlson declined the call, the position was next offered to Johan Enander, who accepted.[6] Enander was one of the leading persons in Swedish America, serving as editor of *Hemlandet* in Chicago and working as a prolific author and public speaker. His ties with the Augustana Synod were also very strong.

Enander's tenure as professor of Swedish lasted until 1893, when he returned to journalism. He does not seem to have fit in the mold of an Augustana professor; in June 1893 the board of directors decided "after a long and thoughtful deliberation" to ask for his resignation due to his "frivolous deportment," including charges of improper behavior with an "American woman" from Moline and "indelicate behavior" toward girls. Enander denied these charges vehemently but left his position in the summer of 1893 for reasons that still seem somewhat unclear.[7] Still, this does not seem to have blackened Enander's name too much in Rock Island, as he was to return to the campus as a speaker on Swedish topics.

Following Enander's resignation, the Reverend Ernst Zetterstrand assumed the professorship in 1895, serving as professor of Swedish until 1901.[8] Zetterstrand seems to have had pedagogical difficulties, and a student from his time noted that he was such a bad teacher that "our class revolted against him."[9] After complaints in 1897[10] and again in 1901, when the senior class "because of a warm zeal for the study of the Swedish language" refused to attend his courses, the Augustana board of directors concluded that it was in the interest of the teaching of Swedish at Augustana that Zetterstrand resign, which he also did at the end of the spring semester in 1901.[11]

Following Zetterstrand's departure, the board considered his replacement. Four candidates were nominated, including S. M. Hill, president of Luther Academy; Professor V. H. Heggström, at the time at Norwegian-American Jewell Lutheran College in Jewell, Iowa, but previously a professor at Upsala College; the Reverend J. G. Dahlberg; and the Reverend Jules Mauritzson. Five rounds of voting were required, but eventually a call went out to Mauritzson, who accepted the position and served as professor of Swedish until his death in 1930.[12]

Born in southern Sweden, Mauritzson graduated from *gymnasium* in Helsingborg in 1886 and during the next three years attended Lund University. He had emigrated in 1896 and served as an Augustana pastor in Iowa before coming to Augustana in 1901.[13] One of the conditions for the job was that Mauritzson had to spend additional time in Scandinavian universities to prepare himself for the position, and he spent the academic year 1902–03 at Uppsala and Christiana (Oslo) universities. At Uppsala he attended lectures and seminars with such leading professors as Adolf Noreen in the Department of Scandinavian Languages and Henrik Schück in the Department of Literature and also had the opportunity to address a gathering of selected Uppsala academics on Augustana College's mission to "be as a bearer of and to promote Swedish culture in America."[14] Mauritzson was also very active in Swedish-American cultural and academic circles. He was one of the founders of and an active member in the American academic organization Society for the Advancement of Scandinavian Studies and served as editor and contributor to several Swedish-language publications published by the Augustana Book Concern.

The way in which Swedish was established in the college clearly shows a concern for the subject, especially after 1890, when a separate Department of Swedish was established. Esbjörn had resigned in protest over what he perceived as a weakening of the subject, and the fact that Enander—at the time, "unquestionably the most influential Swedish-American opinion-maker," according to Barton[15]—was named as the first professor of Swedish is very significant. In many ways Enander was the leading Swedish-American ideologue of the Augustana Synod. The fact that he was called to run the Swedish department at Augustana in 1890 must be interpreted as a way of strengthening the subject; it also lent a great deal of support to Enander's view of what it meant to be Swedish in America. (See chapter 5 for a further discussion of Enander.)

The controversy over Professor Zetterstrand seems to have revolved around issues of personalities. It should, however, be noted that both the synod and the Augustana board of directors considered it important enough to have a well-functioning Swedish department that they studied the matter as closely as they did and eventually, with the interest of Swedish in mind, decided to sever Zetterstrand's connection to the college. A thorough discussion also preceded the choice of Mauritzson as the new professor. The fact that the board demanded that Mauritzson spend additional time in Scandinavian universities to qualify for the position can be seen as a further sign of the significance attached to finding a competent professor of Swedish. Finally, it should be noted that all of the Swedish professors came from within the Augustana Synod itself. Zetterstrand and Mauritzson were ordained ministers in the synod, and Enander was a leading layperson. The selection of individuals associated with the synod ensured that the content given in the Swedish courses at Augustana would remain within the synod's ideological bounds.

CONTENT OF THE SWEDISH COURSES IN THE COLLEGE CURRICULUM

Given the position of Swedish in the curriculum as well as the development of a separate Department of Swedish in the college, the next issue to be looked at deals with what actually was taught in the Swedish courses. What image of Sweden and Swedish cultural traditions was presented to students in the Augustana Swedish courses? An examination of the courses taught dealing with Swedish literature and culture and the textbooks used will shed light on this matter.[16]

In general, a diversification of the Swedish curriculum began toward the end of the nineteenth century, both in terms of topics studied and the textbooks used. The information supplied about the nature of the instruction in the college catalogs, which forms the basis for this analysis, is not uniform, which may account for some unevenness. In the 1880s, the college curriculum included reading and grammatical exercises during the freshman and sophomore years, with the history of Swedish literature studied during the junior and senior years.[17] Swedish literature was studied mainly through several handbooks, and although there is no comprehensive list available for the textbooks used at Augustana, until the mid-1890s a group of three general surveys of Swedish literary history seem to have been commonly used, namely D. A. Sundén and Johan Modin's *Svensk läsebok för elementarläroverken*, Herman Bjursten's *Översikt över svenska språkets och litteraturens historia*, and Claesson's edited version of Bjursten, published as *Svenska språkets och litteraturens historia*.[18] From the mid-1880s, some individual authors and literary works were mentioned in the catalogs. Two leading authors of the romantic movement of the nineteenth century were particularly popular, the Finno-Swede Johan Ludvig Runeberg and Esaias Tegnér. Runeberg's *Fänrik Ståls sägner* and Tegnér's *Fritiofs saga* seem to have been particularly popular texts. These two authors would, as we shall see, remain central in the Augustana Swedish curriculum for several decades.[19] Other individual authors and texts studied in the 1880s included Bernhard Elis Malmström, O. P. Sturzen-Becker (both late-nineteenth-century authors),[20] and the *Edda* from the golden age of medieval Icelandic literature.[21]

In 1891–92, there were some changes in the curriculum, although the basic structure remained, with instruction in reading, writing, and grammatical exercises in the lower classes and Swedish literary history in the higher.[22] In addition to general surveys of Swedish literature and the customary study of Runeberg and Tegnér, a large part of the senior year Swedish curriculum was also devoted to Old Norse literature and culture, including readings of the mythic *Edda* and lectures on *Völuspa*, *Havamal*, and the "civilization of the northmen."

The list of textbooks used in the Swedish curriculum that year reflects this approach, as in 1891–92 it included two volumes of Runeberg's collected works, Tegnér's *Fritiofs saga*, W. E. Lindblad's *Fosterländska minnen*, a Swedish translation of the *Edda,* Snorre Sturlasson's *Konungaboken,* and Viktor Rydberg's *Fädernas gudasagor.*[23] In 1894–95, several individual works by Runeberg and Tegnér were noted, and the list of Swedish textbooks encompassed both the collected works of these two authors as well as Karl Warburg's *Svensk litteraturhistoria* and the previously used reader by Sundén and Modin.[24]

In 1895–96 and 1896–97, the catalogs listed a number of specific courses taught in both the preparatory department and the college. Apart from the linguistic courses, the curriculum offered two survey courses, each covering Swedish literature and history, as well as one course focusing on Old Norse literature. Among individual authors' works, Runeberg's *Fänrik Ståls sägner* and Tegnér's *Fritiofs saga* were again singled out,[25] and in 1898–99 the catalog noted that particular attention was also devoted to Tegnér's poem "Svea."[26]

Through the curricular reform of 1902, the number of courses in the Swedish curriculum increased and included a broader spectrum of authors. The courses in Swedish literary history now encompassed two general survey courses of Swedish literature, one course focusing on the works of Runeberg as well as on nineteenth-century authors Rydberg and C. J. L. Almqvist, and one course called "modern literature" with "the latest of Swedish literature," including works of, among others, August Strindberg, Selma Lagerlöf, Verner von Heidenstam, Gustaf Fröding, Erik Axel Karlfeldt, and Oscar Levertin, all of whom were active during the end of the nineteenth and the beginning of the twentieth centuries. Selected works by Tegnér and the *Edda* were read in a course on composition. The two courses on Swedish history also remained in the curriculum, the first one also covering Swedish geography. In addition, courses in the Norwegian and Danish languages and focusing on selected authors were also introduced.[27] This general pattern remained in force during the following years, with some modifications. In 1905–06, the course on Almqvist, Runeberg, and Rydberg was dropped, but Runeberg was specifically mentioned in other courses.[28]

By 1910–11, the college curriculum included one grammar course; two courses each in Swedish literary and general history; a composition course with readings by Rydberg, Levertin, Lagerlöf, Carl Snoilsky, and Per Hallström; and the modern literature course.[29] In a letter from December 1912, Mauritzson listed the required reading in Swedish that year in both the academy and the college, and the college curriculum included Karl Warburg's *Svensk litteraturhistoria,* Ekerman's *Läsebok till svenska litteraturhistorien,* and Carl Grimberg's *Sveriges historia 1–2.*[30] Warburg's *Litteraturhistoria* seems to have remained in the curriculum and is noted again in 1916–17. In that same school year, the modern literature course was merged with the second survey course. Again, Tegnér and Runeberg were singled out as being especially important from the earlier period; P. D. A. Atterbom, Rydberg, Strindberg, Fröding, Lagerlöf, Heidenstam, and Karlfeldt were selected as representatives of more recent literary developments.[31]

What can be said of the content of the Augustana Swedish courses? First, it should be noted that although a few courses dealt with Swedish history, Swedish literature was central in the teaching of Swedish at Augustana. It was by reading certain authors and their works that Augustana students became familiar with the cultural background of the country from which they or their ancestors had come. Moreover, there are clear parallels between Augustana's Swedish curriculum and that which was taught in contemporary Swedish secondary schools, or *läroverk*. Until the mid-1890s, textbooks by Sundén and Modin, Bjursten, and Claesson were, as shown above, used at Augustana. These books were frequently used in the Swedish *läroverk* during the end of the nineteenth century as well.[32] The introduction of Warburg's *Svensk litteraturhistoria* in the mid-1890s also followed a trend in Sweden, where it started replacing Claesson's *Svenska språkets och litteraturens historia*.[33]

It is also evident that the view of Swedish literature presented to the college students at Augustana echoed to a large extent what was taught in Sweden in the late nineteenth century. The two most popular Swedish authors at Augustana, Runeberg and Tegnér, also played a prominent role in the curricula of Swedish secondary schools in the late nineteenth century. Karin Tarschys, Bengt Lewan, and Bengt-Göran Martinsson have all pointed to the centrality of Tegnér and Runeberg in the Swedish curriculum in the late nineteenth century,[34] and Tarschys has singled out individual texts such as *Fritiofs saga* by Tegnér and *Fänrik Ståls sägner* by Runeberg as especially important.[35] Lars Brink has also pointed to the continued centrality of Tegnér and Runeberg well into the twentieth century.[36]

As shown above, both these authors and specific texts such as *Fritiofs saga* and *Fänrik Ståls sägner* played an important role in the Augustana Swedish curriculum. It has even been noted that students at the college were split in two camps on whether Tegnér or Runeberg was the greatest Swedish author,[37] and in a 1904 publication of "dialogues" for Augustana Synod youth organizations by Augustana minister K. G. William Dahl, the benefits of reading are discussed, with five especially worthy authors identified: Tegnér and Runeberg from the Swedish language and Henry Wadsworth Longfellow, Washington Irving, and William Shakespeare from the English.[38] Tegnér and Runeberg's popularity was not restricted to Augustana College but was equally popular at Gustavus Adolphus College, where Brink, in an examination of the Swedish curriculum at that school, has called them "the most canonized authors."[39]

Tegnér and Runeberg were also well represented in the Swedish-language schoolbooks that were published by the Augustana Book Concern and intended to be used in the instruction in Augustana Synod schools. In addition, the Augustana Book Concern brought out two volumes of Swedish poetry and prose in English translation in 1906 and 1908. Tegnér and Runeberg are by far the dominant authors in both volumes of *Masterpieces from Swedish Literature,* accounting for a third of the total pages devoted to Swedish poetry in one volume and half of the pages in the other volume.[40] Moreover, in 1914, *Fritiofs saga* also appeared in the Augustana Book Concern series of Swedish literature, with vocabularies and commentaries, intended to be used in the Swedish instruction in American colleges and universities, and one year later, Runeberg's *Fänrik Ståls sägner* was published in the same series.[41] In her analysis of *Prärieblomman,* one of the leading literary periodicals and exponents of the Augustana Synod's cultural work, Birgitta Svensson also notes the role that Tegnér played for many of the poems published in the calendar.[42] Other authors studied at Augustana, such as O. P. Sturzén-Becker, Malmström, and, as a part of the expanded Augustana Swedish curriculum after the turn of the century, Rydberg, Lagerlöf, Heidenstam, Fröding, and Karlfeldt, were, as Brink has shown, also a part of the curriculum in Sweden.[43]

The inclusion of Strindberg in the Augustana curriculum may seem surprising, given his controversial status in the Swedish literary canon. Still, this might have been a reflection of the fact that Strindberg had begun appearing in the curricula in the Swedish secondary schools as well from the beginning of the twentieth century, although it took until 1960 before Strindberg reached the position of leading Swedish author in the Swedish secondary schools.[44] Anna Williams has also suggested that Strindberg became more acceptable in Swedish America toward the end of his life.[45] Finally, it is unclear exactly which aspects of Strindberg's works were studied at Augustana, as no individual titles were given in the catalogs.

The Augustana Swedish curriculum thus showed an emphasis on the romantic and idealistic aspects of Swedish literature, with a focus on the nineteenth century, a tendency also visible in Swedish secondary schools at the same time. The textbooks by Sundén and Modin and by Bjursten placed a great emphasis on romantic and neo-romantic nineteenth-century authors. The two leading authors, Tegnér and Runeberg, also represented the romantic and idealistic movement in Swedish literature, with emphases on Swedish and Finnish national feelings. With his background as bishop, there was also a religious dimension to Tegnér's works.[46] The individual authors studied in the Augustana Swedish curriculum after 1900 represented a wider spectrum of literary tendencies, but names such as Heidenstam, Fröding, Lagerlöf, and Karlfeldt were a part of the neo-romanticism associated with the 1890s that emphasized both Swedish patriotism as well as an interest in provincial themes.[47]

It is also possible to discern an interest for the Viking era and its culture at Augustana. A number of works from Old Norse literature as well as lectures on Viking civilization became particularly prominent during the early 1890s. The continued appeal of *Fritiofs saga* in the Augustana Swedish classrooms also suggests an interest in this period, as that work deals with Old Norse themes.[48] Several of the texts by Tegnér and Runeberg studied at Augustana also express national and patriotic feelings, in particular Runeberg's *Fänrik Ståls sägner* as well as poems such as "Svea" by Tegnér and *Fritiofs saga*.[49] This interest in older periods of Swedish literary history has also been noted in the Swedish secondary school curriculum in the 1890s, which, according to Tarschys, was expressed through the study of *Fänrik Ståls sägner* and *Fritiofs saga* but also through such textbooks as Lindblad's *Fosterländska minnen*.[50]

However, even though there were similarities between Augustana's Swedish curriculum and that in contemporary Swedish *läroverk,* the different meaning that this selection of Swedish literature took on in Swedish America must be underscored. Few of the Augustana students had any prior familiarity with Swedish literature of the kind that was taught at Augustana. The Swedish-born students had had little higher schooling prior to their emigration, and to the American-born students Sweden was, by definition, a foreign land, and the Swedish literary and cultural history that was presented to them became something that literally had to be learned. The Swedish literary history at Augustana was idealized and romantic, in which national feelings and an interest in the Viking past and Old Norse literature also played an important role. *Fritiofs saga* and *Fänrik Ståls sägner,* two of the most popular selections from Swedish literature at Augustana, were thus given a new significance in their new, Swedish-American context as they became a part of a Swedish-American tradition at Augustana College, which, in turn, was one important element of Augustana's Swedish-American identity.

SWEDISH ETHNICITY OUTSIDE THE CURRICULUM

The Swedish-American tradition at Augustana was expressed not only through the college curriculum. A number of activities on the campus also provided opportunities for students and faculty to formulate and express a sense of Swedishness as well as to reflect on its significance for the institution. A number of Swedish-related organizations existed on campus; there were meetings and celebrations of different kinds; and Swedish and Swedish-American visitors were received in Rock Island, all of which also provided important ingredients for the Swedish-American identity at the institution. In this section, some of these extracurricular Swedish activities will be examined to provide further answers to the question of what it meant to be Swedish at Augustana College. We will first look at some more general expressions and then examine two of the literary societies on campus.

Visitors from Sweden, Elocution Contests, and Lectures

The Swedish element on campus was made visible by a number of visitors in different capacities from Sweden. These visits were often interpreted as signs of recognition of the cultural work going on among the Swedish Americans by the old country and were important factors in strengthening the position of Swedish at the campus.

The 1901 visit by Bishop von Schéele to the Augustana campus in Rock Island became one opportunity for the college to make its Swedish-American identity visible. Von Schéele was in Rock Island to attend the Reformation festivity at Augustana, which was held for several days beginning on 17 November. The program included several lectures by von Schéele on both religious and Swedish topics, different addresses by representatives of the Augustana Synod, including a greeting "from the daughter church to the mother church" by Eric Norelius, talks on the development of both Augustana College and the Augustana Synod, and a speech on the topic of Augustana as a center of a Swedish-American culture by Professor J. A. Udden of the college's geology department. During the final evening of von Schéele's visit, there was a farewell ceremony in Swedish in the chapel, during which the Wennerberg male chorus sang "Dåne liksom åskan bröder" and the bishop awarded C. E. Lindberg with the Swedish Order of the North

Star. In his remarks, the bishop commented that he was very pleased with the "cultural work" and "expressions of Swedishness" he had encountered at Augustana and promised to convey to the students in Swedish universities that the Augustana students were "worthy descendants of the North."[51]

Another Swedish visitor arrived in Rock Island in April 1902: Carl Sundbeck, who visited the campus as a part of a study trip to America paid for by the Swedish government.[52] A conservative interested in Swedes and Swedish culture outside of Sweden, he embraced the cultural activities he found among Swedish Americans. The speeches he made during his Swedish-American journey as well as his published account of the trip were all highly complimentary to Swedish America in general and to the Augustana Synod in particular.

Upon arriving in Rock Island, Sundbeck recorded his pleasure with having arrived in "the Uppsala of Swedish America."[53] He then gave a speech in the college chapel in which he praised the educational and cultural work at Augustana College, calling the school "the link between the thousands of young people here in America and the country of their ancestors, which they have never visited, but in their hearts still call their own land, their fathers' land."[54] Sundbeck's visit coincided with the first "Founders Day" celebrated on campus.

A visit in November 1904 by Aksel Anderson, a librarian from Uppsala University, provided further opportunities for the Augustana community to express its Swedishness in a welcoming ceremony. Both students and faculty greeted Anderson with speeches and singing—the Wennerberg chorus performed "Hör oss Svea"—and there were cheers for "Sweden in America," "Sweden in the high North," and Uppsala and Lund universities.[55]

Another expression of Swedishness at Augustana was the Swedish elocution contests between Augustana and other Swedish-American colleges. In May 1902, the competition was held in Rock Island, and the judges were all notable Swedish-American authors such as Jakob Bonggren, Ludvig Holmes, and E. W. Olson,[56] the inclusion of which shows the significance attached to the competition. In the following year, the contest was held in Minneapolis and included teams from Gustavus Adolphus College and Bethany College as well; the winning team got a prize and a Swedish flag with the American seal superimposed.[57] In 1904, *Augustana* reported about another elocution competition at Augustana, which now was said to be held in Swedish one year and in English the next. The winner in 1904 was C. P. Peterson; his topic was "the role of the Swedish American in the nation's drama," in which he characterized the creation of an American people as a "quiet, but bitter struggle" between all the different immigrant groups in America and asserted that the Swedish Americans had to play their role in this process as well.[58] *Augustana* commented that the competition was "from beginning to end a show of force of the healthy life of Swedish at the college" and ended with "Long live the wonderful language of our fathers!"[59]

The promotion of Swedishness on the Augustana campus after 1890 was also expressed in public lectures by several prominent Swedish Americans on both Swedish and Swedish-American topics. Examples of lectures by Enander include his talks on Swedish poet and historian Erik Gustaf Geijer in May 1891, an address commemorating the life of Runeberg in February 1904, and a talk on the history and tradition of singing among Swedish university students in February 1905.[60] In March 1900, author and Augustana pastor Holmes gave a talk on "the Swedish Americans in the towns and in the countryside," and in 1911 author and book collector G. N. Swan of Sioux City, Iowa, was invited to give a talk on Holmes and his "significance for Swedish-American literature." In 1914, Swan also presented an address on the topic "Tegnér and his *Fritiofs Saga*."[61]

The Phrenokosmian Society

The Phrenokosmian Society at Augustana College was a literary and debating society of a kind often found at American colleges in the nineteenth century. It started in the same year as the college was founded, and its purpose was to "promote the general welfare" of the student body by discussions, recitations, and elocutions.[62] The membership was open to the entire student body, the society's constitution called for a meeting every week, and the proceedings were held alternately in Swedish and English. Judging from the minutes, the frequency of the meetings varied somewhat, whereas the language requirement seems to have been adhered to.

What can be said about the way in which the Swedish and Swedish-American traditions were articulated in this group up until 1900? The reason for ending my examination in that year has partly to do with the availability of source material. In addition, beginning around 1900 several societies specifically devoted to the study of Swedish came into existence at the college.

The discussions during the society's first fifteen years only infrequently addressed issues related to the college's ethnic background or to the development of the immigrants' heritage in the new homeland.[63] When such topics were discussed, the focus seems to have been on the Swedish language, as on 24 October 1860 when the question posed for discussion was "Are the Scandinavian languages more beneficial than the English for students at Augustana?" or on 11 April 1861, "Are the Scandinavian languages more developed than the English?" Instead, during these early years, members of the society seem to have been mostly concerned with religious and moral issues, such as "Has the written word of God had more influence on the salvation of man than the spoken?" on 7 November 1860 or "Which is more beneficial to man: Poverty or Riches?" on 1 May 1861. A few of the discussions seem inspired by contemporary events: on 23 November 1861, for example, the question discussed was "Who has suffered most at the hands of the whites: Indians or Negroes?"

When the school moved to Rock Island and graduated its first college class in the mid-1870s, the topics of discussion in the Phrenokosmian Society changed considerably. Religious and moral discussions were still frequent, but subjects dealing with Swedish topics were also included, dealing primarily with Swedish literature and history, and we can thus observe a growing sense of a Swedish national feeling in the society. In the literary discussions, the topics reflected the authors who were studied in the Swedish classes in the college. Thus, during the 1870s and 1880s, Tegnér and Runeberg were frequently discussed in the society. "Det eviga," "Svea," and "Kungarne på Salamis" as well as *Fritiofs saga* are examples of works by Tegnér that were read in the society. Frequent selections by Runeberg came from *Fänrik Ståls sägner*,[64] and in 1882, one of the topics for discussion was which of the two authors was the greatest poet.[65] Swedish history was also discussed in the society in the 1880s, although not as frequently as Swedish literature. In 1879, an oration consisted of King Gustav Vasa's farewell address to the Swedish Parliament from the sixteenth century, and one year later another oration dealt with King Gustavus Adolphus's departure for Germany and his participation in the Thirty Years' War.[66]

During the 1890s, literary and cultural topics were the most common subjects of discussion, and several Swedish authors were featured at the society's meetings. Some examples include the 1896 meeting devoted to nineteenth-century historian and poet Geijer and the 1897 discussion of psalm-writer and bishop Johan Olof Wallin, also from the nineteenth century. The Gustavian era of the late eighteenth century, with talks about King Gustav III and authors Johan Henrik Kellgren, Carl Gustaf af Leopold, and Anna Maria Lenngren, was also dealt with several times, and in 1898 the romantic poet Erik Johan Stagnelius was the featured topic.[67] In 1891, the society devoted at least one meeting to Old Norse mythology and literature.[68] A few topics came from the field of Swedish history, such as a discussion of King Gustavus Adolphus and Swedish history during the middle ages and the role of Engelbrekt Engelbrektsson, the leader of an uprising in the fifteenth century. The minutes also note that a "patriotic song" preceded the speech on Gustavus Adolphus, which, typically, was held on the anniversary of the king's death in the battle of Lützen on 6 November 1632.[69] The various provinces of Sweden were also discussed a few times, as well as different provincial dialects.[70]

The members of the Phrenokosmian Society also discussed certain aspects of the heritage of their new homeland, although to a lesser degree than they did their Swedish background. As noted before, the early leadership of the college had encouraged "Americanization," and both American history, geography, politics, and literature were studied in the Augustana curriculum.[71] Although Augustana's Swedish ethnic background received increased attention after 1890, it is clear that Augustana Swedes and Swedish Americans also emphasized their "Americanness" and loyalty to their adopted homeland. Thus, a combination of both Swedish and American elements existed in the Augustana Synod, and the argument was made that no contradiction existed between being a loyal American and at the same time maintaining Swedish cultural traditions.

Some examples will illustrate this point. In 1892, Olof Olsson, the president of Augustana College, emphasized the school's patriotic nature by saying that as citizens of the United States, "we must be faithful and enthusiastic patriots for the land of the free and the brave." This did not, however, preclude the maintenance of the Swedish language at Augustana College, Olsson concluded, asserting that if President Harrison were to come to the campus, he would find "no false Americans" but would instead be "moved" by the "true American civic spirit" at the college.[72] Twenty years later, in 1912, an article in *Augustana* argued that the purpose of the "preservation of Swedishness" was to contribute an important cultural element to the United States, and in 1916 the paper claimed that "America is not only English" but was, in accordance with the country's motto *E Pluribus Unum,* made up of many national groups, of which the Swedish Americans were one.

This American emphasis was also reflected in the Phrenokosmian Society, where notable American historical figures were dealt with. One discussion in 1880 focused on the question "Who was most praiseworthy: Washington, La Fayette, Lincoln, or Grant?"; in 1896, the question was "Who deserves more praise: Christopher Columbus for discovering America or George Washington for defending it?"; and in 1897, the life and achievements of President Lincoln were discussed.[73] Significant events in American history also received attention in the Phrenokosmian Society, such as an 1897 program on "The Revolutionary War" consisting of "patriotic songs," a declamation of "The Declaration of Independence," speeches about the battles of Saratoga and Yorktown, and an 1896 lecture on the Civil War.[74] American and English literature was also discussed, as in a meeting devoted to Longfellow in 1896 and in one to American humor and humorists in 1898, and at least two meetings in the early 1890s dealt with the works of Shakespeare.[75] Contemporary American affairs were also noted a few times, as in a meeting on different American political parties in 1895 and in a discussion of the issue of free silver in 1896.[76]

Swedish and American elements were sometimes directly combined at Augustana. One example is the celebration of Washington's birthday, which the society arranged in 1878. According to the minutes, the celebration took place in the college chapel where "above the speakers, the Banners of the American and Swedish Nations were displayed intertwined. A picture of Washington symbolized the Union." The program opened with "The Star Spangled Banner" and after a short prayer continued with the Finno-Swedish patriotic song "Vårt Land," which was also popular in Sweden. An oration about George Washington by one of the native-born "American" professors followed, and then the program closed with "My Country, 'Tis of Thee."[77] Another such juxtaposition came in the 1897 meeting devoted to "famous battles," where two of the melées discussed were the battle at Hampton Roads from the American Civil War, considered by the participants to have saved the Union fleet, and the battle of Breitenfeld from the Thirty Years' War, in which the Swedish troops were victorious.[78]

An interest in Swedish-American cultural patterns emerged in the society's activities toward the end of the 1880s and in the early 1890s. The term "Swedish American" as a self-description seems to have begun to be used toward the end of the 1880s in the Phrenokosmian Society. In 1888, for example, the society discussed "Swedish-American character traits and their influence on the American nationality," and in 1890, the minutes stated that the society moved that "Our Forefathers' Day ought to be celebrated by the Swedish Americans." Moreover, the 1890s saw the first discussions that dealt with the history of the Swedes in America. In 1893, the reasons for Swedish emigration to and Swedish settlements in America in general were dealt with, and in 1897 the seventeenth-century Swedish colony on the Delaware River was the focus of attention for one meeting. In that same year, one whole evening was also devoted to "the Emigrants," during which different speeches dealt with the preparations and farewells in Sweden, the voyage across the Atlantic, and the first years in America. In 1892, finally, an oration was given to the memory of John Ericsson, the Swedish engineer and constructor of the *Monitor,* the ship that took part in the battle of Hampton Roads during the Civil War.[79]

The sense of a Swedish-American distinctiveness in the Phrenokosmian Society can also be seen from an 1896 discussion of the nature of "Swedish-American youth" and in a meeting two years later when the topic was "A Swedish American and His Duties." In 1898, finally, one evening was devoted to "Swedish-American literature," which featured three authors—Holmes, Enander, and A. A. Swärd—all of whom were closely associated with the Augustana Synod.[80]

It can be concluded, then, that the discussions in the Phrenokosmian Society dealing with Swedish literature, not surprisingly, mirrored much of the instruction in the college's subject of Swedish, with Runeberg and Tegnér taking center stage early on but with a gradual expansion into other authors as well. The evidence from the Phrenokosmian Society also suggests that topics dealing with Swedish literature were frequently discussed at Augustana College as early as the 1870s, which is a further indication of the sustained interest in Swedish at the school, even though the English language was making rapid inroads. In addition, members of the society also discussed topics related to the history and literature of their new homeland. Prominent American leaders, such as Presidents Washington and Lincoln, together with decisive historical events, such as the War of Independence and the Civil War, found their way into the society's discussions.

It is also possible to see the beginnings of a specific Swedish-American awareness in the society, as, beginning in the 1890s, topics of discussion in the society dealt with both the history and cultural expressions of the Swedish-American group. It can be said that the members had begun to see themselves as "Swedish Americans" rather than "Swedes in America." In addition, selected aspects of the Swedish and American pasts were presented at meetings of the society, often dealing with and juxtaposing patriotic or nationalistic symbols from the respective countries, such as famous Swedish kings or leading American presidents.

Svenska Vitterhetssällskapet

Further evidence of the growth of a Swedish-American identity at Augustana College comes from the four student organizations devoted to the study of Swedish and Swedish-American culture that started at the school by the turn of the century.[81] The oldest of these groups was the eighteen-member Svenska Vitterhetssällskapet (The Swedish Society for Belles Lettres), formed in 1896 and dedicated to "the study of Swedish literature and culture"; the group met on a regular basis for discussions of literary topics as well as for readings of original productions. The society also sponsored public lectures on Swedish and Swedish-American topics.[82] A second literary society was Tegnér-förbundet (The Tegnér Society), organized in 1901 to promote the study of Swedish literature. Both groups were primarily intended for students in the college, whereas the third society, Iduna, organized in 1902, was intended for younger students, primarily in the academy. The fourth group was a Swedish debating club, Torgny, organized in 1904.

Little material is preserved from these groups except for Svenska Vitterhetssällskapet, for which there is a book of minutes as well as a publication called *Runan* (The Rune). The latter was a handwritten publication that was read aloud at meetings. On three occasions, the group also published a special Christmas issue, called *Julrunan* (The Christmas Rune). A brief overview of the activities of this group will give an additional view of Swedish-related activities at Augustana College during the years immediately after the turn of the century.

With its eighteen members, the group's name obviously alluded to the Swedish Academy (which also was a topic of discussion in 1905[83]), and the first pages of the society's minute book contain a listing with the signatures of the occupants of each of the eighteen "chairs" in chronological order. The 1911 issue of *Julrunan* also proclaimed that the goal of the society was to work for the preservation of "Swedishness and the Swedish language and literature among the Swedish Americans," adding that "Svenska Vitterhetssällskapet seeks to be to America's Swedes what the [Swedish] Academy is to the people of Sweden."[84]

The society seems to have been particularly active during the decade or so after 1900. In 1900, *Augustana* pointed out that during its early years, the group had been "mis-understood," something that was no longer the case.[85] A retrospective article on the society's history argued that when the group had been founded, the study of Swedish had been on the retreat at Augustana and that many people had feared that the Swedish language would die out. The society had also been met with "resistance" and "ridicule," which, however, changed within a few years as the group developed an energetic program.[86]

During the first years of the century, Svenska Vitterhetssällskapet met regularly and included a business meeting that often, but not always, was followed by a program. In almost all the cases, the program was either a presentation of one or several authors or a discussion of a literary work. An examination of the topics discussed at the meetings and of *Runan* shows that topics dealing with Swedish literature were very common and that the focus was on authors studied in the Swedish curriculum in the college. Runeberg and Tegnér, so popular in the college's Swedish curriculum and in the Phrenokosmian Society, were also discussed in Svenska Vitterhetssällskapet[87] as well as in its publication *Runan*.[88] Other names mentioned in the society's minutes include Levertin, Anna Wahlenberg, Rydberg, Hallström, Karl-Erik Forsslund, Wallin, and Malmström[89] and in *Runan* Georg Stiernhielm, Zacharias Topelius, King Oscar II, and Sigurd (Alfred Hedenstierna).[90] As shown above, some of these authors, such as Levertin, Rydberg, and Malmström, were also studied in the college's Swedish curriculum. Others, such as Forsslund and Sigurd, were also popular authors among those imported by the Augustana Book Concern.

Beginning around 1911, fewer authors were dealt with but in seemingly greater detail. In that year, at least four presentations focused on works by Heidenstam, and in December the society started reading and discussing works by Strindberg, something that continued for more than one year.[91] The minutes from February 1911 stated that special attention would be given to the "national and patriotic" in Heidenstam's writings. In 1914, two meetings each were devoted to Lagerlöf's *Jerusalem* and Tegnér's *Fritiofs saga*.[92] By this time too, Mauritzson, the college's professor of Swedish, was taking a more active part in the society, and meetings were apparently becoming more of a direct supplement to the Swedish instruction at the college.

It is apparent that members of the society sought to promote a certain type of Swedish literature, at least during the first years of the twentieth century. In 1902 and 1903, *Runan* claimed that there were only a few good contemporary authors in Sweden. Good literature, the paper argued, was "idealistic" in nature, a quality lacking in much of what was published in Sweden, and the members of the society were encouraged to instead preserve the memory of the earlier idealistic writings.[93]

Several times, *Runan* spoke of the importance of preserving the Swedish language, literature, and history for the Swedish immigrants and their children in America and of the role that Augustana College and the society played in this process. In November 1902, for example, an article underscored the necessity of maintaining a Swedish cultural heritage, stating that it was indeed possible to be "a good American citizen" while at the same time preserving "one's Swedish language and memories,"[94] and a few months later the society's task of studying Sweden's literary history, especially its "glorious" dimensions such as Tegnér, Runeberg, Frans Michael Franzén, and Geijer, was emphasized, together with the especially great need to convey tradition to those born in America by Swedish parents.[95] In 1906, the paper noted that Augustana College was the "heart of Swedishness in America" where "the pillars of Swedishness in America were reared and educated," a process in which Svenska Vitterhetssällskapet played an important role.[96]

Similar comments were made in conjunction with the establishment of Tegnér-förbundet in 1901, when *Augustana* commented that it was often claimed that the Swedish Americans were becoming Americanized, something that was certainly not true at Augustana. If those who say so, the paper continued, would spend a day among the students here, they would realize that "Augustana College is still the hearth of Swedishness in America, and that it will be difficult to change this."[97]

The society also sponsored literary competitions in the Swedish language. The first suggestion for such a competition was made in 1903, when rules were drawn up, a jury appointed, and monetary prizes adopted for poetry, short stories, and pieces on literary and cultural history. No mention was made of winners in 1903, but it seems as if the competitions continued on a regular basis for a few more years.[98] In 1906, the competition was given high recognition as the jury included the Swedish professors at the three leading Augustana Synod colleges. First and second prizes were awarded in poetry, whereas only a second prize was given for fiction.[99] Two of the winners, C. A. Lönnqvist and J. F. Englund, expressed their thanks in the November 1906 issue of *Runan*.[100] The literary competitions seem to have ended in 1906, as there are no further mention of them in the society's minutes.

The task of preserving a sense of Swedishness at Augustana did not only mean the promotion of national Swedish literature or the Swedish language. As was the case in the Phrenokosmian Society, Svenska Vitterhetssällskapet also showed great interest in specifically Swedish-American cultural concerns. In December 1904, for example, the topic for deliberations was "Our Swedish-American Christmas literature"; in January and February of the following year, the focus was on Swedish-American poet and Augustana pastor A. A. Swärd; and in November 1908, one meeting was devoted to Swedish-American "elocution" and "culture."[101] In 1903 and 1905, *Runan* also included poems by Swedish-American authors, the well-known Augustana pastors Ludvig (pseudonym for Ludvig Holmes) and Teofilus (pseudonym for C. A. Lönnqvist).[102]

The three issues of Svenska Vitterhetssällskapet's special Christmas publication, *Julrunan,* which appeared in 1905, 1911, and 1912, show how Swedish-American cultural concerns were important to the society.[103] An advertisement in *Augustana* for the 1905 *Julrunan* issue also noted that it included contributions from "the leading authors in Swedish America."[104] All three issues included many literary contributions—poems and short stories—the majority authored by Swedish-American authors connected with the Augustana Synod. Contributors included such well-known Augustana names as Lönnqvist, Holmes, Dahl, Carl Kraft, C. W. Andeer, Anna Olsson, and E. W. Olson.

Several of the stories take place in Swedish America. For example, Anna Olsson's 1905 contribution "Babetistera" deals with contacts between Swedish-American Lutherans and Baptists in Chicago and is written in Olsson's typical linguistic style, mixing Swedish dialects and English, and in 1911 Dahl contributed a story about the children Nelly and Peter, also set in Swedish America.[105] A few contributions also deal with the history of the Swedes in America, such as an account of the 1905 Augustana Synod meeting in Stanton, Iowa, or of pioneer life among Swedish immigrants.[106]

Other pieces deal specifically with the nature of cultural developments among the Swedish Americans and are further examples of how a Swedish-American identity was growing stronger at Augustana after the turn of the century. In 1905, Samuel Magnus Hill wondered if a separate "Swedish-American literature" existed, arguing that it was possible to begin to discern such a phenomenon, which reflected the development of life in Swedish America and which was clearly separate from literary developments in Sweden.[107] S. G. Youngert, pastor and editor at the Augustana Book Concern, made a similar point in a reflection on what it meant to be a Swedish American. "It is something more than to be Swedish and also something more than to be American," he stated, incorporating traits that characterized both these peoples, such as the Swedish virtues of honesty, steadfastness, and piety but also the Americans' traits of industriousness, resourcefulness, and courage.[108] A poem by E. W. Olson from 1912, finally, conjured up an image of a Swedish cultural heritage that was preserved in the New World, in harmony with the traditions of the new land:

> In the forests of the North, on the prairies of the West
> still Sweden's children recognize their mother
> and the flag with the dear Swedish colors
> we still hoist next to the Star Spangled Banner.[109]

It is interesting to note that at this time, the Swedish flag had not yet become widely used as a cultural symbol in Sweden. It seems likely that the prevalent use of the American flag in the United States can explain Olson's use of the Swedish flag as a symbol in Swedish America.

The Swedish-American tradition that emerged at Augustana College during the final years of the nineteenth century consisted of several parts. It included elements from a national Swedish culture, stressing the established authors of the romantic era of the nineteenth century and focusing on idealism and patriotism. The American context in which the immigrants and their children existed was underscored as well, and American cultural icons of a patriotic nature were also incorporated in the Swedish-American tradition. Finally, the tradition highlighted a Swedish-American culture, focusing on cultural traits and achievements that were seen as specific to the experience of the Swedish Americans, primarily in the Augustana Synod.

The role of ethnicity was thus strengthened at Augustana College around the turn of the century. The previous relative lack of interest in the institution's ethnic background was replaced with not only an interest in certain dimensions of Swedish, and to some extent American, culture but also a clear emphasis on precise Swedish-American cultural patterns. Given the centrality of Augustana College within the Augustana Synod, the Swedish-American tradition that developed at the college became an important part in the synod's Swedish-American identity.

THE AUGUSTANA STUDENT BODY

The preceding discussion has illustrated the position and the nature of what I have called a Swedish-American tradition at Augustana College. In this section, the question of the nature of the student body at Augustana College that was exposed to this tradition will be addressed.

In chapter 2, the dominance of the Augustana Synod in Swedish America was discussed and some tentative answers given to the question of who the

Augustana Swedish Americans were, based on observations about the geographical, generational, and social characteristics of the Augustana Synod, synod statistics, census data, and contemporary observations by synod members. Still, the source material available for the synod as a whole makes it difficult to more precisely establish dimensions such as generational composition and social and geographic background.

Sources are, however, more abundant for Augustana College, and an intensive analysis of the student body at Augustana College will further illuminate the question of Augustana's specific character in Swedish America. Questions to be addressed include the ethnic and generational dimension of the student body, the social background of the Augustana students, and the geographical recruitment patterns of the college. An attempt will also be made to trace the careers of graduates of the college in order to discuss the college's role for social mobility among the Augustana Swedish Americans and to see to what degree the Augustana graduates played a part in the larger Swedish-American community.

For this study, a number of different sources have been collected in a database and used in the analysis. The most important sources are the printed catalogs for Augustana College from 1871 to 1914, in which all students are listed by name and class in the college, and the forms each student completed upon registering at Augustana. The registration forms usually include information about birth year, birthplace, place of residence, father's occupation, church affiliation, and previous education.[110] Additional information about the students has been gathered through a number of sources: the official annual of the Augustana Synod, *Korsbaneret; The Augustana Ministerium,* a directory of all ordained pastors in the Augustana Synod; and the booklet *Who Is Who among the Alumni?* which traced the further careers of the Augustana graduates, published in 1923.[111]

A total of 1,433 students who matriculated at Augustana College between 1871 and 1914 have been recorded and form the basis for the following discussion. The completeness of the sources is, however, uneven, and the information is much more complete during the first decades of the period than during the latter. Some variables are also more complete than others, such as birth year and place of residence. The latter is noted in 96 percent of the cases. Father's occupation is available in roughly two-thirds of the cases throughout the period. During the first two decades, more than 70 percent of the students noted their father's avocation, whereas this is true of only 56 percent of the students between 1900 and 1914. The figures are similar for the students' further careers and for the generational classification. In no case, however, can one discern a systematic tendency in the way in which the information is missing. Instead, as time progressed, the data collected by Augustana College when its students registered each year became less precise, something which was also true for the church records maintained by the synod.

Most of the data about birth years, birthplaces, and fathers' occupations has been gathered from the registration forms. It is important to note that not all of the students in the database graduated from the college. Only a little fewer than half of the students attended their senior year at Augustana, leaving a very large group of persons who for some reason left the school after less than the full four years. A small caveat concerning the occupational category "farmer" is also necessary. This term, or the Swedish-American version of it *(farmare)*, is by far the most common word used to indicate that the student's father was working the land—both in Sweden and in the United States. It is used in almost 90 percent of the cases in which students indicated that their fathers tilled the soil. Other categories are used much less frequently: *lantbrukare, bonde,* or *jordbrukare* in 7 percent of the cases and *hemmansägare* in less than 5 percent. The word "farmer" in the U.S. context suggests landownership, but, given both the commonality of the word "farmer" in American English and a desire to raise one's social status, it is almost certain that some Augustana students had fathers in Sweden who were not landowners, although they were noted as such.

Generational and Ethnic Composition

Generational composition has, as noted in chapter 1, been an important factor in the discussion of the nature of ethnicity and ethnic identity. An assessment of the generational and ethnic makeup of the Augustana students, and its changing nature over time, is thus of great importance for our further discussion.

The students of Swedish background have been divided into two general categories: first-generation and second-generation Swedish Americans. First-generation students were Swedish-born, while second-generation students include American-born students of at least one parent (usually the father) born in Sweden. In addition, those students who had typically Swedish-sounding names, lived in typical Swedish-American cities and areas, and had some kind of affiliation with the Augustana Synod (such as being a member of an Augustana congregation or previously having attended another Augustana Synod academy or college) have also been included in this group. The use of these criteria makes it possible that some third-generation Swedish Americans (that is, American-born of at least one Swedish-born grandparent) might have been included, as the available sources do not make their identification possible.

In addition, those students who were clearly not of Swedish background have been grouped separately as "non-Swedish." Here, names, religious affiliation, and places of residence have been important in the classification.

During the entire period 1871–1914, Augustana College was clearly dominated by students with a Swedish background. Only 13 percent of the student body was non-Swedish, mainly consisting of students from the urban area known as the Tri-Cities in Illinois and Iowa where Augustana College was located. Among the students of Swedish background, the number of students born in Sweden and those born in the United States of Swedish-born parents were of roughly the same size, with 45 percent born in Sweden and 42 percent born in the United States.[112]

The generational constitution of the student body did, however, vary significantly over time, as can be seen in table 2. Since the normal course of study lasted four years, it was possible to be enrolled in the college during two decades, and some students have thus been counted twice. This does not, however, affect our reading of changes in the generational makeup at the college.

During the 1870s and 1880s, the Swedish-born students constituted about three-fourths of the student body. During the following decades, a decline in the number Swedish-born students started. During the first decade of the twentieth century, about a third of the students had been born in Sweden, and between 1910 and 1914, the figure stood at 14 percent. The American-born students of Swedish background increased as the Swedish-born declined. Before 1890, about 20 percent were born in the United States, but by 1900, the American-born students constituted a majority of all students at Augustana College. The non-Swedish part of the student body, finally, also grew, in particular after the turn of the century. At the end of the period, the non-Swedish students at Augustana constituted about a fifth of the student body.

In terms of generational shifts, it is obvious that the decades around the turn of the century were of crucial importance at Augustana College, and they stand out as the period when the American-born generation established a dominance at Augustana. This generational shift can also be seen elsewhere

TABLE 2. GENERATIONS AT AUGUSTANA COLLEGE, 1871–1914 (PERCENTAGES)

	1871–79	1880–89	1890–99	1900–09	1910–14
Swedish-born	75	73	51	30	14
American-born	22	20	40	57	64
Non-Swedes	3	7	9	13	22
Total	100	100	100	100	100
N	146	303	325	310	266

Source: Augustana Student Data Base

in the college, and it is telling that the first American-born president of the institution, Gustav Andreen, assumed office in 1901.

The shift of generations at Augustana College does not coincide with the course of Swedish immigration to the United States. Roughly a third of all Swedish immigrants landed on American shores after 1900, when the number of Swedish-born students at Augustana College rapidly grew smaller. It is thus apparent that Augustana College was much less attractive to the immigrants of this later phase, something also observed for the synod as a whole.

Geographical Recruitment Patterns

The geographical recruitment patterns of the Augustana students can also be analyzed in order to characterize the student body. An analysis of the data for the first- and second-generation Swedish-American students at the college shows that five states in the Midwest accounted for more than three-fourths of the students. The state with the largest percentage was Illinois, from which a third of the students came, followed by Iowa (15 percent), Minnesota (14 percent), Nebraska (7 percent), and Michigan (6 percent).

A comparison with the general settlement patterns for the first- and second-generation Swedish Americans in 1910 shows that the Augustana students had a distinct geographical background. Three-fourths of the Augustana students came from the five most popular states, while these states accounted for only half of the total Swedish-American population. Moreover, in 1910, the states of New York and Massachusetts ranked as numbers three and four among the Swedish Americans, with 11 percent of that population. Only 3 percent of the Augustana students came from these two eastern states.[113]

The recruitment patterns thus show that Augustana students primarily came from the midwestern states. Moreover, the patterns also show a considerable stability throughout the period under investigation, as the five leading midwestern states were as dominant during the second decade of the twentieth century as they were during the 1880s. Augustana's location in the heart of the Midwest, on the border between Illinois and Iowa, is, of course, one factor that can help explain the geographical origins of the students.

However, it also seems possible to speak of a recruitment tradition at Augustana College, where students kept coming from primarily those midwestern states that formed the nucleus of the Swedish settlements when Augustana College had been founded during the early phase of the Swedish mass-immigration. Moreover, the recruitment patterns were not affected by the generational shift at the college. As we have seen, the student body was largely dominated by the second generation after 1900, and in 1910 the midwestern Swedish Americans, from whom Augustana recruited heavily, were to a large degree American-born. In Iowa and Nebraska, for example, which were in second and fourth place among the home states of Augustana students, more than 60 percent of the Swedish Americans were American-born.[114] Thus, in the old Swedish-American heartlands, the propensity to go to Augustana was passed down from one generation of Swedish Americans to the next.

Social Background of the Augustana Students

A lively scholarly discussion in social history concerning the social stratification of individuals exists, and a number of classification schemes has been advanced, depending on such factors as theoretical starting points, the nature of the source material, and the need for comparisons. In the present analysis of the social background of the Augustana students, a slightly modified version of a classification scheme that was developed at Uppsala University in the 1970s is used. The scheme aims to place the individuals on a socioeconomic scale, where unskilled laborers are found at the bottom and wealthy property owners at the top. This scheme also corresponds with the classificatory system that developed in the United States in the 1960s and 1970s with the advent of the "new social history."[115]

The social background of those Augustana students who enrolled in the college between 1871 and 1914 can be seen in table 3. The dominant occupational group among the fathers of the Augustana students was clearly the farmers, to which almost 40 percent of the students belonged. The second largest category was group I, high white collar, which was followed by group IV, skilled and semiskilled workers, and group II, low white collar. The smallest group represented among the Augustana students was the unskilled laborers, to which only 8 percent belonged.

TABLE 3. SOCIAL BACKGROUND OF MATRICULATING AUGUSTANA STUDENTS, 1871–1914 (PERCENTAGES)

Group	Swedish-born	American-born	Non-Swedes	Total
I (high white collar)	5	31	40	22
II (low white collar)	7	16	31	15
III (farmers)	57	31	16	39
IV (skilled and semiskilled workers)	18	16	13	16
V (unskilled laborers)	13	6	0	8
Total	100	100	100	100
N	345	413	114	872

Source: Augustana Student Data Base

There were, however, some major differences among the students of Swedish and non-Swedish background. Although the numbers are considerably smaller for the non-Swedish students, it is clear that they came from a much more urban and white-collar background than did the Swedes or Swedish Americans. Over 70 percent of the non-Swedes belonged to groups I and II, and 85 percent of them lived in Illinois, almost exclusively in the urban area in which Augustana College was located. Over 10 percent of the non-Swedish students had fathers who were ministers in a local American congregation, and other common parental occupations included merchants, physicians, and attorneys. Thus, the non-Swedish students tended to come from fairly well-to-do, often professional American families in the area, to whom Augustana College was the closest institution of higher education. It is also significant that a fairly small number of the non-Swedish students actually graduated from the college. Only 25 percent of those students who have been classified as non-Swedish attended their senior year at Augustana. It was very common for these non-Swedish students to enroll at Augustana for one or two years only.

There were also noticeable differences among the students of Swedish background. Although the category of farmer was a dominant parental occupation for both the Swedish-born and the American-born students, it was much more significant for the Swedish-born, where more than half of the students were found in this category. Only a third of the American-born students came from farming homes. Moreover, almost a third of the fathers of the Swedish-born students were skilled or unskilled laborers, whereas the corresponding figure for the American-born was about a fifth, suggesting that the college provided an opportunity for intergenerational social mobility among Swedish Americans.

Thus, the American-born students of Swedish background at Augustana were also much more frequently represented in the higher categories than were their Swedish-born peers. Almost half of them have been classified as high or low white collar, whereas the corresponding figure for the Swedish-born is 12 percent. It should, however, be noticed that a large group of Augustana pastors is included in the figures for high white collar fathers for the American-born group and constitute as much as three-fourths of all the fathers of American-born students in group I.

The classification of an Augustana pastor as high white collar raises a potential problem. As the Augustana Synod was struggling to get organized, the training of the Augustana pastors was, especially during the first couple of decades, not as rigorous as for the ministers within the Church of Sweden or for other denominations in the United States, which suggests that they should be included in a lower category. It seems likely that the social prestige of an Augustana minister was less than that of a minister in the Church of Sweden (although Sten Carlsson has shown that an Augustana degree does not seem to have been a major handicap for returning Augustana pastors seeking a career in the Church of Sweden[116]), but it is also probable that the Augustana pastor did enjoy a great deal of respect in the Swedish-American communities, particularly in rural areas. Other common parental white-collar occupations among the American-born students included merchants, teachers at Augustana College, and clerks.

There is also a clear shift in occupational background, over time, among both the Swedish-born and the American-born students of Swedish background, as can be seen when the figures for the period 1871–99 and 1900–1914 are compared in table 4. The analysis is based on a decennial breakdown of the student body, and some students attending Augustana during two decades have been counted twice.

TABLE 4. SOCIAL BACKGROUND OF MATRICULATING AUGUSTANA STUDENTS, 1871–99 AND 1900–14 (PERCENTAGES)

Group	Swedish-born 1871–99	Swedish-born 1900–14	American-born 1871–99	American-born 1900–14	Total 1871–99	Total 1900–15
I (high white collar)	3	17	27	32	11	30
II (low white collar)	6	8	10	20	8	18
III (farmers)	58	47	40	26	52	29
IV (skilled and semiskilled workers)	20	14	19	14	19	14
V (unskilled laborers)	13	14	4	8	10	9
Total	100	100	100	100	100	100
N	356	51	187	286	543	337

Source: Augustana Student Data Base.

There was a significant difference in the social background of Augustana students before and after 1900. Before the turn of the century, over half of the students at Augustana came from farming homes, while after 1900 less than a third belonged to that category. Similarly, the share of students from white-collar backgrounds (groups I and II) increased from 19 percent during the period before 1900 to almost half after the turn of the century. As was shown in table 3, the social composition of the students is linked to the generational classification, and the quickly growing number of American-born students of Swedish background explains the growing number of students of white-collar background at the school. Augustana College thus developed from an institution that, before 1900, primarily attracted students born in Sweden of an agricultural background to a school that, after the turn of the century, was dominated by American-born students, the great majority of whom were of Swedish background and, to a large degree, came from white-collar homes.

Further Careers of the Augustana Students

What occupations did graduates of Augustana College take up, and to what extent did these occupational choices remain within the sphere of the Augustana ethnic institution? These questions will shed light the social mobility within the group of Augustana students and the significance of Augustana College for maintaining the cohesiveness of the ethnic group.

To establish the further careers of the Augustana students, lists of graduates and their occupations have been used, which were published in the college catalogs at some intervals and in a booklet from 1923 published by the Augustana Alumni Association. In addition, the *Augustana Ministerium* has been utilized. The listings in the catalogs and the Alumni Association publication included only those persons who graduated from the college, which, as noted above, was a little less than half of the enrolled students. Especially during the early years, many of the nongraduating students continued in the seminary and can thus be traced in the *Augustana Ministerium*. Except for the Augustana ministers, those students who left the college prior to their senior year are not included in the following discussion. It should finally be noted that among those students who did attend their senior year at Augustana, 17 percent have not been identified.

These caveats noted, the evidence suggests that the Augustana students found their future jobs in the white-collar categories. Almost all of the students who have been identified—95 percent—were employed in the high white collar category, while the remaining persons had low white collar jobs. It is, however, again important to notice that the great number of ministers in the Augustana Synod among the college graduates is included in the high white collar figure, as almost 70 percent of the identified students became ministers in the synod.

Some differences among the Swedish-born, American-born of Swedish background, and non-Swedish student categories exist. The dominance for the white-collar occupations was equally strong among all three categories, but among the Swedish-born students, the position of minister in the Augustana Synod was by far the most popular occupation, including 85 percent of the identified Swedish-born students. Other common occupations among the Swedish-born students included college professor, public school teacher, and physician.

The occupational panorama among the American-born students of Swedish background was more varied. Almost half of them were ordained in the

Augusta Synod, while the remaining students found jobs in other professional white-collar employments such as physician, university professor, public school teacher, lawyer, and private businessman. The non-Swedish students, finally, constituted only 5 percent of all the identified students. The most popular occupation for them was public school teacher, followed by private businessman, physician, and lawyer.

Another way of looking at the subsequent careers of the Augustana students is to try to ascertain what influence they may have exercised both throughout Swedish America at large and within the Augustana sphere of Swedish America. As Augustana College was the leading institution of higher learning within the Augustana Synod and in many ways functioned as a cultural "motor" for the synod as a whole, it is of great interest to see how actively associated with Augustana the graduates of the school became. For the present analysis, I have defined a category of "Augustana occupations," which includes the Augustana pastors, teachers at colleges or academies operated by or associated with the synod, and a few journalists at newspapers with well-known Augustana sympathies.

This analysis shows that both students born in Sweden and those born in America of Swedish background demonstrated a strong propensity to remain within the Augustana sphere of Swedish America, as about three-fourths of the students did so following their graduation from the college. There are some differences between the Swedish-born students and those born in America of Swedish background. Almost 90 percent of the Swedish-born students remained associated with Augustana in their later lives, whereas the figure for the American-born was 58 percent.

The very large number of Augustana graduates who became ministers in the synod accounts for many of the "Augustana occupations" among the college graduates. Among the Swedish-born with Augustana occupations, the pastors constituted almost all the cases. The American-born students with Augustana occupations also include more than three-fourths of Augustana ministers among their alumni. It should, however, be noted that there was also an increasingly large number of teachers at Augustana-affiliated institutions among this group, approximately 20 percent. In a comment from 1918 on the further careers of the graduates of synod colleges, *Augustana* also noted that of the 740 ministers in the synod in that year, only 11 were not educated at a synod school. These graduates of one of the denomination's colleges were, in *Augustana*'s words, spiritual leaders of more than 300,000 congregation members but were also, together with the college professors, spearheading "the cultural work which is the unifying force for our people."[117]

It is thus clear that a very large number of Augustana graduates went on to an active professional life within the Augustana sphere of Swedish America. Most of them became ministers within the synod at a time when an ethnic church like the Augustana Synod was important in more than spiritual matters. Local Augustana congregations scattered all over the American continent became linguistic and cultural safe havens as well, supporting a number of social and cultural activities such as Sunday schools, youth groups, and other undertakings. In most of these settings, the Augustana pastor held a key position. In addition, it was often the local Augustana pastor who encouraged the young and promising members of his congregation to apply for admission to Augustana College, thus further strengthening the ties between the Swedish-American youth and the institution of higher learning in Rock Island.

It is very difficult to determine to what extent the Augustana graduates played a role in the Swedish-American community outside of Augustana. It is, however, not unlikely that the fairly large numbers of professionals, such as physicians, lawyers, businessmen, and the like, who resided in places with large Swedish-American populations achieved positions of relative prominence and influence within their respective local Swedish-American communities. An Augustana graduate lawyer or physician in Lindstrom, Minnesota, in Rockford, Illinois, or on the Near North Side in Chicago were almost bound to play an important role in his or her local Swedish-American context. This was also noted by the synod's official paper in 1918, which pointed to the fact that in "dozens of our communities" there were prominent doctors and lawyers who had been "reared in our congregations and [who] studied in our colleges."[118]

The case study of the student body at Augustana College shows that the 1890s was a particularly important decade at Augustana College. During that decade, the institution underwent a generational transformation so that by the turn of the century, the school was dominated by American-born students of Swedish background. The generational shift also coincided with a change in the students' social background, as students from agricultural backgrounds before the turn of the century were replaced by students of parents from white-collar professions after 1900.

During the first phase of Augustana's history, the Swedish immigrants who were attracted to the college, as well as to the synod in general, came from rural and agricultural backgrounds in Sweden. Given the roots of the Augustana Synod in the Swedish low-church revival of the nineteenth century, it also evident that many of the students came out of that tradition as well. A number of students also came to the college and seminary from Swedish schools associated with the revival, such as Fjellstedtska skolan in Uppsala. (Thirty students in the Augustana Student Database noted that they had previously attended one of the schools associated with the Swedish revival. Almost half [fourteen] had come to Augustana from Fjellstedtska skolan in Uppsala. The majority of these students attended Augustana during the 1870s and 1880s.) During the college's second phase, American-born students were in the majority, most coming from a nonagricultural background and belonging to what could be called a Swedish-American middle class. The most common parental occupation for the American-born students in this category was Augustana pastor, but there were also fair numbers of professionals, such as physicians, lawyers, and academics.

We have also observed a considerable geographic stability among the Augustana students, as the majority came from the traditional Swedish settlement areas in the Midwest, both before and after 1900, which also suggests that the college, like the synod, had difficulties in attracting students from the more urbanized and secularized post-1900 waves of Swedish immigrants.

The analysis of the later careers of the students shows that the Augustana graduates remained largely within the Augustana sphere of Swedish America. To a considerable degree, they actively contributed to the various activities of the Augustana Synod by working in the congregations, colleges, academies, and benevolent institutions and within the publication endeavors. In this way, the ethnic institution recruited new members from within its own ranks, thus ensuring a significant social and ideological continuity.

Several conclusions can be drawn in assessing the role of Swedish-American education, and in particular that which we have observed at Augustana College, in the construction of a Swedish-American identity. First, it is clear that the role of Swedish ethnicity at Augustana College changed considerably over time, and two phases can be distinguished: one before and one after circa 1890. The school developed from a small institution with primarily Swedish-born and Swedish-speaking students from an agricultural background in the 1870s and 1880s to a larger college with a majority of American-born students of Swedish background with limited Swedish-speaking ability and from white-collar family backgrounds after 1890.

During the first phase, the maintenance of a Swedish ethnicity does not seem to have been an issue of major concern. The sense of Swedish identity was weak both in Sweden and at Augustana at this time, and the focus was on teaching the students English and on becoming "Americanized," in President Hasselquist's words. Still, Swedish was taught at the school, and the content of the curriculum largely mirrored that of the Swedish secondary schools. The sense of Swedishness as it existed at Augustana during this early phase, however, seems to have been defined in terms of the use of the Swedish language, as shown by the discussions about the possibility of graduating from the school without having studied Swedish.

After 1890, when the college was dominated by American-born Swedish Americans, Swedish ethnicity became much more pronounced at Augustana College. A separate Department of Swedish was created in 1890, several student organizations devoted to the study of Swedish culture were founded, Swedish visitors were greeted at the campus, and lectures on Swedish topics were presented. The maintenance of this tradition now also became one of the central parts of the school's mission.

During the second phase, a Swedish-American tradition thus developed at the school in which the Swedish ethnicity was culturally defined and which, for American-born students without any direct experiences of Sweden or Swedish culture, became something that had to be studied and learned. In this way, we can say that Augustana College went from being a Swedish institution to a Swedish-American institution.

Second, it is also obvious that the concern for Swedishness was linked with the concern for religion. Between 1882 and 1890, the subjects of Christianity and Swedish were taught by the same professor, and Christianity was the only subject that still required a reading knowledge of Swedish (because of the use of Swedish-language textbooks) at a time when the use of Swedish as a medium of instruction had declined in other subjects. Also, evidence from various official levels in the synod from the years under examination points to how the maintenance of the Augustana Synod's religious heritage was seen as particularly dependent on the maintenance of a Swedish ethnicity. Bishop von Schéele, for example, noted in his visits both the school's commitment to the Lutheran faith and its Swedish identity.

Third, the development of the Swedish-American tradition at Augustana played an important role in defining a specific Swedish-American identity. Even though the curriculum in Swedish literature at Augustana College to a large degree seems to have echoed curricular developments in Sweden, both in terms of books used and authors studied, the Swedish-American context in which it functioned gave it a different meaning than it had in Sweden. At Augustana, the Swedish-American tradition as it was presented through the college's Swedish curriculum was embedded in Swedish-American circumstances, removed from the Swedish cultural milieu. In that sense, authors like Tegnér and Runeberg and their works, the study of the Icelandic sagas, visits by prominent Swedes, or choir concerts took on a meaning specific to the Augustana's Swedish-American cultural context. The idealized view of Sweden, with an emphasis on romanticism, patriotism, and idealism, that was presented at Augustana could also be said to be representative of the Augustana Swedish Americans, thus providing them with characteristics from their ethnic background that added significant parts to their identity in America.

Finally, we have also seen that the Swedish-American tradition at Augustana not only included elements from a national Swedish cultural tradition but also had a multiple approach, through which Swedish, American, and Swedish-American elements were merged. The topics of discussion in the Phrenokosmian Society or in Svenska Vitterhetssällskapet show how a Swedish-American identity was emerging, consisting of selected aspects from the members' two cultural backgrounds and also focusing on the new specific cultural patterns that were developing in Swedish America. In February 1906, C. M. Olander contributed an article to the student newspaper on "Patriotism at Augustana," arguing that even more emphasis ought to be placed on this specific Swedish-American identity and reminding his readers that we must "neither be Swedes, nor Americans but *Swedish Americans*" (emphasis in original).[119] And still in 1919, when immigrant and ethnic cultures were coming under attack in the aftermath of World War I, the first issue of Svenska Vitterhetssällskapet's *Runan* argued that although modern Americans were prone to talk about "America first, America last, America forever," it was still the case that the United States was not "one single integer" but "the sum of all immigrant cultures" and that it was the members' "duty as true Americans to bring forth to the altar of our new homeland, as our most precious gift, the best of Swedish culture."[120] These elements also became important ingredients in the Swedish-American identity that was emerging within the Augustana Synod at the turn of the century.

In 1897, Andreen, who would assume the presidency of Augustana College and Theological Seminary in 1901 and then remain in office until 1935, provided a good illustration of how, by this time, Augustana College was seen as central in creating and propagating a specifically Swedish-American identity. Significantly enough, Andreen was American-born, and in a speech given in Stockholm about growing up in a Swedish-American community on the prairies of Illinois, he described how he had learned about Sweden, its glorious history, its nature, and its folk legends through accounts from his parents and other Swedish immigrants so that a "shimmer from sagas was imbued in the image of the old father country." Andreen also told how his understanding of what it meant to be Swedish and Swedish American had been furthered by his enrolling as a student at Augustana, echoing the experiences of Charley Washington in the play mentioned in chapter 1. Swedish-American schools like Augustana College, Andreen stated, provided the vehicle through which the Swedish-American youth could be taught to "keep the valuable things we own . . . the best which we have inherited from a rich history and a historic church."[121]

In a letter to C. A. Swensson at Bethany College in Kansas from 1897, Andreen further elaborated this point by arguing that the Augustana Synod schools must be centers from which this educational program is spread, "filling our people with love for our language, our history, our church, our activities—in one word *our* heritage." This particular heritage cannot be taught or conveyed through the regular American colleges and universities, Andreen continued. Thus, it becomes a central purpose for the Augustana Synod schools to ensure that the specific Swedish-American heritage is maintained and passed on to the students at these institutions. At our colleges, Andreen concluded, "one becomes . . . such a thoroughly dedicated *(inbiten)* Swedish American that it never goes away."[122]

5

Reading, Writing, and Identity Formation in Swedish America

In 1916, Vilhelm Berger, a journalist, author, and astute observer of Swedish-American conditions, published an article on the significance of the Augustana Synod among the Swedish Americans in which he maintained that the synod had become the "strongest bulwark of Swedishness in the New World." Apart from the work carried out in the individual congregations, two factors are mentioned specifically by Berger as especially important in the synod's work for Swedishness: its educational efforts and its publishing endeavors.[1]

Berger's observation about the significance of the publishing (and reading) of Swedish-language materials for the maintenance of a sense of Swedishness in America points to an important link between the spread of printed materials and the rise of an ethnic or national feeling. This chapter will focus on the role Swedish-language publications in the United States played in the forming of a Swedish-American ethnic identity, particularly on what the Swedish immigrants and their children in America read and on the different kinds of publications that were brought out in Swedish America and within the Augustana Synod.

There is a long history of publications written in languages other than English in the United States, and immigrant or ethnic literatures emerged within almost all immigrant and minority groups in America. They have been unevenly studied, in many cases from within the groups themselves or by scholars from the respective homelands as an extension of their national literatures. Only rarely have they been seen as a part of American literature. In recent years, attempts have been made to integrate and view these literatures as a part of the larger American literary history, as is the case with Orm Øverland's study of Norwegian-American literature, *The Western Home*, where the opening sentence announces that "[T]his is a history of American literature."[2] Immigrant and ethnic literatures can thus be seen from different perspectives, but as work by, among others, Øverland, Werner Sollors, and Øyvind Gulliksen shows, they can help us increase our understanding of the historical linguistic and cultural diversity in America as well as provide opportunities for the study of questions related to issues such as multilingualism, the role of ethnic cultures in American life, and national and ethnic identity formation.[3]

To what extent the act of reading a book, poem, or journal in the Swedish language in America influenced the individual reader, beyond the obvious effect of strengthening language retention, is a question that may of course be raised. But it could be argued, as Brent Peterson has done in his analysis of the nineteenth-century German-American family magazine *Die Abendschule* (The Evening School) published by the German-American Lutheran Missouri Synod, that the readers of such a publication in some ways were influenced by what they read. Peterson concludes that "[r]eading affected the lives of the readers whose inherited culture was no longer adequate for the situation in which they found themselves" and that the narratives published in *Die Abendschule* and read by German Americans "contributed to the formation of an acquired consciousness—and specifically one variety of German-American consciousness."[4] Similar studies of the connection between ethnic literature and identity formation exist, for example, for Italian-American and German-American theater, Polish-American travel narratives, and Chinese-American literature.[5]

From the field of Swedish-American literature, Anna Williams uses the case of Swedish-American journalist and poet Jakob Bonggren to show that he managed to establish himself in Swedish-American cultural circles, and Williams uses his writing to illustrate how it contributed to establishing a sense of Swedish distinctiveness in America. Bonggren as a "literary leader" contributed to the construction of a Swedish-American identity or "ideology," as Williams calls it.[6]

The question of the role that a print culture played for the emergence of a more general sense of community and identity is well known and provides a useful parallel for the study of the formation of ethnic identities. Benedict Anderson's now-classic study *Imagined Communities*, for example, provides a forceful argument for the "ideological" importance of "national print-languages" for European nationalism in the nineteenth century, and he points to how a gradual codification and establishment of national languages and the spread of printed matter in a codified national language were crucial in forging national sentiments for several European nations.[7]

SWEDISH-LANGUAGE READING MATERIALS IN THE UNITED STATES

Previous scholarship in Swedish-American history has only cursorily dealt with publishing and printing in Swedish America. The subject has usually been treated in connection with discussions of Swedish-American literature, and Oliver Linder's overview of Swedish-American literature from the 1920s devotes only two paragraphs to the publishers in Swedish America. Göran Stockenström has discussed the Swedish-American publishing houses briefly in an article,[8] the Augustana Book Concern and the Chicago-based Engberg-Holmberg have been analyzed by Nils Hasselmo and Raymond Jarvi,[9] and Lars Wendelius has analyzed the publishing ventures in Rockford, Illinois.[10] The most comprehensive treatment so far is Williams's discussion of what she calls "the Swedish-American literary institution." Her study provides a comprehensive picture of the ways in which the Swedish-language literature was produced, distributed, and read in Swedish America.[11]

Source materials for the publishing enterprises are not abundant, and little archival material has survived from any of the publication ventures. Most companies published catalogs of their books and other imprints with some regularity, but only some of these have survived. The book catalogs give an in-depth review of the different Swedish-language items that were available in the United States. The majority of the books listed in the catalogs and sold through the Swedish-American publishing houses were not printed in the United States but imported from Sweden. At times, the imported books were listed together with those items actually published in the United States, making it difficult to distinguish between imported literature and original Swedish-American materials. In addition, two historical overviews by E. W. Olson and the Augustana Book Concern provide supplementary information.

Audience

The Swedish population in the nineteenth century exhibited a high degree of literacy. The Reformation in the sixteenth century had emphasized the need for individuals to be able to read and understand the word of God. The Church Law of 1686 prescribed that all persons should learn to read and write, and in 1842 a compulsory basic school was introduced, which, especially after some decades, began to be important for the further development of Swedish literacy. There has been some discussion about how well the Swedes could read: did their reading involve a genuine process of understanding unknown writings, or was it more of a recognition of already well-known texts? Recent scholarship does suggest that the majority of the Swedish people had a fairly good reading ability when the mass-emigration to America began.[12]

Moreover, one dimension of Sweden's economic and social transformations in the nineteenth century meant that the growing bourgeoisie in the country also changed Swedish literary production and consumption. A literary market was created, and in the middle of the nineteenth century the number of books and periodicals published in Sweden increased drastically.[13] Even though the emigrants came from social groups in Swedish society that would not have been great consumers of literature, it has nevertheless been shown that a number of books were printed in large editions and read by substantial numbers of Swedes. Religious literature, such as the hymnal and catechism, were important, but gradually stories, many of a moralizing nature, became more widespread.[14] The basic reader for the compulsory school, *Läsebok för folkskolan*, which was first published in 1868 and reprinted in ten editions until 1910, was crucial in stimulating reading habits among its audience of those attending the primary schools.[15] The Swedish immigrants who arrived in the United States beginning in the latter part of the nineteenth century were thus fairly literate and had some experience with reading on a regular basis. They constituted a large potential Swedish-language literary market in the United States. As immigration came to a halt in the late 1920s and as the retention of the Swedish language dropped considerably in the second and drastically in the third generations,[16] one can assume that this market started dwindling by the 1930s. The different bibliographies and book catalogs also indicate that the heyday of Swedish-language publishing in the United States occurred between 1885 and 1925.

Newspapers and Periodicals

The most significant Swedish-language publications that appeared in the United States were periodical publications—newspapers, journals, annuals—and the Swedish-American press was particularly important in this context. As early as 1922, Robert Park underscored the significance of the foreign-language press for the adjustment of the ethnic group into American society, but the foreign language press's emphasis on materials specific to the needs and interests of the ethnic group helped promote group loyalty and cohesiveness, something that has also been noted by students of the Swedish-American press.[17]

Almost all Swedish-American newspapers were weeklies. The first Swedish-American newspaper was *Skandinaven* (The Scandinavian), published in New York between 1851 and 1852. In 1855, the far more successful *Hemlandet. Det Gamla och Det Nya* (The Old and New Homeland) was started in Galesburg, Illinois, by prominent Augustana pastor T. N. Hasselquist. The paper moved to Chicago after a few years and was one of the leading Swedish-American newspapers until 1914, when it merged with *Svenska Amerikanaren* (The Swedish American). Throughout its history, *Hemlandet* was closely associated with the Augustana Synod, and one of its most influential editors was Johan Enander.

By the beginning of the twentieth century, hundreds of newspapers, magazines, and journals had been established all over Swedish America. The newspapers and magazines followed the settlement patterns of the Swedish ethnic group, and the center for the Swedish-American press became Chicago, where according to one estimate 187 Swedish-language periodicals were published.[18] Numerous publications appeared in Minnesota, on the East Coast (New York City; Jamestown, New York; and Worcester, Massachusetts), and on the West Coast (San Francisco, Los Angeles, and the Seattle area). The only major newspaper in the South was *Texas Posten* (The Texas Post), which was started in Austin in 1896 and continued to be published until 1982.[19]

A number of periodicals were also published in Swedish America, although much fewer in number than the newspapers. A few titles were specifically geared toward literary and cultural subjects, such as *Ungdomsvännen* (The Friend of Youth) and *Prärieblomman* (The Prairie Flower) published by the Augustana Synod. The official organ of the Augustana Synod, *Augustana*, was also a major Swedish-American periodical.[20]

The same social, cultural, and religious divisions that prevailed in Swedish America in general and that have been discussed in chapter 2 also shaped the attitudes contained in the newspapers and periodicals. There were newspapers and periodicals associated with the various segments of Swedish-American opinion as well as with more independent ones.[21] The differences in attitude between the Augustana-oriented *Hemlandet* and the secular *Svenska Amerikanaren* with regard to both cultural and ethnic issues are an often-cited example of the variety of opinion within the Swedish-American press in particular and in the Swedish-American community in general.[22]

It is hard to estimate precisely how many Swedish-language newspapers and periodicals were published in North America. Many appeared only for a short while, and mergers with other papers make it difficult to trace individual papers. In 1910, Swedish-American journalist Axel Söderström recorded 1,158 periodicals,[23] a figure that Ulf Beijbom has lowered to about 650 newspapers and magazines. Of these, 35 percent were weekly newspapers, 54 percent weekly or monthly magazines, and 11 percent annuals, calendars, or Christmas publications of different kinds.[24]

Most of the newspapers were local, with fairly small circulation figures of a few thousand copies. In 1915, *Vestkusten* (The West Coast) in San Francisco and *Texas Posten* in Austin both claimed around 4,000 copies, and newspapers in cities like Moline, Illinois, and Ispheming, Michigan, had even lower circulation figures.[25] A small group of newspapers had a much larger and wider circulation, with a readership extending beyond the immediate boundaries of the city of publication. Included here are, for example, the Chicago papers *Svenska Amerikanaren* and *Svenska Tribunen* (The Swedish Tribune) and the Minneapolis paper *Svenska Amerikanska Posten* (The Swedish-American Post), with publication figures of well over 50,000 copies each week during the second decade of the twentieth century.[26] In 1915, *Svenska Amerikanaren* had the highest circulation among the Swedish-American newspapers, with more than 75,000 copies. The largest periodical, *Augustana*, had a circulation of some 21,000 copies each week in 1915.

The total circulation for the Swedish-American press in 1910 was just over 660,000 copies. This made it the second largest of the foreign-language presses in the United States at that time, well behind the German-language press with over 3,000,000 copies recorded but ahead of the Norwegian- and Yiddish-language presses with 423,000 and 321,000 copies respectively.[27]

Books

The main source for Swedish-language books in the United States was the many bookstores that carried Swedish books and catered to a Swedish reading audience. Swedish book dealers and booksellers existed throughout the United States, mainly in the urban areas where they were a part of the Swedish ethnic communities. The number of bookstores is not known, but Wendelius has recorded several Swedish bookstores in Rockford around the turn of the century, and for 1880 Beijbom has noted eight "paper, book and music dealers" in Chicago.[28] The Augustana Book Concern (henceforth ABC) maintained bookstores in Rock Island, Minneapolis, New York, and Chicago, and over the years Engberg-Holmberg acquired outlets in Moline, St. Paul, and Boston. Other well-known establishments included Dahlén's in New York, Andrew Lundborg's large bookstore in Worcester, and Svenska Bokhandeln in San Francisco.[29] Mail order also seems to have been quite common.[30]

The bookstores were not the only channel of distribution for Swedish-language books in the United States. It was also common to buy books through many of the Swedish-American newspapers and religious publishing houses or in businesses where not only books and paper products but also tobacco, steamship tickets, jewelry, and household appliances were available.[31] In fact, there was a considerable overlap between authors, publishing houses, newspapers, and booksellers. Frequently, a Swedish-language publishing house also maintained a bookstore for its own and imported titles. Sometimes the publisher even assumed the role of author and marketed his or her own products in the bookstore.[32] A well-known example of the latter combination was the bookstore, publishing house, and general business Dalkullan operated in Chicago under Anders Löfström. Löfström imported and sold books and published the popular calendar and almanac *Dalkullan,* which appeared until at least 1942.[33]

The fact that a Swedish book market existed in the United States was not lost on commercial interests in Sweden, and as Johan Svedjedal has shown, several attempts were made by national Swedish booksellers and publishers to find outlets for their products in America.[34] Two of the major Swedish publishing houses even established their own branches in the United States, Bonniers in 1910 in New York and Åhlén & Åkerlund in 1912 in Chicago. In 1911, 10,000 copies of Åhlén & Åkerlund's popular Christmas magazine, *Julstämning,* were sold in Swedish America, and in September the following year the company shipped more than 60,000 copies of both "dime-novels" and more expensive books to its outlet in Chicago.[35] Eventually, however, the interest for Swedish books in the United States tapered off, and, in Svedjedal's words, the "rush" for the "un-mined gold field" in Swedish America that the commercial booksellers and publishers in Sweden had hoped for never materialized.[36]

Publishers

Readers in Swedish America did not have to rely only on imported publications; a great number of Swedish-language items were also printed and published in the United States. It is impossible to assess exactly how many Swedish-language titles were published and in how many copies, as no comprehensive bibliography of Swedish-American imprints exists. However, some estimates exist for specific publishers. Hasselmo has calculated that the largest publisher of Swedish-language materials in North America, the ABC, published 746 Swedish-language titles in about 3.3 million copies between 1891 and 1920. It should be noted that a title may have been reprinted several times during the time period and that the number of original titles would thus be smaller.[37] The fiftieth anniversary publication for the major publishing house in Chicago, Engberg-Holmberg, listed 185 published titles between 1877 and 1909.[38]

The bibliography of the Tell G. Dahllöf collection of Swedish-language imprints in North America provides the best overview of what has been published in Swedish in the United States. Although the collection is far from complete, it is both geographically and ideologically comprehensive in that it includes publications from all over the United States as well as from a large variety of organizations, denominations, and publishing houses. Arnold Barton has called the bibliography the "most comprehensive and useful catalogue of Swedish imprints in America ever published."[39]

The Dahllöf bibliography records 343 different Swedish-language publishing houses and printing outlets in the United States from the mid-nineteenth century on. Several types can be discerned. First, there are a few of what can be called established Swedish-American publishing houses, with a fairly broad publication policy, including religious materials, fiction, schoolbooks, and the like. Included here are the ABC, Engberg-Holmberg Publishing Company, Anders Löfström's Förlag of Chicago, Rasmussen's of Minneapolis, and the two Swedish publishers, Bonniers in New York and Åhlén & Åkerlund in Chicago. Although the ABC, and to a lesser extent Engberg-Holmberg, had a denominational affiliation and a large part of their publications was religious, they also published nonreligious books. Of all these publishers, the ABC was the largest. During a discussion in the Swedish-American press about what kind of literature should be imported to Swedish America from Sweden, the radical paper *Svenska Socialisten* (The Swedish Socialist) identified the ABC, Engberg-Holmberg, and Rasmussen's as those publishers and book dealers that had dominated the market prior to the advent of Åhlén & Åkerlund and Bonniers around 1910.[40]

A second group of publishers was made up of the different Swedish-American denominations themselves. Denominational publications composed one of the major categories among Swedish-American imprints, making up 40 percent of the entries in the Dahllöf bibliography: 28 percent of the publications were theological texts (Bibles, catechisms, devotional literature), and 12 percent were related to the life of the denomination (minutes, anniversary publications, and the like). In Chicago, the Mission Covenant Church and the Swedish Methodists maintained Missionsförbundets Bokhandel (later the Covenant Book Concern) and the Swedish ME Book Concern. The Swedish Baptists used publishing outlets in Chicago and Minneapolis.[41] In addition to these more or less official denominational publishing houses, many other printing offices also published and printed religious literature.

A third printing outlet was made up of the Swedish-American newspapers, which published among other things so-called premium books *(premieböcker)*. These were handsomely printed and bound volumes of a fairly popular character that were given away as incentives to potential subscribers to the newspaper. *Svenska folkets tidning* (The Swedish People's Paper) in Minneapolis, for example, published many premium books, including August Strindberg's *Giftas*, Zacharias Topelius's *Fältskärns berättelser,* and several of Pehr Thomasson's and Herman Bjursten's works.[42] Many authors also used the printing offices of the newspapers to publish privately printed books. Several of Berger's publications appeared in this way at Nordstjernan's printing offices in New York.[43]

Finally, many smaller print shops and publishers published Swedish-language imprints in the United States of a highly varied kind. In Chicago alone, the Dahllöf bibliography lists some forty print shops or publishers with two or fewer titles, many of which seem to have been supported by individuals or organizations.[44]

The practice of issuing lengthy series of fiction, which became prevalent in Sweden from the mid-nineteenth century, also seems to have caught on in Swedish America.[45] In Minneapolis, Rasmussen's and J. Leachman & Son brought out long series of popular Swedish fiction. Rasmussen's series was called Svenska Folkböcker (Swedish Popular Books), appearing as a subgroup of Skandinavisk National Bibliotek (Scandinavian National Library), while Leachman's run was known as Svensk-Amerikanska Biblioteket (The Swedish-American Library). Little bibliographical information is available for these series, but the titles in the series were often included on the back or inside back covers of individual books. *Svenska folkets tidning* had its Svenska nationalbiblioteket (Swedish National Library), which by June 1898 had issued 119 installments.[46] During the first years of the twentieth century, Engberg-Holmberg in Chicago published several historical works and seems to have had a series called "romanticized Swedish historical stories,"[47] and around the same time Löfström at Dalkullan in Chicago catered to those especially interested in detective stories.[48]

What Was Available

An analysis of the books sold in Swedish America has to rely on the catalogs of the Swedish-American bookstores. As noted above, no systematic collection of such catalogs exists, and the following discussion is based on an examination of surviving catalogs in different libraries in the United States and Sweden. Catalogs from Swedish-American book dealers have been located in the Royal Library of Stockholm, the Uppsala University Library, the Tell Dahllöf Collection of Sueco-Americana in the University of Minnesota Library, and the library of the Minnesota Historical Society. As can be expected, imported books from Sweden, or pirated editions of Swedish originals, strongly dominated. Most Swedish booksellers in America did carry some Swedish-American imprints, but they made up a small minority of the titles available. It is not always possible to distinguish which books were imports, American reprints, or original Swedish-American imprints, although evidence suggests that the imports dominated heavily. A catalog from Engberg-Holmberg from the 1870s listed over 2,700 different titles, of which only 23 were the publishers' own items.[49] The rest were imported from Sweden. Although the publication of Engberg-Holmberg titles increased toward the turn of the century, the company's own books always remained a small share of the books distributed through Engberg-Holmberg. No complete listing of the number of titles published at Engberg-Holmberg exists, but no more than 200 books seem to have been brought out prior to 1910.[50] This figure strongly points to the great significance of the imported books from Sweden.[51]

The same tendency can be observed in other Swedish-American bookstores, such as Nya Svenska Bokhandeln in St. Paul, I. T. Relling & Co. in Chicago, A. Österholm & Co. in New York City,[52] and the Swedish bookstores in Rockford.[53] The great majority of the Swedish popular fiction in these bookstores was not published in the United States but imported directly from Sweden. Similarly, in the 1912 catalog from the ABC, about 60 percent of the listings were Swedish imports.[54]

What kind of literature, then, was read in Swedish America? Judging from catalogs of various book dealers, a great variety of books in Swedish was available in the United States on such subjects as religion, education, history, geography, music, and theater and in the form of schoolbooks, dictionaries, cookbooks, how-to books, and almanacs. Stockenström has observed that history and education were particularly frequent categories and that while fiction was available, it made up no more than 15 percent of the total number of books sold.[55]

An examination of the fiction and poetry sections of Swedish-American book catalogs reveals a notable difference between the religiously oriented and the secular book dealers. Fiction, and especially the mass-market-oriented popular fiction that emerged in Sweden (and in the United States as well) in the second half of the nineteenth century, was a problem for religious groups in Sweden. The Swedish religious revival movement actively promoted the reading of "good literature" of a Christian nature.[56] One representative sent out by the National Evangelical Foundation in 1857 reported that he had to struggle against the tendency among Swedes to read what he called "books and newspapers of a harmful nature," among which he included "fairy tales and stories of different kinds."[57] As the Swedish-American denominations had strong roots in the revival movement, similar attitudes toward literature and reading were found in the Swedish-American churches and were reflected in the literature available at the religiously oriented Swedish-American book dealers. The ABC literary profile will be discussed in this respect in greater detail below.

The selection of Swedish-language fiction in the nondenominational bookstores was, as Stockenström has pointed out, dominated by popular literature, including novels, romances, detective stories, and the like.[58] Historical romances with themes from Swedish history and stories, anchored in a particular province in Sweden, were especially common. An examination of the most popular Swedish authors of fiction in catalogs from Rasmussen's in Minneapolis, Dalkullan and Engberg-Holmberg in Chicago, and Österholm's in New York from around the turn of the century yields a group of particularly well-selling authors. By far the two most popular writers were J. O. Åberg (276 titles) and Thomasson (138 titles), whose romanticized historical romances and accounts of life in rural Sweden were available in great numbers in the Swedish-American bookstores.[59] They were followed by several authors of popular Swedish fiction, including Emilie Flygare-Carlén, Marie Sophie Schwarz, Sara Pfeiffer (pseudonym Sylvia), and Alfred Hedenstierna (pseudonym Sigurd). Authors like Flygare-Carlén, Hedenstierna, and Schwarz wrote in a romantic vein, often focusing on a particular province or area in Sweden.[60] As little information is available on the sales of books, it is difficult to determine the degree to which these books were read. Still, Kermit Westerberg's study of a Swedish-language lending library in St. Paul confirms the popularity of these authors among Swedish-American library patrons in that city. The authors with the highest circulation figures were Bjursten, Flygare-Carlén, Schwarz, Thomasson, and Åberg.[61]

The popularity of these authors in Swedish America is hardly surprising, as they were read extensively in Sweden as well, and over 250 titles by Åberg and over 160 by Thomasson were published between 1860 and 1900.[62] Lars Furuland has noted that Thomasson was probably the most widely read author of Swedish fiction before Strindberg (43,000 copies of his *Kung Oskar och skogvaktaren* were printed in numerous editions), and in 1866 a Swedish magazine commented that emigrating peasants in Gothenburg would buy a Bible, a hymnal, and works by Thomasson before boarding the ship.[63] In his study of Swedish family magazines in mid-nineteenth-century Sweden, Eric Johannesson also shows how some of the authors found in the Swedish-American bookstores were also among the most frequent contributors to the Swedish family magazine *Svenska Familjejournalen* (The Swedish Family Journal), including Flygare-Carlén, Schwarz, and Pfeiffer.[64]

Similar conclusions have been reached in analyses of books in various lending libraries in Sweden. An examination of the most frequently borrowed books in a local library in central Sweden in the 1880s shows that Thomasson and Hedenstierna were particularly popular and that the kind of historical and biographical works by, for example, Åberg that were so common in Swedish-American bookstores were also frequently read in Sweden.[65]

It should also be noted that a number of popular authors of non-Swedish background had their works translated into Swedish, at times imported from Sweden, and read in Swedish America, such as the French authors Eugène Sue, Alexandre Dumas, and Paul de Kock, who were well represented in the Swedish-American bookstores. These authors were also widely read in Sweden at the time, although not always viewed with approval. The middle-class-oriented *Svenska Familjejournalen* criticized works by Sue, Dumas, and de Kock as "dangerous" and "inflammatory."[66] The same also seems to have been true elsewhere in Europe. In France, *Les Mystères de Paris* (Mysteries of Paris) and *Le Juif Errant* (The Wandering Jew) by Sue were "explosive successes" and printed in totals of 60,000 and 50,000 copies respectively before 1850.[67] In Ulster, novels by de Kock were controversial and, according to J. R. R. Adams, viewed "with horror by the right-thinking people of Britain."[68] It seems fair to assume that these sentiments would have been shared by many leading representatives in Swedish America as well. In Swedish America, the above-mentioned titles by Sue were available in Swedish translations as *Paris mysterier* and *Den vandrande juden* through Dalkullan in Chicago in 1910.[69]

The most important source of Swedish-language fiction and poetry was, however, the Swedish-American press, where the serialized stories, which could run for several months, were particularly important.[70] In 1930, readers of two Swedish-American newspapers in Moline and Rock Island indicated that the serials were the second-most popular feature in the newspapers, rivalled only by news from Sweden and Swedish America.[71] Unfortunately, no systematic study of the kind of literature that was made available to Swedish-American newspaper readers exists. It seems likely, however, that the same patterns that have been noted in the Swedish-American bookstores and in the publishing houses also characterized the literary selection in the Swedish-American press. In her study of *Svenska Amerikanaren,* Williams also notes that the most frequently serialized Swedish authors in that newspaper were Flygare-Carlén, Georg Starbäck, Schwarz, and Sigge Stark (pseudonym Signe Björnberg), a selection that seems to confirm this assumption.[72]

If the fiction and poetry available in selected commercial Swedish-American bookstores are taken as an indication of what was read in Swedish America, then popular fiction, often with a historic and local attachment, was particularly well liked. This selection also mirrors general reading habits of popular literature in Sweden at the time. Many of these bookstores and publishing outlets were thus responding to literary demands from the Swedish-American community, and their sales policies can thus be assumed to be largely commercially motivated.

It is also clear, however, that bookstores and publishing outlets associated with one of the Swedish-American denominations showed much more deliberate publishing and import policies. Here it is possible to find publishing profiles that show fairly precise notions of what kind of reading matter was desirable or undesirable. Obviously, some of the boundaries were determined by the religious dimensions of the bookstore or publishing house. As the significance of ethnicity increased toward the turn of the century, it is also possible that ethnic cultural considerations came to be important as well. This question will be discussed in greater detail below with regard to the ABC.

THE AUGUSTANA BOOK CONCERN: A BRIEF HISTORY

The annual meeting of the Augustana Synod in 1889 was held in Rock Island and Moline. At this synodical meeting, several years of work toward creating a publishing house owned and operated by the Augustana Synod came to fruition, as it was decided on 18 June to establish a board of publication, the purpose of which was to "achieve better uniformity in the use of textbooks in the parochial schools and our colleges and to publish and supply such books and newspapers that the synod may deem suitable."[73] In September 1889, the Lutheran Augustana Book Concern (from 1904, the Augustana Book Concern) was formally incorporated in the State of Illinois, remaining the official publishing house of the Augustana Synod until the merger of the synod into the Lutheran Church in America in 1962.

The ABC was not the first publication endeavor associated with the Augustana Synod. Discussion about publishing activities had begun as early as 1854, six years prior to the establishment of the Augustana Synod when the early Augustana leaders L. P. Esbjörn, T. N. Hasselquist, and Erland Carlsson discussed the need for a Swedish-language newspaper promoting the religious interests and needs of the Swedish immigrants.[74] As noted above, in 1855 Hasselquist had started the newspaper *Hemlandet,* and four years later Svenska Lutherska Tryckföreningen (the Swedish Lutheran Publication Society in the United States) had organized in Chicago for the purpose of publishing *Hemlandet* as well as "books of general usefulness, especially Christian books and above all those of the Lutheran confession."[75] This organization never turned a profit, and in 1872, the ownership was transferred from the Augustana Synod to the board of Augustana College and Theological Seminary for the financial benefit of this institution.[76]

In 1872, the Augustana Synod found itself in a serious economic situation. Faced with the choice of continuing to operate the educational institutions or the publication activities, the synod leaders opted for the former. They sold off *Hemlandet* to Johan Enander and G. A. Bohman in Chicago, and the Swedish Lutheran Publication Society, which had been the Augustana Synod publication outlet since 1859, was sold to the firm Engberg-Holmberg, also in Chicago. The synod guaranteed not to publish any further newspapers that could be seen as competitors to *Hemlandet,* and representatives of Engberg-Holmberg claimed that the synod would not be able to start another publishing house again. Still, following the move of Augustana College and Theological Seminary to Rock Island in 1875, several private publishing enterprises were started, such as Ungdomens Vänner (The Friends of Youth) in 1877. In 1889, the synod as a whole decided to reestablish a formal publication enterprise.[77] The organization of the ABC resulted in a prolonged conflict with Engberg-Holmberg, who claimed that the synod had forfeited its publishing rights through the sale of the Swedish Lutheran Publication Society and that Engberg-Holmberg should be considered the synod's official publishing house. This conflict would characterize much of the relationship between the ABC and Engberg-Holmberg for almost the next three decades. Following several years of negotiations, the much larger ABC bought Engberg-Holmberg in 1917.[78]

The ABC quickly established itself as a major force in Swedish-American publishing. Due to the lack of a comprehensive Swedish-American bibliography, it is difficult to determine the exact size of the ABC in relationship to other publishers, but Williams identifies the ABC and Engberg-Holmberg as the two leading publishing houses.[79] These two are also the leading publishers in the Dahllöf bibliography, with 354 titles recorded for the ABC and 154 for Engberg-Holmberg,[80] thus pointing to the dominant position of the ABC on the Swedish-American book market.

By 1910, the ABC also operated bookstores in Rock Island, St. Paul, New York City, and Chicago as well as a mail order service, through which the publisher's own books were available in addition to significant numbers of imported books from Sweden.[81] Its strong position is also shown by the fact that it was the only Swedish-American publisher that was a member of Svenska Bokförläggareföreningen (The Swedish Publishers Association).[82]

What Was Sold and Published

By the turn of the century, the ABC had become the dominant Swedish-American publisher as well as a major importer of Swedish-language books. How did the ABC fit into the larger picture of the Swedish-American literary institution sketched above? What kinds of books were sold and published by the ABC, and what does this tell us about the view of Swedish literature and culture presented by the ABC?

An examination of the Swedish-language books available for sale through the ABC shows that it had its own literary perspective. An analysis of the 1912 ABC catalog reveals that, as noted above, 60 percent of the titles were imported from Sweden. In the category of Swedish fiction and poetry, the

ABC placed almost all its emphasis on the established authors from the latter part of the nineteenth century. Authors frequently represented in the commercial Swedish-American bookstores, such as Thomasson and Åberg, were conspicuously absent at the ABC.[83] The most popular authors in the 1912 catalog included Topelius (30 titles), followed by Oscar Levertin (27), Mathilda Roos (21), Viktor Rydberg (18), Verner von Heidenstam (14), Selma Lagerlöf (10), Johan Ludvig Runeberg (7), Carl Snoilsky (7), and Esaias Tegnér (6).

The Swedish literature available through the 1912 ABC catalog was thus much more of an "elite" nature than in many other bookstores. It was the more established and critically acclaimed authors who were presented to prospective Swedish-American readers. This focus on authors established in the Swedish literary canon is also evident from an announcement that the ABC had become the sole American seller of the edition of the collected stories by Lagerlöf published by Bonniers in Stockholm, as well as by an advertisement for the twenty-five-volume Sveriges Nationallitteratur (Sweden's National Literature), a multivolume series of Swedish literary history that was underway in Sweden.[84]

The ABC's focus on established nineteenth-century Swedish authors is also reflected in several anthologies of Swedish literature published at the ABC around 1900. Enander brought out two books of poetry, *Eterneller och vårblommor* (Evergreens and Spring Flowers) (1892) and *Ur svenska sången* (From Swedish Songs) (1901), which, according to the prefaces and advertisements in the ABC catalogs, were geared toward youth clubs and literary societies among the Swedish Americans.[85] The circulation was small, with the total number of copies for each title coming to 2,000.[86] Both volumes include principally Swedish national poetry from the nineteenth century with an emphasis on romantic, historical, and patriotic pieces. *Eterneller och vårblommor,* for example, includes poetry by, among others, Johan Olof Wallin, K. M. Malmström, Carl David af Wirsén, and C. W. Böttiger and a number of "historical" selections by Erik Gustaf Geijer ("Manhem," "Odalbonden," and "Vikingen") and Tegnér (selections from "Svea" and *Fritiofs saga*).[87] In the commentaries that accompany the poems, Enander also asserts that the different poems embody various Swedish national character traits, such as the unbroken freedom of the Swedish peasant as embodied in "Odalbonden" or the fact that the Viking journeys described in "Vikingen" were "the school of our fathers, the emigration of our old fatherland during ancient times."[88] The pieces in *Ur svenska sången* are similar, but, as will be shown below, its selection of poems was not uncontroversial, which resulted in a discussion in the Swedish-American press about the ABC's literary perspective.

Given this literary focus, it should come as no surprise that the ABC's selection of established Swedish literature excluded some examples of modern writers, in particular representatives of the more realistic and radical literature of the so-called modern breakthrough. One of its most notable representatives, Strindberg, had only one title in the 1912 catalog—*Sagor,* a collection of literary fairy tales—while his more controversial works were missing. Strindberg's work was available elsewhere in Swedish America. A. Österholm in New York and Nya Svenska Bokhandeln in St. Paul, for example, each listed eight Strindberg titles around the turn of the century, and Svenska Folkets Tidning in Minneapolis published the controversial *Giftas* in 1888, which went through three editions in two years.[89] In the same way, few of the female authors of the Swedish 1880s were represented in the ABC catalog.[90]

Let us finally examine the publication profile of the ABC. What kinds of reading matter did the ABC publish under its own imprint? My examination covers the years 1890–1919, during which period a total of some 3.9 million copies were printed. The Swedish-language imprints dominated greatly, accounting for 81 percent of the total copies printed. As Hasselmo has shown, the number of English-language publications began to grow in earnest only after 1915. Prior to that year, only 9 percent of the copies printed at the ABC were in English, and it was not until after 1920 that the number of English-language titles and number of copies printed at the ABC exceeded those in Swedish.[91]

All information concerning the publications of the ABC has come from the annual reports of the ABC between 1890 and 1919, which were printed in the synod's minutes each year. The 948 titles have been grouped in twenty-three categories according to contents, which forms the basis for the following analysis. As many titles were reprinted, the total number of copies has been chosen to indicate the relative sizes of the groups. The identification of each publication is not always easy as no systematic bibliographic references were given in the reports. In most cases the circulation figures were included, but they are missing for thirty-one titles. The information from the annual reports has been supplemented with data from the printed ABC catalogs and with individual books with ABC imprints missing from the annual reports but located in various libraries. It is thus likely that some ABC imprints are missing from the ABC database. Still, it provides the best approximation that we have of the ABC imprints. Printed ABC catalogs exist in the Evangelical Lutheran Church in America Archives in Chicago, in the Royal Library in Stockholm, and in the Uppsala University Library.

Given the ABC's role as a denominational publishing house, it is only natural that religious publications serving the needs of the growing church body were significant. Just over 50 percent of all copies printed at the ABC between 1890 and 1919 belonged to what can be called denominational publications. Religious music was the most important group, accounting for 17 percent of all the copies published at the ABC between 1890 and 1919. Included here were various hymnals and songbooks, including the very popular *Hemlandssånger*. Its popularity was particularly pronounced before 1900, when it was used as a hymnal in the Augustana congregations and represented over two-thirds of the copies printed in the category of religious music. Sunday school materials accounted for about 10 percent of the total copies published and were followed by a group including Bibles, New Testaments, and catechisms, making up some 5 percent of the total.

Not quite half of the ABC publications were of a nondenominational nature. This is a high figure in comparison with other Swedish-American denominational publishing houses. Both the Mission Covenant Book Concern and the Baptist Publication Society published very few nonreligious publications,[92] whereas by 1910 the ABC had clearly developed a publishing profile that went beyond the more direct denominational needs of the church body. The nondenominational publications can be divided into several categories. The largest was almanacs, which accounted for 16 percent of the total ABC copies printed between 1890 and 1919, followed by stories primarily intended for children and youth (14 percent), schoolbooks (10 percent), and various literary periodicals (6 percent). Some national Swedish literature was also reprinted at the ABC (1 percent), as was a small group of original Swedish-American fiction and poetry (half a percent) and books about Swedish America (1 percent). Those publication categories that were particularly important for the ABC's role in shaping Augustana's Swedish-American identity will be discussed in chapter 6.

Suitable Reading Material

In 1908, *Augustana* carried an article stating that Swedish Americans ought to read "good, elevated *[uppbygglig]* literature."[93] In the same year, the position of a literary editor was established at the ABC, whose duties it was "to encourage the authorship of such works as it may be in the best interest of the Book Concern to publish."[94]

As has already been suggested, a vision of suitable reading matter existed in the synod, and it thus becomes important to identify what the Augustana Synod meant by "good" literature that would be in the "best interest" of the denomination. The synod's view of literature must be seen against the background of the general attitude toward culture and education within the Augustana Synod, in which, as has been underscored earlier, the religious dimension, and more precisely the Lutheranism associated with the synod, was fundamental. Upholding and promoting what were perceived as basic Christian values was, as we have seen, a very important concern for the synod leadership.

The ABC made clear several times its specific position regarding suitable reading materials. In his annual report to the synod in 1884, President Erland Carlsson pointed to complaints from Minnesota and Kansas where the "bad newspapers and magazines" had gained influence among Swedish Americans. He not only voiced concern over the non-Christian tendencies in these publications but also pointed to the danger associated with reading the serialized novels in these newspapers and magazines that "inevitably destroy a person's sense of right and wrong." He stated that it was the duty of parents, pastors, and the churches to ensure that "good and Christian" books and magazines were read.[95] Carlsson noted with pleasure, however, that youth organizations "guided by a true Christian spirit" had been formed in the synod, which provided its members with lending libraries that contained "good books."[96]

This attitude remained one of the basic elements in the Augustana Synod's view of literature. In 1893, *Augustana* warned against the kind of literature that appealed to the "lack of morality and materialism" among Swedish Americans, instead advocating reading materials that were founded on Christian religion and that had played a very important role in "the moral and intellectual growth of the Swedish-American people."[97] As noted above, fifteen years later, *Augustana* cautioned against reading "cheap and sensational" books and maintained that Swedish Americans ought to read "good, elevated literature."[98] In 1910, when the ABC published *Ett klöfverblad* (A Clover Leaf) by Margarete Lenk, a story for children, *Augustana* recommended it strongly as a "healthy and simple story" in a time when so much material "of a doubtful nature, especially for the youth" was being published.[99] Again in 1912, "bad literature" was called a threat to the church and the reading of novels dangerous, as it diverted attention from "serious subjects."[100]

A further example of the process of how the ABC sought to promote "good literature" appropriate for Swedish-American readers comes from the discussion in 1913 about "trash literature" *(smutslitteratur)*—sensational and popular fiction—sparked by attempts by the two Swedish publishing houses Bonniers and Åhlén & Åkerlund to gain a foothold in the Swedish-American market. Protests were heard in many quarters of Swedish America, including the Augustana Synod, against this kind of fiction that these publishers imported, and an appeal was published in *Svenska Journalen* (The Swedish Journal) in Rockford in early 1913 calling for writers of higher quality, such as Gustaf Fröding, Heidenstam, Lagerlöf, and Strindberg.[101]

Karl-Otto Bonnier of Bonniers publishing house responded to the Swedish-American accusations, saying that Bonniers simply marketed what Swedish America wanted, an "older literature," including August Blanche, Flygare-Carlén, and Schwarz. Erik Åkerlund added that this was not the first time his publishing house had been attacked by Swedish Americans, suggesting that part of the reason was fear of competition on the part of the ABC. He also noted that the ABC had refused to publish advertisements for Åhlén & Åkerlund's Christmas magazine *Julstämning* in 1912, of which a substantial part of the 300,000 copies printed had been set aside for the Swedish-American market.[102]

A quick response appeared in *Augustana,* which pointed out that the synod agreed that a great deal of undesirable literature promoting free love and drunkenness and attacking religion was imported to Swedish America.[103] But *Augustana* did not abide by all the suggested replacements made by *Svenska Journalen,* noting that "many of Strindberg's works cannot be recommended to our people." Concerning *Julstämning, Augustana* admitted that advertisements had been refused but cited aesthetic grounds rather than commercial for their exclusion. Many of the illustrations in the magazine were of such a nature that *Augustana* found it highly surprising that they were considered suitable for distribution in Sweden, concluding that no members of the Augustana Synod could "tolerate *Julstämning* on their parlor tables." (*Augustana* may well have been referring to the colored illustrations by Anders Zorn and others of dancing and bathing women, sometimes not fully clothed.)

The situation does not seem to have been resolved, and three years later, in 1916, the issue was discussed by the executive committee of the board of directors of the ABC when it was stated that an ABC Christmas magazine was "urgently needed" in order to "obviate the evil influence of certain Swedish Christmas magazines with very offensive contents" that were imported to Swedish America every year. It was also decided to publish such a Swedish-American Christmas magazine, to be edited by E. W. Olson, on the staff of the ABC. The magazine, which was to be "adapted to the needs of the Swedish Americans in general without regard to their church affiliation," would "furnish a literary publication of good moral tendency" and contain articles of interest to Swedish Americans, dealing with "their history, their cultural progress and matters of similar import."[104] Contributors were carefully selected and the title *God Jul* (Merry Christmas) settled upon.[105]

God Jul became a Swedish-American Christmas magazine.[106] A number of leading Swedish-American authors and artists contributed to the publication, both from within and without the Augustana sphere in Swedish America, suggesting both the degree to which a Swedish-American identity had developed in the Augustana Synod by 1916 and the leading cultural position the synod had in Swedish America. It included artwork by Olof Grafström, G. N. Malm, Henry Reuterdahl, and Birger Sandzén, and literary contributions came from Bonggren, David Nyvall, E. W. Olson, Ernst Skarstedt, Mauritz Stople, and Leonard Strömberg. Some contributions specifically dealt with what it meant to be Swedish American and will be discussed in chapter 6.

Selecting Reading Material

Because the Augustana Synod had a vision of the kind of proper or suitable reading material that it wanted its members, and especially youth, to read, the process through which these reading materials was selected is important to analyze. The workings of this process can be observed in the screening of suitable manuscripts at the ABC as well as in discussions following the publication of certain books. One example is the publication of a book of poetry by the well-known journalist and editor of *Svenska Amerikanaren* in Chicago, Jakob Bonggren, who submitted a manuscript for a book of poetry in 1899. As Williams has shown, Bonggren was one of the leading persons in the Swedish-American cultural circles at this time, and to publish a book of his poetry would clearly have strengthened the Swedish-American profile of the ABC.[107] Following the submission, a committee was appointed to "edit the manuscript,"[108] and in July 1900, the ABC encouraged Bonggren to send in the poems he would like to publish to "the official scrutinizer S. G.

Youngert," who would then determine which of the poems "from the point of view of the ABC ought not to be published."[109] No versions of the manuscript have survived, but it seems likely that Bonggren's text did undergo some kind of a screening process. The ABC decided to publish the book in 1901,[110] and it appeared under the ABC imprint in 1902 as *Sånger och sagor* (Songs and Sagas).[111] Apparently, the publishing house was pleased with the publication, as the book was kept in stock at the ABC at least until 1912.[112]

An example of a publication rejected on the grounds of not being suitable comes from 1901 when the former science professor at Augustana, Joshua Lindahl, at the time living in Cincinnati, offered the ABC translations into English of *Singoalla* by Rydberg, an offer that was rejected because works of this nature were not considered to be "within the sphere of activities of the Augustana Book Concern."[113] It was not explicitly stated why this was the case, but one factor may be that *Singoalla* partly deals with forbidden love between a married man and a young, seductive Gypsy girl.[114]

Another example of the gatekeeping function that ABC exercised comes from a 1902 discussion about the publication of *Ur svenska sången,* an anthology of Swedish songs and poetry from 1800–1850 edited by Enander, offered to the ABC in 1889, and published shortly before Christmas 1901.[115] According to the preface and the advertisements in the Swedish-American press, this "poetic reader" was intended to be read and used in "Swedish-American homes, youth groups, and literary societies."[116] The book was fairly widely reviewed in the Swedish-American press, and a debate ensued about the selection of poems that had been included. The Chicago-based *Fosterlandet* (The Native Land) criticized Enander for having excluded some of "the most beautiful" poems by the poet and bishop Frans Michael Franzén because they dealt with drinking both champagne and beer. In this way, Enander showed a bias, *Fosterlandet* argued, favoring those groups who advocated abstinence of alcohol.[117] On the other hand, two other leading papers in Chicago, *Hemlandet* and *Svenska Amerikanaren,* found no problems with the selection of poems in the book. *Hemlandet* emphasized that the selection of poems was "carefully done" and recommended the book "warmly" to "youth groups, literary societies, homes and schools in Swedish America."[118] A similar opinion was expressed by "J. B." (Jakob Bonggren) in *Svenska Amerikanaren,* who stated that the selection of poetry was "good and done with care" and that the book would satisfy a "felt need among us Swedish Americans."[119]

A week after the first reviews had appeared, the discussion continued in *Svenska Kuriren* (The Swedish Courier) another Chicago paper, where *Fos-*

terlandet's criticism against the book was noted. *Kuriren* defended Enander's job as an editor, claiming that he had only done what the publisher—the ABC—had wanted the editor to do. He had been given the task of putting the book together "following the same principles that the synod wishes to implement in all the education of the youth that it sees as its mission to educate," *Kuriren* wrote.[120] These principles, *Kuriren* continued sarcastically, obviously included the "exclusion" of all pieces from the first half of the previous century that expressed "joy of life," contained even mild swear words, or hinted that all "fermented beverages," except for weak beer *(svagdricka),* would have an exhilarating effect. These biases were to be expected, as Enander followed only "the Augustana perspective" *(Augustanasynpunkten)* in his editing policy. Had he been able to act independently, without having to pay attention to the views of the Augustana Synod, *Kuriren* was convinced that he would not have given "such a terribly mutilated view of Swedish poetry." A week later, *Kuriren* commented further on the issue of including poems in which champagne was drunk, asking if it did not seem strange for Augustana ministers, who at the recent banquet in honor of Bishop von Schéele had been seen "happily consuming one glass of champagne after the other," to impose different moral standards for their parishioners.[121]

The book was also reviewed in *Augustana,* which presented it in a very positive manner, specifically stating that Enander's selection of poetry was "the best from the time period in question" and that the book would be a suitable anthology for Swedish-American youth and societies and educational institutions.[122] *Augustana* also responded to the criticism by *Fosterlandet,* defending the exclusion of certain poems. It is notable that a newspaper "for church and home" would lament the fact that poems such as "Gode gosse, töm glaset" and "Champagnevinet" were missing. "We consider it a strength *[en verklig förtjänst]* that the collection is free from drinking songs, and only contains such poems that can be read both at home and in church, or in company where 'church and home' are revered."[123]

Fosterlandet responded to both *Augustana* and *Svenska Kuriren*. To *Augustana*'s criticism that *Fosterlandet* condoned drinking songs, the paper said that "fiction and poetry ought to be able to be what they are and not be subjected to arbitrary excising and interpretations in such a biased manner that every single piece could be read in church." *Augustana*'s opinion that "church and home" required the elimination and annotation of poetry by Wallin and Franzén was rejected, and the paper repeated its position:

Reading, Writing, and Identity Formation

"[L]et our people get our Swedish literature un-mutilated! Let young and old themselves choose what suits them!"

In response to *Kuriren*, *Fosterlandet* maintained that Enander as editor had not been unduly influenced by the ABC, as *Kuriren* had claimed. The paper asserted that it knew for a fact that the ABC had published the manuscript just as it had been received from Enander. The selections in the book had thus been made by Enander and should not be seen as an attempt by the Augustana Synod to "strangle or mutilate the Swedish poetry." Moreover, *Fosterlandet* wondered how it was that anyone who wished could order books by "the other Swedish poets," from Carl Michael Bellman to Fröding, through the ABC, if the ABC was engaged in such vicious attacks against Swedish poetry. *Fosterlandet* also pointed to the recently published volume of the literary annual *Prärieblomman* where "the Augustana Synod poet par excellence" Ludvig Holmes had a poem, which, although devoted to the "glory of coffee," also "praises 'Spiritus Stimulus.'"[124]

Enander himself finally commented on the debate in *Augustana* a few weeks later, saying that, although those poems that had been excluded could well have a literary and artistic value, they were "less suitable" for a book intended to be used in "homes, churches, schools, youth associations, and literary groups."[125] Further, he noted that he knew that the ABC "did not approve" of such songs nor "would have been willing to publish or distribute" them and that it thus would have been impossible to publish a book along the lines that his critics wanted. And, said Enander, "I am convinced that if *Ur svenska sången* had included such 'gems' as Franzén's drinking songs, both I and the publishing house would have been just as much criticized as we have been now." It is also worth noting that in the preface to the book, Enander stated that he had avoided those poems that included words and expressions that may seem "offensive" in certain circles in order that the book may be useful for *"all countrymen"* (emphasis in original).[126]

The debate over *Ur svenska sången* illustrates the fact that a "special perspective" existed within the Augustana Synod regarding the nature of suitable reading matters, especially in a publication that was directed toward the home and the young. Poems that could be seen as endorsing drinking were not suitable—not even if they were written by a Swedish bishop—and thus not possible to publish, as both Enander and *Augustana* pointed out. The debate also shows that the secularly oriented newspaper *Svenska Kuriren* used this discussion as an opportunity to attack the view on literature and culture in general in the Augustana Synod, claiming that it sought to "mutilate" Swedish poetry.

It is not surprising that *Hemlandet* gave the book a very positive review, as the paper was closely allied with the Augustana Synod. It is perhaps more noticeable that *Svenska Amerikanaren*, *Hemlandet*'s old rival and antagonist, which in the past had been very critical of the cultural narrow-mindedness in the Augustana Synod, also treated the book in positive terms and approved of the selection of poems. This can partly be explained by the fact that, as Williams has pointed out, the "cultural gap" between *Svenska Amerikanaren* and the Augustana Synod by this time was beginning to grow smaller.[127] Moreover, it should be noted that the reviewer in *Svenska Amerikanaren* was the same Jakob Bonggren who had had his *Sånger och sagor* published by the ABC six months prior to the review.

The significance attached to the process of selecting suitable ABC publications eventually resulted in the decision to establish a position of literary editor at the ABC. Such a position had been discussed in 1894, when the need to ensure that "only truly good works" were published had been noted.[128] But it was not until the annual meeting of 1907 that the synod created the position of literary editor at the ABC, and Pastor C. J. Bengtson was appointed to the job in 1908.[129]

The literary editor was to review manuscripts submitted to the ABC and recommend to the board on the suitability of publication. In judging the various manuscripts, the editor considered both literary and financial aspects of the publications. An example of the latter comes from 1909, when the manuscript "Ungdomsbilder i biblisk belysning" (Youth Pictures in a Biblical Light) by E. J. Werner was considered to be "a credit to the author" but hardly economically viable to publish.[130]

Bengtson served as literary editor for two years, then was replaced by Pastor O. V. Holmgrain, who had served as assistant editor at the ABC. Two other applicants had applied for the job, but the executive committee of the ABC did not feel that either one was suitable and therefore picked Holmgrain, who was considered the best candidate because of his "many years of experience of literary questions, sound judgement in literary matters, and general expertise and suitability."[131] Holmgrain remained as literary editor until 1918.

Publishing activities were an important part of the work of the Augustana Synod. Its publishing house, the ABC, became the dominant Swedish-

American publisher as well as a major bookseller of imported and domestic titles. The preceding discussion has shown that the ABC developed a definite literary profile in which religious and moral concerns were important, both in terms of the books published and of the books sold in the ABC bookstores. In terms of books imported from Sweden, the most frequent authors represented the established elite authors from the latter part of the nineteenth century, while many of the authors of Swedish popular fiction of the time, widely read in both Sweden and Swedish America, were excluded at the ABC. Apart from religious publication for denominational use, the publisher's own publication list included almanacs, stories for children and youth, and schoolbooks, as well as a small amount of original Swedish-American fiction, poetry, and books about Swedish America.

The analysis of the discussion about the kind of books sold and published shows the significance that the ABC attached to its publication profile. Suitable reading matter for Swedish Americans was a part of the cultural struggle in Swedish America, and the ABC functioned as a gatekeeper. We have seen how the publishing house carefully selected the books to be sold and published, in this way maintaining an "Augustana perspective" on literature, as critics labeled it in the debate over *Ur svenska sången*. Religious and moral considerations set boundaries for what was considered acceptable and what was not. In this way, the literary selections at the ABC provided a restricted number of literary building blocks that became an important element in the Augustana Synod's Swedish-American identity.

6
The Augustana Book Concern as a Source for Swedish-American Identity

The religious dimension in the publication profile of the ABC was not only important in terms of denominational publications; as noted earlier, the general Christian tenor that informed the Augustana view of culture and education also set an ideological framework for its nondenominational publications. In his 1901 annual report to the synod, President Eric Norelius also noted that the Augustana Synod was a "civilising" force among Swedish Americans. He characterized the Augustana Synod as the only denomination that, through schools, literary activities, and maintenance of a Swedish Lutheran faith, had done anything significant for the "maintenance of Swedish language, literature and spirit *[anda]*" in the United States.[1]

This statement is a reflection of the fact that the "ethnic element" in the Augustana Synod in general was beginning to be emphasized around the turn of the century in what I have called the second phase of the synod's history. In chapters 3 and 4, we saw how a Swedish-American tradition was taking form at Augustana College after circa 1890 in its curriculum, student societies, and the like. We will now examine the specific role of the ABC in the creation of a Swedish-American ethnic identity in the Augustana Synod, or what can be called the "ethnic element" in the ABC publishing profile. This will be done through an analysis of several types of ABC publications that were especially important for shaping the Swedish-American identity. As in chapter 5, the discussion of titles and circulation numbers is based on a compilation and analysis of book catalogs and annual reports of the ABC publications.

An analysis of the ethnic element at the ABC will rely on three types of publications: stories for children and youth, schoolbooks, and publications specifically dealing with Swedish-American topics. One of the main concerns of the Augustana Synod was keeping the children who were growing up in America as members of the denomination. Given the secular and mainstream American cultural environment, keeping youth within the religious and cultural confines of the synod became a serious matter. As we have seen, the synod supported a great number of activities directed toward the youth, in which various forms of instruction—such as Sunday schools, confirmation schools, parochial schools, as well as the academies and colleges—were important elements. In addition, special youth organizations were started, promoting both religious and ethnic loyalties.[2]

The publications at the ABC that were directed toward children and youth included a wide array of magazines, books, and pamphlets. The youth publications are a good source for examining the ideas that the synod considered to be important for the socialization of the young. The ABC publication list shows that publications for the youth were one of the main concerns of the publishing house. The classification of the various titles as reading matter for children or youth is not always obvious, but my main rule has been to follow the ABC's own guidelines. When a book contains a subtitle such as "readings for the young" or something similar, I have automatically grouped it as reading for children or youth. Stories in book form made up 14 percent of all the copies published between 1890 and 1919 (538,000 copies). Of the copies printed, 81 percent were in Swedish, and it was not until after 1910 that any significant number of stories in English for children and youth were published.

In addition, at least six literary serials or annuals directed especially toward juvenile readers existed, which appeared either once—usually before Christmas—or several times per year, containing literary selections of varied nature. These made up almost 5 percent of the total copies published, accounting for 177,500 copies. This figure excludes *Prärieblomman*. Finally, the ABC published a number of monthly or semimonthly magazines directed at children and youth, which went out in quite large editions, averaging between 20,000 and 30,000 copies per issue.

A second category of publications that can be assumed to have had a more direct role in the promulgation of a Swedish-American identity consists of schoolbooks, including readers of both an elementary and a more advanced nature, as well as anthologies of selected Swedish fiction and poetry. Schoolbooks constitute an obvious example of how values are transmitted from generation to generation, and it can be argued that they are important elements in the construction and maintenance of national identities.[3] The creation of an ethnic identity is in some ways parallel to the socialization process in schools, and one can thus assume that similar processes were at work here. Schoolbooks also made up the fourth largest category of publications at the ABC, behind stories for children and youth, accounting for some 10 percent of the total copies printed. All of the schoolbooks that will be examined were published in Swedish.

A final group of publications related directly to Swedish-American culture. Included here are original Swedish-American literature, titles dealing with different aspects of Swedish-American history, and books reflecting on the nature and character of Swedish America. Contributors and authors in this group include established Swedish-American writers and opinion makers such as C. W. Andeer, Jakob Bonggren, Johan Enander, Oliver Linder, Johan Person, and Anna Olson. In addition, *Prärieblomman* and *Ungdomsvännen* also contained material that merits their inclusion in this category of the ABC publications.

It is this group of publications at the ABC that most explicitly deals with Swedish-American culture and the issue of what it meant to be Swedish in America. Still, it must be underscored that it made up only a fraction of the ABC imprints—just 1.5 percent. *Sånger och sagor,* the 1902 collection of poetry by Bonggren, was printed in a run of 2,500 copies and remained in stock for at least a decade, and *Prärieblomman,* which was considered a show window for Swedish-American culture, never exceeded 3,000 copies.[4] Though quantitatively a small group of publications, they are, from the point of view of how a Swedish-American identity was formed in the Augustana Synod, of great qualitative interest. In the remaining parts of this chapter, these three categories of publications will be examined in greater detail.

STORIES FOR CHILDREN AND YOUTH

Books

Virtually none of the books published at the ABC for children were written by Swedish-American authors. They were instead either reprints (or, toward the end of the period, translations into English) of national Swedish children's literature or translations into Swedish (or sometimes English) of non-Swedish materials.

Since the ABC was the largest Swedish-language publishing house in the United States, one could assume that large quantities of national Swedish children's literature would have been published. However, the position of the national Swedish literature was surprisingly weak, as only about 15 percent of the copies printed where the national origin of the author can be established was Swedish. The identification of the national origin of the author is not always easy. In many cases when the author's name is not given, the books have been classified based on translation information. In this way, 54 percent of the national origin of the children's literature published at the ABC has been established. The most popular authors from Sweden were Mathilda Roos, whose books appeared in 12,000 copies (of which 10,000 were in English translation), Elisabeth Beskow (better known under her pseudonym, Runa) with 14,000 copies (of which 6,000 were in English translation), and Emily Nonnen with 15,000 copies.

Rather, translations of German authors into Swedish (and to a lesser extent English) dominated among the books for the young at the ABC. More than two-thirds of all the children's books printed (for which the background of the author is known) were of German origin.[5] The top three authors, who accounted for almost half of the copies printed, were Margarete Lenk, who was printed in 33,000 copies (of which 5,000 were in English translation), Nikolaus Fries with 21,000 copies, and Minna Rüdiger with a total run of 12,000.

As Margareta Hamrin has pointed out, the children's literature published in Swedish America did not reflect the intensive debate about children's reading going on around the turn of the century in Sweden, and stories containing elements of fantasy were very rare in Swedish America.[6] Most of the authors mentioned above tended to write books conveying a basic message of Christian morality to their readers, in which traditional moral values such as being content, obeying one's elders, doing good deeds, and so on, prevail, and which in many cases end with the protagonists finding salvation in God. The stories exhibit the same characteristics that Åke Kussak has found in his analysis of the short stories published by Svenska Missionsförbundet in its various publications after 1910, with an emphasis on the Christian faith and "how to become a Christian and how to act as a Christian."[7] Of the German authors at the ABC who can be found in the standard encyclopedia of German children's literature, all are described as having written stories with religious tendencies, and several of them were published at German religious publishing houses.[8]

How closely did the ABC follow the publication profiles of similar religious publishing houses in Sweden? Did it merely mirror what was being done on the other side of the Atlantic, or did it choose to pursue a more independent policy? We have seen that the share of national Swedish children's literature was relatively small at the ABC. Translated children's literature dominated in Sweden from 1870 until 1920 as well, even though the German share of translations in Sweden was gradually replaced by English-language originals at the turn of the century.[9] Many of the authors and, to some degree, titles that came out at the ABC were also published in Sweden, primarily by Evangeliska Fosterlandsstiftelsen (EFS) but also by other religiously oriented publishing houses.

At EFS, the literature for children and the young was dominated by translated works,[10] and the top three German writers at the ABC—Lenk, Fries, and Rüdiger—were also frequently published by EFS. During the decades around the turn of the century, twenty-one titles by Lenk, sixteen by Fries, and nine by Rüdiger appeared in Sweden, with the great majority by EFS.[11] Of these titles, two by Lenk and Fries and one by Rüdiger also appeared at the ABC. The figure might be higher, as some of the books might have been published under different titles in Sweden and at the ABC. Moreover, several of the ABC titles are collections, which may have been put together by the ABC under its own title.

Still, the majority of the titles by Lenk and Fries as well as a number of other authors at the ABC do not seem to have been published in Sweden. Moreover, a physical examination of those titles published in both countries shows that the American editions are not just American republications of the Swedish editions.[12] The translations were done in the United States and, judging by the names or initials of the translators given, usually by someone associated with the ABC or Augustana College. In at least one case, the ABC preceded EFS in bringing out a Swedish translation of one of the German titles, later published in both countries.[13]

This suggests that the ABC maintained an independent publication profile in the selection of individual titles, although it quite naturally operated within a similar cultural sphere as did, for example, EFS in Sweden. It also seems likely that the ABC was influenced by the publication profiles of other Lutheran publishing houses in the United States. The large number of translations from German were inspired by German-American Lutheran publishing houses in the United States. One such example is Fries's *Irrlichte*.

Eine Erzählung, which was published in Pelcher, Pennsylvania, in 1880 and was brought out at the ABC in 1904 as *Vid fyrelden.*

Literary Serials and Annuals for Children

Six different serials or annuals in Swedish aimed at the younger readers have been identified in the ABC publication list. No complete runs of these literary serials have been located, and my analysis is therefore based on incomplete material. The ABC annual reports do not always include the literary serials, which makes it hard to compute the size of the editions and to establish exact years of publication. The best holdings of the literary serials exist at the Swenson Swedish Immigration Research Center at Augustana College in Rock Island and in the Royal Library in Stockholm.

Four of the serials—*Julklockorna* (The Christmas Bells), *Juvelskrinet* (The Jewel Box), *Blommor vid vägen* (Roadside Flowers), and *Lekkamraten* (The Playmate)—were published mainly before the turn of the century and appeared in print runs of between 9,000 and 14,000, totals considerably smaller than for those titles published after 1900. *Julklockorna* was a Christmas annual, *Juvelskrinet* and *Blommor vid vägen* contained "stories for children," and *Lekkamraten* included "illustrations for the young with text."[14] The content in these publications was heavily religious and in rather simple language, obviously directed at fairly young children.

Around the turn of the century, two new serials were started that reached much larger editions, *Nytt bibliotek för barn och ungdom* (New Library for Children and Youth) and *Vid Juletid. Vinterblommor samlade för de små* (At Christmastime. Winter Blossoms for the Young). In both serials, the language was considerably more advanced than in those published before the turn of the century, the intended audience being young persons with a good basic knowledge of Swedish. Their content was also of a different nature. *Nytt bibliotek,* published at least between 1906 and 1915, appeared in a minimum of 47,000 copies and contained a number of short stories, mostly of an edifying and religious nature, and a few poems. Although all authors have not been identified, those who have—including Josef Grytzell, Anna Lybecker, Karl Karlsson, Lina Sandell-Berg, and Sigrid Wiedemann—were active in the sphere of religious publishing for children and youth in Sweden and associated with denominations such as EFS or Svenska Missionsförbundet.[15]

Vid Juletid, published between 1896 and 1910 with a total run of at least 72,000 copies, was an even more ambitious publication. It was edited by professors of Swedish at Augustana College, first Ernst A. Zetterstrand and, from 1904, Jules Mauritzson. A Christmas magazine similar to those published in Sweden at the turn of the century, *Vid Juletid* in fact drew heavily on texts from those Swedish magazines, and many of its contributions were *Kunstmärchen* by such well known contemporary literary fairy tale authors in Sweden as Beskow, Hugo Gyllander, Hedvig Indebetou, Amanda Kerfstedt, and Harald Östenson. Most of these fairy tales had already been published in Sweden, and although there was a basic tone of Christian morality to many of the stories, they were much less explicitly religious than the contributions in the other magazines discussed.[16] *Vid Juletid* thus showed a high cultural profile in comparison with the other periodicals and was the Christmas magazine that was most like its Swedish counterparts.

It should be noted that other American denominations also published periodicals for children with didactic, moral, and religious content similar to that found among the Augustana publications. According to Barbara Snedeker Bates, over 200 denominational periodicals for children were published between circa 1840 and 1960, reaching millions of children. This is, however, an area of research within which relatively little work has been done.[17]

How did these publications for children and youth relate to the creation of a sense of Swedishness at the ABC? First, the language aspect must be stressed. By reading these books and magazines, young Swedes and Swedish Americans were given an opportunity to learn or to maintain the use of the Swedish language. Some publications, such as books by Roos or Lenk and *Vid Juletid*, required a good command of the Swedish language, which thus contributed to the use and knowledge of a more advanced level of Swedish in America.

Second, some are set in a Swedish milieu. This is of course particularly true of the contributions by Swedish authors but also visible in some of the collections of stories.[18] A few collections also include Swedish-American settings, such as *Vid Jesu krubba* from 1908, where a Christmas story contrasts a wealthy but non-Christian Swedish-American family in Chicago with a much poorer but pious one in the same city.[19] Although the moral and religious elements in the stories undoubtedly were most significant, the Swedish or Swedish-American geographical settings also singled out and placed Swedish and Swedish-American milieus in special circumstances for the readers, helping create a frame of reference in which Sweden and Swedish America were natural elements.

Finally, it is important to note that certain fairly well-known Swedish authors for children were also introduced into the Swedish-American cultural milieu, especially through *Vid Juletid*. Among all the periodical publications for youth, *Vid Juletid* was clearly the most ambitious and included contributions that went beyond the basic Christian morality that appeared in many other works. Several contemporary national Swedish authors were represented in the journal, who thus also became a part of the Swedish-American cultural tradition.

SCHOOLBOOKS

As noted above, schoolbooks were the fourth largest category of publications at the ABC and a close second after stories for children and youth among the nondenominational publications. The category includes elementary Swedish language books, primers for various grades, anthologies of Swedish literature, and a few titles to be used in the instruction of Swedish at the college and university level. The great majority of the publications were in Swedish, and those few titles that appeared in English were the Swedish college and university textbooks.

The publication of these schoolbooks was of great significance for the Augustana Synod; indeed, it was one of the motives behind the establishment of the publishing company in the first place. When a board of publication was appointed at the synod meeting in 1889 and empowered to buy the then privately owned Augustana Book Concern on behalf of the synod, one of the main reasons given was, as noted above, to "achieve better uniformity in the use of textbooks" in the schools associated with the Augustana Synod.[20] Moreover, during the ABC's first decade, schoolbooks made up the leading category on the ABC publication list, both in terms of number of titles and number of copies. These books were thus significant both as they assisted in the maintenance of the Swedish language and in helping the more advanced readers shape a view of Sweden and Swedish America. In the following sections, we will pay particular attention to the role these schoolbooks played in the forging of a Swedish-American ethnic identity in the Augustana Synod. The main focus of the analysis will be on the primers, as these were printed in the largest number of copies. Although the elementary language books were printed in many large runs as well, their contents focused exclusively on linguistic exercises, material that is not of particular use for a content analysis. The two anthologies of Swedish literature that were at least partly intended to be used in schools—Enander's *Eterneller och vårblommor* and *Ur svenska sången*—have already been discussed in chapter 5.

The first primer at the ABC was *Församlingsskolans läsebok* (A Primer for the Congregational Schools), edited by Anders Bersell, professor of Greek at the college, and meant to be used in the Augustana congregational schools. The matter of suitable textbooks was brought up at the synod meeting in 1890 when it was decided that the synod would publish its own primer.[21]

Församlingsskolans läsebok became one of the most venerable titles at the ABC; from its first publication in 1890 it was reprinted sixteen times—the last in 1915—and appeared in more than 38,000 copies. As far as can be determined, the book remained virtually unchanged through all the printings. In 1898, the title page notes a second edition and the book is one page longer than the previous printings.[22] No texts, however, have been changed, and the preface notes that the only alterations concerned the usage of the new spelling rules in Sweden according to Sundén's principles.

In 1897 Bersell brought out another primer called *Barnens andra bok för skolan och hemmet* (The Children's Second Book for Schools and Homes), which, according to the preface, was intended to complement *Församlingsskolans läsebok,* since the latter was sometimes considered to be too advanced, especially for younger children. With the publication of *Barnens andra bok,* however, the editors proudly noted that there now existed a "relatively complete series of Swedish school-books" to be used by the Swedish-American children as they were learning to use and love "their fathers' resounding language."[23] *Barnens andra bok* was also printed in a large edition: it appeared in fifteen printings between 1897 and 1914 in a total of 57,800 copies.

After the turn of the century, a series of three primers appeared: *Första läseboken för skolan och hemmet* (The First Primer for Schools and Homes), *Andra läseboken för skolan och hemmet* (The Second Primer for Schools and Homes), and *Tredje läseboken för skolan och hemmet* (The Third Primer for Schools and Homes). The first two were edited by Hulda Magnusson and first appeared in 1908 and 1910; Augustana Swedish professor Jules Mauritzson brought out the third in 1917. Both the Magnusson books were aimed at children learning Swedish and contain simple reading exercises. *Tredje läseboken,* which appeared in one printing of 2,000 copies, however, assumes a good reading knowledge of Swedish, as it includes a number of selections from poetry, fiction, and historical writings, and although it was aimed at the congregational schools, the publishers felt that "the Swedish youth in America" and "Swedish Americans of all ages" could read and enjoy this book.[24]

The two schoolbooks published by the ABC that best lend themselves to a content analysis from an ethnic point of view are thus *Församlings-*

kolans läsebok and *Tredje läseboken*. In the following sections, they will be analyzed and compared. Their dependence on similar Swedish primers will also be discussed.

Församlingsskolans läsebok

An examination of *Församlingsskolans läsebok* shows that it was obviously inspired by similar primers in Sweden, perhaps most prominently *Läsebok för folkskolan* (A Primer for the Elementary Schools), which was used in the nineteenth-century Swedish elementary schools.[25] This primer first appeared in 1868 in 25,000 copies, and within the next two years another 75,000 copies were printed. These high circulation figures meant that *Läsebok för folkskolan* in its many editions became very influential in shaping reading habits and minds of generations of Swedish school children.

The book was carefully edited by prominent academics and teachers; even the minister of education, F. F. Carlson, took an active part. The object of the book was to cover most of the fundamental subjects in elementary school, and it therefore included sections on Swedish and world geography, nature, and history, as well as pieces on natural phenomena, technical inventions, and the like.[26] The book also included fictional reading selections with stories, fables, and poetry. According to Lars Furuland, the primer sought to instill a sense of national feeling in its readers. A number of selections from Swedish literature and history helped create a "national canon of persons and events" that was rooted in the romanticism of the nineteenth century, in part emphasizing what was seen as the ancient Swedish virtues of freedom and independence associated with the Swedish peasantry as well as exalting Swedish nature and the different provinces.[27]

The name of the Augustana primer alludes to its Swedish counterpart, especially as the Swedish book was almost always referred to as *Folkskolans läsebok* instead of its actual title. In the preface to *Församlingsskolans läsebok,* the editor also notes that "there is no lack of primers for Swedish elementary schools" but that the present volume is still needed since there is no book that is especially suited for "our congregational schools in this country."[28] The purpose of the book is to include selections that are "suitable for our Swedish-American circumstances" and that "have a clean, moral character" and emphasize "positive Christian" aspects.[29] The ABC catalog from 1900 further states that the selections have been made so that a "domestic viewpoint is kept, so that nothing appears strange or alien to the young readers."[30] Similar points were made in various advertisements in the press at the time

Augustana Book Concern

of publication.[31] To ascertain the nature of a book "suitable" for "Swedish-American circumstances," it will be useful to compare the two primers.

Församlingsskolans läsebok includes two parts: spelling exercises followed by shorter or longer texts. There is a gradual progression in difficulty in the reading section, beginning with a simple piece on "The Child" and ending with a fairly advanced item on Henry Wadsworth Longfellow. The primer is slightly more than half the size of its Swedish counterpart and includes a similar division into geography, history, natural phenomena, and so on, as well as shorter stories, fables, and poems.[32] At least thirteen of the items are direct copies or, in a few cases, modified versions of pieces from *Läsebok för folkskolan,* sometimes with slightly different titles, mostly shorter poems, and often with a religious touch.[33] Other pieces that were borrowed, often in an abbreviated form from the Swedish primer, include short biographies of historical figures or events, such as the emperor Charles the Great, the Crusades, and Esaias Tegnér.[34] Furthermore, a number of the items in *Församlingsskolans läsebok* have the same titles as in *Läsebok för folkskolan,* particularly pieces dealing with different animals, such as elephants, reindeer, and camels. Although the texts are different and mostly shorter in the American primer, there are no substantive differences in the mode of presentation between the two books, as they both give a straightforward presentation of the subject matter at hand.

There are, however, some major differences between the books. Roughly half of the selections in *Församlingsskolans läsebok* are stories and poems, while they make up only about a fourth of the items in *Läsebok för folkskolan.* Slightly more than a third of the pieces in *Församlingsskolans läsebok* deal with geography, natural phenomena, or geology, whereas almost half of the items in the Swedish book are found in these categories. Finally, historical and biographical pieces, both Swedish and general, make up not quite a third of the selections in the Swedish book but only about a tenth in the Swedish-American primer. The Swedish-American primer thus places much more emphasis on selections with a general moral and religious content, with inspiring stories of how faith in God or good behavior is rewarded. Very few of the selections from Swedish literature of the kind included in *Läsebok för folkskolan* have been identified in *Församlingsskolans läsebok.*

As noted above, the Swedish primer became important in shaping a Swedish national feeling by emphasizing Swedish nature and certain aspects of Swedish history and literature. A similar national element can also be found in *Församlingsskolans läsebok,* although to a lesser extent. The emerging national element in *Församlingsskolans läsebok* shows a duality in that the book includes a number of selections that deal with both Sweden and the United States. Evidently, the editors of *Församlingsskolans läsebok* wanted to make sure that the intended readers among the Swedish-American youth were exposed to both the Swedish and American cultural heritages.

This emerging duality is also found among the selections dealing with history, famous persons, and general cultural phenomena. The Swedish historical selections include pieces on ancient Swedish history (the Stone, Bronze, and Iron Ages), the Viking voyages, the Swedish patron saint Erik, the Christianization of Finland, Ansgar (the first missionary to Sweden), Engelbrekt Engelbrektsson (a political leader of the 1430s), the Reformation, and the kings Gustaf Vasa and Gustavus Adolphus. Two prominent authors are given short biographies, Georg Stiernhielm and Tegnér; two pieces on the Swedish language, one descriptive and one laudatory poem, and the poem "Sverige" by Erik Gustaf Geijer are included; and in addition to the entry on Swedish geography, the reindeer and the Lapps (Sami) are also presented.

The selections dealing with the cultural background of the adopted homeland include biographical sketches of Christopher Columbus, George Washington, Benjamin Franklin, Washington Irving, Abraham Lincoln, and Longfellow. There is also a general description of American geography, a piece on Niagara Falls and Yellowstone Park, and entries on two American animals, the buffalo and the prairie dog. It is interesting to note that *Församlingsskolans läsebok* devotes very little attention to Swedish-American experiences. Only one item in the book deals specifically with such a theme, namely an overview of the history of the Swedish Lutheran Church in America, which was the Augustana Synod itself.

Many of the themes that deal with the Swedish background in *Församlingsskolans läsebok* can be found in *Läsebok för folkskolan* as well, although the entries in the Swedish-American primer are often modified and shortened. This is the case with the items on ancient Swedish history, Ansgar, St. Erik, Stiernhielm, and Tegnér, where parts of the text have been borrowed verbatim. It should be noted that a mild criticism of Tegnér in the Swedish primer—regarding different opinions of his role as bishop[35]—has been omitted in the American book. The discussions of Engelbrekt Engelbrektsson, Gustav Vasa, and Gustavus Adolphus share the same basic assumptions in the two books, and all three figures are portrayed in very positive terms: as noble, intelligent, and guarantors of freedom, independence, and religion. *Församlingsskolans läsebok* tends to put a somewhat stronger emphasis on the religious dimensions. In it, Gustav Vasa, who was said to have become by the grace of God as powerful and wise as King David, is praised for saving the country from slavery and carrying out the Reformation, and Gustavus Adolphus is hailed for his bravery, steadfastness, and defense of religious liberty.[36]

None of the pieces dealing with the American cultural background are found in the Swedish primer. The historical biographies of Washington, Franklin, and Lincoln all emphasize their significant contributions to the new homeland of the readers of *Församlingsskolans läsebok*. A keyword for all three figures is "freedom": Washington, with the help of God, led the English colonies to freedom from England; Franklin, as the "noble citizen," worked for freedom of the slaves; and Lincoln, finally, was the "instrument of God" in saving the United States in its times of trouble and defending the freedom of both the nation and the slaves.[37] The two American authors highlighted for the Swedish-American audience, Irving and Longfellow, are both characterized as the "best" and most popular writers of prose and poetry in the United States, writing in a simple and clear style yet also with "depth" (Irving) and "compassion" (Longfellow).[38]

The choice of the Swedish cultural symbols in *Församlingsskolans läsebok* is perhaps not surprising. Almost all of the Swedish symbols could also be found in Sweden at the time, and the American primer can thus be said to reflect the situation in Sweden. Still, in our comparison with *Läsebok för folkskolan,* we can note that fewer Swedish cultural symbols are included in the American primer. Also, there is a clear emphasis on religion and freedom, as Swedish-American readers learned about the accomplishments of Ansgar and St. Erik in bringing Christianity to Sweden and Finland respectively, of Engelbrekt Engelbrektsson and Gustav Vasa in defending the freedom and independence of Sweden, and of Gustav Vasa and Gustavus Adolphus in promoting the Lutheran faith at home and abroad. The poets Stiernhielm and Tegnér receive special notice. The concern in America for preserving the Swedish language may partly explain the inclusion of Stiernhielm, as one of his main contributions was his importance for the development of the Swedish language.[39] As noted above, the primer also includes two pieces on the Swedish language itself, one of which is a poem by Enander glorifying the language.[40] Tegnér is praised as Sweden's greatest poet and was, as we have seen, together with Runeberg, among the most popular authors both at Augustana College and in the Swedish secondary schools in the late nineteenth century.

The choice of American historical symbols is not surprising either. Washington, Franklin, and Lincoln were among the most important symbols of American nationhood around the turn of the century. Ruth Elson has shown how important these persons were in mainstream American primers at the time,[41] and Peter Karsten has charted the rise and fall of American "patriot-heroes" in the nineteenth century with similar results.[42] Of the three, Lincoln receives the greatest attention. This corresponds to a growth in Lincoln's popularity at the expense of Washington and others during the end of the nineteenth century.[43] Regarding the American authors included, it should be noted that Longfellow enjoyed a great deal of prestige in Swedish America, as he both visited Sweden and translated some of the works of Tegnér into English,[44] which the entry in *Församlingsskolans läsebok* duly notes. Augustana College president Olof Olsson used him in justifying the study of the Swedish language at Augustana College in the 1890s, when he rhetorically wondered if "it reduce[d] the honor of Longfellow that he appreciated Swedish as one of the cultured living languages."[45]

Tredje läseboken

Quite a different picture is presented in *Tredje läseboken för skolan och hemmet,* which was brought out by the ABC in 1917, some twenty-five years after *Församlingsskolans läsebok* first appeared.[46] This book was the third and most advanced in a set of Swedish primers published by the ABC after 1908 and was targeted not only at schools but also at a larger Swedish-American audience. The two earlier books had been edited by Hulda Magnusson, but when she submitted the manuscript for the third book, the literary editor at the ABC, Oscar Holmgrain, reported that the manuscript was not suitable.[47] Instead, it was decided that Jules Mauritzson be engaged as editor and make a selection of materials as he saw fit.[48] The new manuscript was submitted in early 1917, and after some discussions of revisions (necessitating an extra meeting of the executive committee of the ABC board), the manuscript was finally approved.[49]

More than any of the other schoolbooks published by the ABC, *Tredje läseboken* is oriented toward building a sense of Swedish-American identity. The 326-page volume consists of three sections: the first, roughly a third of the book, includes a selection of stories and poems; the second, slightly less than half of the book, deals with the "Swedish people in old and recent times"; and the third and shortest section, about a fifth of the content, includes contributions "from America."

The stories and poems in the first section are mostly Swedish. In Mauritzson's selection of materials, two national Swedish primers by Bertil Hammmer and Anders Wallgren, *Första läseboken* and *Andra läseboken*,[50] seem to have been a source of inspiration for *Tredje läseboken*'s first section, and four items are specifically noted as being based on these books. The dependency particularly on *Andra läseboken* is in fact even greater, as three-fourths of the selections in the first section of the Swedish-American primer also appear in *Andra läseboken*.[51] Authors represented in this section include, for example, Zacharias Topelius, Karl-Erik Forsslund, and Anna Maria Roos, well-known names in literary selections for children in turn-of-the century Sweden.[52] It is, however, noticeable that a few selections by Strindberg in Hammer and Wallgren's *Andra läseboken* were not included in the Swedish-American primer. Strindberg's name was still controversial, and few of his works were available at the ABC.

The section dealing with Swedish history and culture includes historical and biographical items as well as a few selections of poetry. The historical selections are almost all based on national Swedish textbooks in history for the elementary school, notably those by Carl Grimberg and Anders Fryxell. A comparison between *Tredje läseboken* and Grimberg's *Sveriges historia för folkskolan* shows that eight selections in the American book are based on Grimberg's. The American versions are slight modifications of the Swedish originals, most commonly shortened versions. No particular tendency seems evident in the modifications, except perhaps in the part dealing with Swedish life during the ninth century: the American entry omits a section on the pagan religion in Sweden.

The view of Swedish history presented to the prospective Swedish-American readers in *Tredje läseboken* emphasizes the Viking Age, Engelbrekt Engelbrektsson, Gustav Vasa, and Sweden's Age of Greatness during the seventeenth century. Religion was still important, as Ansgar, St. Birgitta (a Swedish saint from the Middle Ages), Martin Luther, and the nineteenth-century hymn-writer Johan Olof Wallin are featured. Other prominent individuals from Swedish history are Jonas Alströmer, Carolus Linnaeus, Per Ling, Peter Wieselgren, and Alfred Nobel. Two authors are also highlighted through biographical sketches and examples from their literary production, Anna Maria Lenngren and Tegnér.

The third section in *Tredje läseboken* includes contributions that, according to the table of contents, come "from America." In this context, America actually means Swedish America, as all of the selections deal specifically with the history and circumstances of Swedes in the New World. This is a marked difference from *Församlingsskolans läsebok,* which only includes one such selection. In addition, the items dealing with Anglo-American mainstream culture found in *Församlingsskolans läsebok* are also missing in *Tredje läseboken.*

It is thus largely a view of Swedish-American conditions that is presented in *Tredje läseboken.* However, the longest contribution, taking up more than a fourth of the section, deals not with the Swedish-American community of the nineteenth and twentieth centuries but with Swedes in America in the seventeenth century in the New Sweden colony.[53] The selections are drawn from a national Swedish primer for elementary school children written by Märta Edqvist, which dealt with various aspects of the history of the Swedish church.[54]

In *Tredje läseboken,* readers are presented with a romanticized version of the history of the colony, set in 1691 when the old colony had passed into the hands of the English. The story takes place in the house of Carl Springer, a Swede who had arrived in the area after Sweden's loss of the colony. Springer has invited a group of Swedes, including one of the original colonists, Peter Rambo, to greet the Swedish visitor Anders Printz, the nephew of Johan Printz, the first governor of the colony. Rambo relates stories of the early years of pioneer hardship for the colonists and asserts that the Indians were treated fairly by the Swedes, since, as he puts it, "we were Swedes, and Swedes respect the rights of others."[55]

Springer tells the visitor of the churches built in the colony and of its religious life. Unfortunately, no minister is left any longer to conduct services. Moreover, the Swedes are forgetting their language, and Springer wishes that there were "school teachers and Swedish books available."[56] The remaining Swedes on the Delaware River had written to Sweden asking for assistance but had not received a response. Anders Printz is moved by what he hears and promises to do what he can upon returning to Sweden.

The story also gives a picture of an "Indian camp" that Printz visits.[57] In very positive terms, the Indians tell of their friendship with the New Sweden colonists and speak with particular reverence of Pastor Campanius Holm, who translated the catechism into Lenapi. Printz is amazed by the thought that, at one time, both children in Sweden and Indians in their wigwams had been studying the Swedish catechism. Upon returning to Sweden, Printz acts on the behalf of the Delaware Swedes, and the story ends in 1697 with the arrival of three ministers from the Church of Sweden for the old Swedish churches in the area, which the Swedes see as the answer to their prayers.

There is a historical background for this story. Carl Springer and Peter Rambo lived in the New Sweden area at the end of the seventeenth century and had appealed to Sweden for new ministers to the old Swedish churches. Anders Printz did visit the old colony in 1691, and a group of new ministers from the Church of Sweden did land in Delaware in 1697. The significance of this story is that it establishes a continuity and kinship between the prospective readers—turn-of-the-century Swedish Americans—and the Swedish colonists on the Delaware River and their descendants. First of all, in the story the New Sweden colony is characterized as a historical link between the two groups, suggesting a much longer Swedish history in America than that of the recent phase of immigration. Moreover, the similarities between the two groups of Swedish migrants is further underscored through the portrayal of the colonists and their life in old Swedish Delaware as pioneers who had struggled against harsh conditions but succeeded in building a prosperous community. The parallels to the Swedish immigration of the nineteenth and early twentieth centuries are obvious. The positive attitude toward the Indians expressed by the colonists also reflects favorably on the Swedes both of the seventeenth and nineteenth centuries. Finally, it is interesting to note that the immigrants in the story, the descendants of the New Sweden colony in 1691, are concerned about the same issues that were confronting the Swedish-American community in general and the Augustana Synod in particular around the turn of the century, namely how to maintain the language and religion of their Swedish ancestors.

After the section on New Sweden, *Tredje läseboken* moves on to nineteenth-century Swedish America. A chapter is devoted to the inventor John Ericsson, who is portrayed in very positive terms, emphasizing his role as the designer of the *Monitor,* which headed off the attacks by the Confederate *Merrimac* at the battle of Hampton Roads in 1862 during the American Civil War.[58] According to *Tredje läseboken,* this achievement was greeted with great joy and made Ericsson known as "the liberator of four million slaves."[59] The primer also notes that although Ericsson was a true American patriot, he also remained loyal the country of his birth and requested that he be buried there.

The primer also includes an account of how "our fathers" participated in the Civil War as well as a description of Swedish pioneer life in rural Minnesota in the 1870s.[60] The latter piece depicts the hard work of the homesteading immigrants, emphasizes the importance of the arrival of a Lutheran pastor, and portrays how the monthly services turned into joyous festivities for the entire community.

Three pieces deal specifically with the history of the Augustana Synod: one an overview of the synod's history, one an account of life at the Augustana Deaconess Institute in Omaha, Nebraska, and one a humorous account of student life at Augustana College.[61] The two final pieces in the book deal with life among contemporary Swedish Americans. The first is a narration of Christmas celebrations among Swedish Americans in the fictitious rural community of Bethlehem, while the last item in *Tredje läseboken* describes a Fourth of July celebration among Swedish Americans somewhere on the prairies.[62]

The schoolbooks published by the ABC served several purposes. One important aim of the more elementary ABC books and primers was obviously to teach Swedish-American children to read and write Swedish. A second objective, especially in the more advanced books and in particular *Församlingsskolans läsebok* and *Tredje läseboken,* was to provide children with edifying reading and to teach them about various subjects.

In *Församlingsskolans läsebok,* the greater emphasis is on edifying reading of a religious and moral nature, but the book also includes a number of selections that deal with geography, natural phenomena, history, and culture. In the latter pieces, it is possible to discern a duality in emphasis, as conditions in both Sweden and the United States are presented. Prominent leaders of the respective countries are featured, and values such as freedom and religiosity, said to be typical for the two countries, are underscored. *Församlingsskolans läsebok* from 1890 thus provided its Swedish-American readers with cultural elements from both Sweden and the United States that, when juxtaposed, formed the foundation for the identity of the Augustana Swedish Americans.

The history and culture of the Swedish Americans themselves play a small role in *Församlingsskolans läsebok*. Only one piece deals explicitly with Swedish-American conditions, namely a section on the history of the Augustana Synod. In this respect, *Tredje läseboken* is markedly different. Here, those pieces that deal with the United States are all concerned with Swedes in America, beginning with the New Sweden colony and extending to contemporary Fourth of July celebrations among Swedish Americans. *Tredje läseboken* provides its readers with cultural ingredients for an identity that are drawn from a joint Swedish and Swedish-American cultural repertoire. In 1917, Augustana's version of a Swedish-American identity was not rooted only in Sweden and in the United States, as it had been seventeen years earlier in *Församlingsskolans läsebok*. Now cultural expressions and patterns focusing on Swedish America itself were important elements of the ethnic identity, suggesting an important shift in the way the Augustana Synod had begun to perceive of a Swedish-American identity in the intervening years.

A parallel movement was simultaneously underway among the Norwegian Americans. Schoolbooks of a similar nature to those discussed in this chapter were also published by different Norwegian-American Lutheran synods. Anne Hvenekilde has shown how, as in the Augustana Synod, the different synods' views of culture and religion were reflected in these books. With regard to the role these books played for a Norwegian-American ethnicity, Hvenekilde shows how the ethnic dimension gradually became more important. Before circa 1900, she notes little material about Norway or Norwegian America that could be used as a basis for an ethnic identity in Norwegian-American primers. After that time, however, a shift took place, and the primers became exponents for Norwegian-American ethnicity, primarily through a literary and historical perspective.[63] Thus, there seems to be a parallel among Lutheran groups in Norwegian America to developments in the Augustana Synod, as the schoolbooks after the turn of the century played a more explicit role in shaping an ethnic identity among the immigrants.

SPECIFICALLY SWEDISH-AMERICAN—ORIENTED PUBLICATIONS

The ABC also published a number of titles that dealt directly with Swedish-American conditions and that are specifically useful for an analysis of the Swedish-American identity at the ABC. Publications in this category can be divided into Swedish-American literature, Swedish-American history, and works that reflected on the nature of the Swedish-American community. In addition, the two cultural and literary periodicals *Prärieblomman* and *Ungdomsvännen* frequently dealt with Swedish-American topics and can thus also be included in this category. Quantitatively, this group of publications includes few titles, published in small editions. Qualitatively, however, these books were significant. They provided both the authors and the publishing house with an opportunity to articulate their opinions about Swedish America and what it meant to be a Swedish American, and these publications thus became the exponents of the new Swedish-American culture that was being created in the United States. Included are both original

Swedish-American literature and texts dealing with the life and history of Swedish America.

Swedish-American Literature

Although it made up no more than 1 percent of the total copies published at the ABC, Swedish-American literature was one qualitatively important category of Swedish-American publications at the ABC. These Swedish-language imprints included works of poetry and fiction, and the authors represented were a fairly small group of persons, most of them associated with the Augustana Synod. We have already encountered some of these names in the analysis of the discussions of Swedish-American culture in both the Phrenokosmian Society and in Svenska Vitterhetssällskapet at Augustana College. Eric Johannesson and Anna Williams have shown that an awareness of the existence of a distinct Swedish-American literature had developed by the turn of the century, and the ABC was one of the leading publishers of this kind of literature.[64]

The first title was published in 1897 and was a selection of poetry called *Ludvigs dikter* (Ludvig's Poems) by Ludvig Holmes, an Augustana pastor. The collection appeared in a fairly modest run of 950 copies. Holmes was the leading author of Swedish-American literature at the ABC and brought out two more volumes of poetry.[65] He has been characterized as the "national poet" of the Augustana Synod and was the author of a number of commemorative poems written especially for different Augustana jubilees. He was also recognized as a major literary figure in Swedish America by contemporaries who wrote histories of Swedish-American literature.[66]

During the next two decades, a small group of authors was to follow Holmes at the ABC, most of them connected with the Augustana Synod in some way, often as ministers or professors at a synod college. The Reverend C. W. Andeer brought out several collections of short stories that dealt with life in Swedish America in general and in the Augustana Synod in particular, such as *I brytningstid. Skisser från det svensk-amerikanska folklifvet* (In Changing Times. Sketches from Swedish-American Life) from 1904 and *Augustanafolk. Bilder och karaktärer ur vårt kyrkliga arbete* (Augustana People. Pictures and Characters from Our Religious Work) from 1911, with a second volume appearing in 1914.[67] As already discussed, in 1902, the collection of poetry *Sånger och sagor* by the editor of *Svenska Amerikanaren* and leading Swedish-American author Jakob Bonggren was published by the ABC.[68] Another Augustana pastor, C. A. Lönnquist, published two volumes of poetry in

1907 and 1916,[69] and Anna Olsson, daughter of Augustana president Olof Olsson, brought out her *Från solsidan* (From the Sunny Side) in 1905 and in 1917 her well-known account of life on the Kansas prairies, *En prärieunges funderingar* (Thoughts of a Prairie Child).[70]

In 1913, the ABC established a publication series of Swedish-American literature called Svensk-amerikansk vitterhet (Swedish-American Belles Lettres), which can be seen as a further sign of the significance attached to this genre. The board of the ABC decided to publish each year "a literary work by some Swedish-American author of good repute." Two manuscripts were discussed as the first volume in this series, one by Johan Person and one by Oliver Linder.[71] Eventually the ABC settled for Linder's *I Västerled* (In Western Lands),[72] which, according to advertisements for the book, was particularly suitable since it dealt with Swedish America and was characterized by "a Swedish-American temperament." Linder was described as a "typically Swedish-American" author and as one of the first who had "naturalized his Swedish pen and consequently is able to give us something genuinely Swedish American in his writings."[73]

Swedish-American Literary and Cultural Periodicals

As noted above, the ABC published two periodicals between 1900 and 1918 that were of great importance for the maintenance and formulation of a Swedish-American ethnic identity. The first was the annual *Prärieblomman*, which appeared shortly before Christmas each year. The first issue of the calendar, which appeared in December 1899, was published by the Chicago-based group Vitterhetens vänner (Friends of Culture), in which journalists and authors Anders Schön and Johan Enander, who were both associated with the Augustana sphere in Swedish America, played an important role.[74] In April 1900, the calendar was offered to the ABC, which decided to take on the publication and appointed Schön editor. The second issue of the calendar was published in December 1901.[75] Schön remained editor of *Prärieblomman* until it ceased publication in December 1913.[76] Its circulation was between 2,000 and 3,000 copies per year.[77]

In her study of *Prärieblomman*, Birgitta Svensson argues that the calendar became an exponent for a "Swedish-American ideology." Svensson shows that the majority of the writers in the calendar were leading Swedish-American authors, such as Bonggren, Enander, Schön, and Ernst W. Olson, and that, although some contributions to *Prärieblomman* dealt with national Swedish topics, the main emphasis was on Swedish-American themes, with a noticeable emphasis on Swedish-American history.[78] *Prärieblomman* also became an important vehicle for the Swedish Americans to demonstrate to Sweden how a separate Swedish-American culture had developed in the United States, and Svensson calls the calendar a "cultural manifestation toward Sweden."[79]

Ungdomsvännen was a monthly publication started by two Augustana pastors in St. Paul in 1898. A year later, it, too, was offered for sale to the ABC, which assumed responsibility for the magazine from 1900. The first editor appointed by the ABC was S. G. Youngert, an Augustana pastor who was also active within the ABC.[80] Youngert remained editor until 1913, when the responsibility was shared by Holmgrain and E. W. Olson.[81] From 1915, Olson assumed the sole editorship, a post he held until April 1918, when he was forced to resign over a controversial article that was claimed to show disloyalty during the ongoing world war.[82] In October the same year, the magazine was officially discontinued.[83] At its peak in 1912, it had a circulation of close to 10,000 copies, but two years later the figure had declined by half.[84]

Ungdomsvännen contained more varied material than *Prärieblomman*, focusing on Swedish and Swedish-American topics but also on other motifs, such as religion, history, literature, and cultural topics, and there were both Swedish and Swedish-American contributors. (No systematic study of *Ungdomsvännen,* such as Svensson's for *Prärieblomman,* exists, and it has not been possible to conduct a complete examination of *Ungdomsvännen* within the framework of this study. Evidence from the journal will instead be given to illustrate the general developments.) The articles were grouped under different headings, such as "Edifying Articles," "Poems," "Sketches, Stories, and Articles of General Nature," and "Biographies." *Ungdomsvännen* was also richly illustrated.[85] It was, as indicated by its name, aimed toward the youth of the Augustana Synod and, in contrast to *Prärieblomman,* seems to have been more inwardly directed toward the Augustana Synod rather than toward the rest of Swedish America or Sweden.

The magazine maintained a balance between religious articles and articles of a more general cultural nature, which varied over time. The religious element was more dominant during the magazine's first decade of publication, but with the change of editorship in 1913, the new management recommended that *Ungdomsvännen* become "a purely literary magazine" and that a new journal be started for reports from religious youth groups that had previously been included in *Ungdomsvännen.* Following a "lengthy discussion," the ABC board of directors agreed that the material dealing with religious youth groups be discontinued but also stated that *Ungdomsvännen* would remain "a positively Christian literary magazine."[86] The following year, when the magazine's low circulation figures were discussed, the board of directors once again emphasized the journal's religious dimension, stating that it should include more articles of a Christian nature and more by writers from the Augustana Synod.[87] In 1917, two new sections of specifically religious materials were also added: "Our Christian Faith and Doctrine" and "Our Field of Work."[88]

Both *Prärieblomman* and *Ungdomsvännen* were discontinued due to a lack of interest among its readership. Birgitta Svensson suggests that *Prärieblomman* may have suffered from the competition with *Ungdomsvännen* but also underscores economic difficulties.[89] *Ungdomsvännen*'s circulation figures declined after 1912, making it economically difficult to continue publication. In 1917, the ABC board of directors decided to circulate a questionnaire to all pastors and others interested in order to solicit ideas about the future of the magazine.[90] The questionnaire showed that a majority of the respondents were dissatisfied with the magazine, as it was perceived as "too advanced" and difficult for its intended readership.[91] This decline in subscriptions, taken together with the accusations of disloyalty to the war effort, sealed the fate of *Ungdomsvännen*.

Swedish-American History

A few titles dealing with Swedish-American history were also published by the ABC, most of them authored by the synod's official historiographer, Eric Norelius. In 1891 he brought out his monumental *De svenska lutherska församlingarnas och svenskarnes historia i Amerika* (The History of the Swedish Lutheran Congregations and of the Swedes in America), which contains a wealth of information about the early phase of the immigration of Swedish Lutherans and of the Augustana Synod.[92] Norelius was scheduled to bring out a second volume within a few years, but it took until 1916 and many reminders, including a visit by a delegation from the publisher to Norelius's home in Vasa, Minnesota, before it finally appeared.[93] Norelius was also the author of a biography of T. N. Hasselquist, the dominant figure during the early years of the Augustana Synod, published in 1900.[94] In conjunction with the fiftieth anniversary of the Augustana Synod in 1910, the ABC also published two overviews of the synod's history—one in Swedish and one in English—as well as an account of the celebrations in Rock Island.[95]

Enander's 1892 book *Nordmännen i Amerika eller Amerikas upptäckt* (The Norsemen in America or The Discovery of America) occupies a special place among the historical works published by the ABC. This book was published in conjunction with the World's Fair in Chicago, called the "Columbian Exposition" in commemoration of the 400th anniversary of Columbus's landing in the New World. In the face of all the focus on Columbus, the author draws attention to the Viking journeys to North America around the year 1000, making the claim that the "Norsemen" were the first Europeans to reach the American continent.[96]

Reflections on Swedish America

The ABC also published three books that reflected on the lives and times of those in the Swedish-American community, one by a Swedish visitor and two by Swedish-American journalists. The first book was written by Carl Sundbeck, who, as noted in chapter 4, visited Swedish America in 1902 and was received with particular warmth by the Augustana Synod. In 1903, Sundbeck offered a book manuscript of his journey to the ABC, and after a very positive evaluation by C. J. Bengtson, the book was accepted for publication.[97] It appeared in 1904 under the title *Svensk-amerikanerna. Deras andliga och materiella sträfvanden* (The Swedish Americans. Their Spiritual and Material Developments),[98] and according to Arnold Barton, the book became a "bestseller" on the Swedish-American market,[99] giving a highly positive account of conditions among Swedish Americans. In particular, it was very complimentary to the Augustana Synod, suggesting that the synod provided the best support for Swedishness in America.[100]

The two Swedish-American books were Person's *Svensk-amerikanska studier* (1912) and Vilhelm Berger's *Svensk-amerikanska meditationer* (1916).[101] Both Person and Berger were well-known journalists in Swedish America, and their respective books are collections dealing with Swedish-American topics.[102] The articles explore a variety of subjects, such as the history and social, cultural, and political characteristics of the Swedish immigrant community as well as its future.

Berger also published his book *Vårt språk*—a collection of articles on the Swedish language in America and how it had been influenced by English—at the ABC in 1912.[103] It was one of the first studies of the development of the Swedish language in America. Berger was clearly interested in getting the book published at the ABC, as he had already begun correspondence with ABC board member G. N. Swan on the topic in 1910.[104]

A Swedish-American Identity at the ABC

What do these relatively few publications dealing with specific Swedish-American topics tell us about the significance of the ABC for the construction of a Swedish-American identity? First, the time dimension should be noted, as these publications appeared during the second, post-1890 phase of the history of the Augustana Synod, corresponding to the renewed emphasis on ethnic identity visible elsewhere in the synod as well at this time. Holmes's first volume of poetry from 1896 was followed by several volumes of Swedish-American poetry and fiction over the next twenty-odd years. In 1900, the ABC also took over the publication of the two leading cultural periodicals, *Prärieblomman* and *Ungdomsvännen,* and beginning in 1904, three books reflecting on the nature of the Swedish-American community by Sundbeck, Person, and Berger were published. The series on Swedish-American literature was established in 1914, and shortly thereafter *Ungdomsvännen* tried to raise its literary and cultural profile.

Second, many of these books show an awareness of a distinct Swedish Americanness, suggesting that a new set of cultural patterns had developed in America, different from those in Sweden. Holmes's first volume of poetry from 1896, for example, is dedicated to "the Swedish-American youth," which he identifies as a group of persons with roots in both Sweden and America and who "love" both countries equally.[105] In his poem "The Swedish American," included in *I Västerled* from 1914, Linder speaks of an emigrant from Sweden who has become a Swedish American, "keeping the bonds of memory" with the land of his parents but at the same time building his home in America, which has become his new homeland.[106] Holmes also points to the cultural developments taking place in America in an article from 1903, "En hälsning till det gamla landet" (A Greeting to the Old Country). There he describes how a new Swedish culture had developed in America, which, because of its separation from Sweden, had grown particularly strong.[107] In 1913, Augustana pastor Alfred Bergin also concluded that "Swedish America is a reality" and that the Swedish Americans constituted a "respectable nation." Swedish America was not a geographic entity, Bergin continued, but was made up by a common language, religion, and press and existed "wherever the Star Spangled Banner flew."[108]

Examples can also be found of how Swedish America was conceived of as a new nation and Swedish Americans as a new people. As discussed in chapter 1, Person noted in his *Svensk-amerikanska studier* how the eight-day Atlantic crossing laid the foundations for the transformation of the

Swedish immigrants into "a Swedish-American people." Although not fully understood by either the Americans or the Swedes, the Swedish-American people had "a common language, common memories, common traditions, and common interests," which, according to Person, were "neither Swedish, nor American . . . but a combination of both." As long as these attributes existed in America, Person concluded, a Swedish-American people would exist.[109] Person's ideas were explicitly endorsed in a preface to the book by E. W. Olson, editor at the ABC. He wrote that too many uniform accounts of Swedish America had been published but that the ABC could without hesitation recommend Person's book, as it was written by a knowledgeable Swedish American.[110]

In his work on the Swedish Americans from 1904, Sundbeck had also spoken of a "Swedish-American nationality" containing "the best of both the old and the new homelands."[111] To Sundbeck, the future of the Swedish-American nationality depended on the existence of a religious movement, namely the Augustana Synod, and he identified three particularly important dimensions of the cultural work of the Augustana Synod: the Lutheran religion, the Swedish language, and Swedish cultural traditions (*svensk bildning*).[112]

Similar sentiments were expressed in an article in *Ungdomsvännen* in 1905. The author (who used the pseudonym E-n, probably Johan Enander) argues that since the Swedish Americans had established themselves economically in America, conditions existed for the development of a Swedish-American culture or, in his words, the creation of "a new Swede." We are fortunate, he says, to be the "heirs of freedom and personal independence" as Americans and the children of the "peculiar creative talents of the North" as Swedes. This made Swedish Americans one of the "best equipped" cultures of the world, as they had developed a "harmonious cultural combination" of both American and Swedish traits. The American elements in this identity included independence and industriousness, while the Swedish contributions encompassed Nordic honesty, preservation, and faith.[113]

As we have seen, the Christmas magazine *God Jul* was started in 1916 to provide a specifically Swedish-American Christmas publication and included many leading Swedish-American authors and artists as contributors. The first issue featured an article by David Nyvall, a leading educator in the Mission Covenant Church, called "Bort med bindestrecket?" (Shall We Do Away with the Hyphen?), in which Nyvall discusses the advantages of being a hyphenated "Swedish-American" in ways similar to those of Holmes or Person. Those who wished to do away with the hyphen would become orphans and familiar with only one culture, Nyvall argued, ignorant of either their Swedish background or of the conditions in the new country. By retaining the hyphen, however, a balance could be struck that would allow the Swedish Americans to affirm both their American and Swedish backgrounds, much like the "harmony of a rainbow."[114]

The focus on a specific Swedish-American experience can also be seen in some of the Swedish-American fiction published by the ABC. One illustrative example is *I brytningstid,* the collection of short stories by Augustana pastor Andeer, published in 1904. Most of the stories take place in Swedish America, often in rural settings with the local Augustana Lutheran church playing a significant role, where life is portrayed in very positive terms. A common theme in these stories is the attraction that the good life in Swedish America has, and several stories deal with how unhappy protagonists of the stories, often Swedes or recent Swedish immigrants, find happiness in Swedish America and become "good Swedish-Americans."[115]

The story "The Swedish-American" specifically shows the superiority of Swedish America over Sweden. Arvid Norén, a Swedish-American college professor, returns to the village where his father had been a crofter before emigrating to America. He is received with great disdain by a group of Swedes, who think Swedish Americans are nothing but rabble. Still, Norén gets the better of his hosts, as the Swedish-American professor is highly educated, eloquently defends America and Swedish America, and speaks better French, German, Italian, and Latin than the Swedes. Before he returns to America, Norén falls in love with young Anna Stjärnfält, on whose estate Norén's father had worked. Despite the differences in social status, Anna's father, Count Stjärnfält, agrees to their marriage, as he has taken a great liking to the upstanding Swedish American, and the happy couple leaves for America.[116]

The American side of the Swedish-American identity was less often featured in the ABC publications, but it was dealt with in some articles in *Ungdomsvännen.* In 1903, an address by Olof Olsson, the former president at Augustana, on the nature of "true Swedish-American patriotism" was published, which claimed that although the Swedish Americans from a religious, cultural, and linguistic standpoint had ties to Sweden, they were without any doubt loyal to the American Republic and its form of government.[117] Some of the relatively few American topics in *Ungdomsvännen* often focused also on the political or civic dimensions of American life, such as articles on the

Declaration of Independence, George Washington, American presidential elections, and the centennial of the American national anthem.[118]

Reading was important in Swedish America. As most Swedish immigrants were literate, a Swedish-American literary market developed in the United States during the second half of the nineteenth century, replete with newspapers, periodicals, books, bookstores, and publishing houses. Most books available in Swedish America were imported directly from Sweden, but a number of Swedish-American publishing houses also existed. The Swedish-American reading patterns followed the cultural and ideological divisions within the community, and there was a noticeable difference between the secular and religious spheres.

The ABC was one of the most important building blocks in the creation of a Swedish-American identity within the Augustana Synod. As has been noted, it was the largest Swedish-American publishing house as well as a major importer of Swedish-language reading materials to the United States. The literary profile of the ABC must, like the general cultural work in the synod, be seen as one part of the interaction of religion and nationality. Obviously the immediate concerns of the synod were religious, and they defined its ideological framework. This emphasis is also evident at the ABC. Almost half of its publications were directly geared toward synodical use, and the religious element was also a basic determining factor for the nondenominational publications.

Thus, it became possible to establish a sense of Swedish-American identity at the ABC, and much of the reading material provided by the publisher became an important ingredient in the Swedish-American ethnic identity that emerged within the Augustana Synod. We have also seen that this process began during the years around the turn of the century, when a stronger emphasis on the Swedish element also can be found elsewhere in the Augustana Synod.

Three categories of publications have been analyzed: publications for children and youth, schoolbooks, and books specifically dealing with Swedish-American conditions. The publications for children and youth cannot be said to have contributed directly toward the growth of a Swedish-American ethnic identity. Their main contribution was rather indirect, through promotion of the language and general references to Sweden and to Swedish milieus. It is instead among the latter two categories that the growth of an explicit Swedish-American identity can be more directly observed. Through the schoolbooks, Swedish, American, and Swedish-American cultural traditions were presented, and in *Församlingsskolans läsebok,* for example, Swedish-American students could read about Swedish historical figures such as Gustav Vasa and Gustavus Adolphus as well as the American presidents Washington and Jefferson. Increasingly, the schoolbooks also included materials dealing with the specific conditions and history of the Swedish immigrants and their children in America.

The concern for specific Swedish-American conditions was also clearly manifested in the third group of publications—those dealing directly with Swedish America. Stories by Andeer on life in Swedish America, accounts of Swedish-American history, reflections on what it meant to be Swedish American by leading Swedish-American authors, or high-profile literary and cultural publications such as *Prärieblomman* or *Ungdomsvännen* suggest a conscious effort on the part of the ABC to assist in the process of shaping a Swedish-American identity in the Augustana Synod. This meant that the opportunities for Swedish-American cultural work increased within the general cultural and religious boundaries of the synod. It is possible to speak of a cultural opening-up that took place within the synod, which made it possible for a Swedish-American identity to be formulated, an identity in which the religious and ethnic elements complemented each other.

Finally, it can be noted that the nature of the Swedish-American identity and views of Swedish America that were expressed through the publications at the ABC became influential also outside the Augustana sphere of Swedish America, and, as the cultural struggles in Swedish America from the 1870s and 1880s were abating, it was Augustana's definition of what it meant to be Swedish American that was becoming dominant.[119] Nyvall's article in *God Jul,* expressing his views on the dual heritage of the Swedish Americans and the desirability of maintaining this identity, is one example of the similarity of opinion between the Augustana Synod and the Mission Covenant Church.[120]

Another example is the inclusion of Bonggren's *Sånger och sagor* on the ABC publication list, which might seem surprising, given Bonggren's earlier antagonistic position toward the Augustana Synod.[121] Still, as Williams has shown, Bonggren had by the turn of the century abandoned his more radical and anti-clerical positions and had instead approached the cultural views of the Augustana Synod. The selections in *Sånger och sagor* included poetry of a nature much more acceptable to the synod.[122] The book was also favorably advertised in *Augustana,* where Bonggren was called one of the "foremost" Swedish-American authors and his writings "true poetry" both in terms of form and content.[123]

A final example is the cultural magazine *Valkyrian* (The Valkyrie), published from 1897 to 1909 in New York. According to Gunnar Thander, the Augustana Synod exercised a similar influence on the content of *Valkyrian*, which Thander maintains was started as a secular alternative to publications in the Augustana Synod, especially *Prärieblomman*.[124] Still, several prominent Augustana authors, such as Holmes, Andeer, and Swärd, also contributed to *Valkyrian*,[125] and Thander concludes that although the journal sought to establish a cultural distance from the Augustana Synod, this proved difficult. The synod affected *Valkyrian's* attempt at creating its separate Swedish-American culture and, according to Thander, instead became "willing promoter" of the Augustana's view of Swedish-American culture.[126] The fact that the ABC purchased *Valkyrian* in 1910 is also suggestive of the proximity between the journal and the ABC.[127]

7

Putting the Past to Use: The Creation of a Swedish-American History

As noted in chapter 1, myths of origin and descent and a sense of a shared history are important in the construction of both national and ethnic identities, and Kathleen Conzen has argued that a fundamental part of ethnicity is the sense of "commonality that results from being part of the same extended conversation about where we came from and how we got where we are."[1] According to John Bodnar, American history is full of examples of minority groups "mounting spirited defenses of their own versions of the past,"[2] which, as Raymond Breton has observed, entail a "reconstruction of the past and/or the creation of a mythical past" and can thus be literally created or fictitious (that is, with no empirical grounding) or be reconstructions, in which the meanings of past events are redefined.[3] Orm Øverland has also called attention to the ethnic pasts and the way in which they functioned. He identifies three kinds of "homemaking myths"—myths of foundation, myths of ideological gifts, and myths of blood sacrifice—that developed among immigrant and ethnic groups in late-nineteenth- and early-twentieth-century America and were used by them in their interactions with the American host society and with other ethnic groups. These myths provided the immigrants with an opportunity to stake their claims in America and as Americans by affirming their ethnicity and their ethnic pasts while at the same time arguing that their ethnicities were central in making them American and in building an American identity. Being ethnic thus meant that the immigrants and their children were being American.[4]

In this chapter, the process by which Swedish Americans in the Augustana Synod fashioned a past for themselves and its significance for the construction of their identity will be discussed. As the Augustana Swedish Americans set out to construct a Swedish-American historical tradition, they were able to draw on three main sources, namely the historical traditions of Sweden, the United States, and Swedish America. Taken by themselves, these traditions could be seen as referring to the separate histories of Sweden, the United States, and Swedish America. By using a combination and selection of these histories, however, the leaders of the ethnic group created a new historical tradition, which we can call a Swedish-American history. This history was specific to the needs of the Swedish immigrants and their children in the United States and must thus be seen from the American and Swedish-American context in which it was created and presented and as a part of the creation of Swedish-American homemaking myths.

Early on, a strong sense of history developed in the Augustana Synod. Already during the synod's first decade, a "Committee for Historical Documents" was active, collecting "historical information on our diverse parishes and settlements, of value to the history of our Synod," with Pastor Eric Norelius as the driving force.[5] In 1869, Norelius was appointed "historiographer" of the synod and eventually wrote both a massive two-volume study of Swedish Lutheran settlements in the United States and a biography of T. N. Hasselquist.[6] Moreover, in 1893 the synod discussed a proposal of forming a "Swedish-American academy of history and antiquities" based on the Swedish Academy in Stockholm, but nothing came of the initiative. In 1897, the synod considered historical work to be of such significance that it encouraged its membership to send source materials for "the study of the history of our church and people" to the college in Rock Island, where archival and library collections also began to grow.[7]

A sense of history was also nurtured through the leading Augustana literary and cultural publications *Prärieblomman* and *Ungdomsvännen*, with many historical and biographical articles. As discussed in chapter 6, the ABC also played an important role as publisher of a number of works dealing with different aspects of the synod's history and the general history of the Swedes in America. Historical celebrations and anniversaries at Augustana College and throughout Swedish America also provided opportunities for historic manifestations of a different kind.

Johan Enander played a crucial role in the formulation of a Swedish-American history, both for the Augustana Synod and for Swedish America in general. His writings will thus be of great importance in the analysis of the creation of a Swedish-American history. Born in Sweden in 1842, he emigrated at the age of twenty-seven in 1869, having attended the *läroverk* in Vänersborg for a few years. He enrolled at Augustana College with the intent of becoming a minister, but after a brief time he was appointed editor of the Augustana Synod's most influential newspaper, *Hemlandet*. In 1872, he, along with G. A. Bohman, bought the paper and remained editor and owner until 1890. He served as professor of Swedish language and literature at Augustana College from 1890 to 1893, edited *Svenska Journalen* in Omaha, Nebraska, from 1893 to 1896, and took over *Hemlandet* again from 1896 to his death in 1910. Enander also served as editor of the family magazine *När och fjerran* (Near and Far Away) from 1877 to 1879. He worked actively within the Republican Party and was in 1889 appointed U.S. minister to Denmark, a post he could not accept for medical reasons.[8]

Enander's significance was thus great both within and outside the Augustana Synod. Ulf Beijbom has called him the Synod's "foremost layman,"[9] and when he died, one obituary recognized his importance by saying that "one of the chieftains of Swedish culture has fallen" who had devoted his entire life to "the preservation of Swedishness in America" and to whom "being a Swedish American was second only to being a human being."[10] It is also worth noting that there was a direct link from Enander to the next generation of Swedish-American historians and activists, as Amandus Johnson, writer and historian, was inspired by a lecture by Enander in 1903 at Gustavus Adolphus College in Minnesota when Johnson was an undergraduate. It aroused his interest in the New Sweden colony, and he spent much of his life writing about it and became the prime mover behind the American Swedish Historical Museum in Philadelphia.[11]

MYTHS OF FOUNDATION: THE EARLY PRESENCE IN AMERICA

Of the three types of homemaking myths identified by Øverland, the myth of foundation seems to have been particularly important among the Swedish Americans, and they actively sought to establish an early presence, both on the North American continent and in what was to become the United States. This was, of course not something unique to Swedish immigrants but took place among other immigrant groups and among Americans in general. Beginning in the final decades of the nineteenth century, for example, a number of organizations that attached significance to connections with early American history were founded, including the Colonial Dames of America, the Society of Mayflower Descendants, the Sons of the American Revolution, and the Daughters of the American Revolution.[12]

Being First on the North American Continent

The issue of the European "discovery" of America has always played an important role in promoting the status of different American immigrant and ethnic groups. Several groups, including the Croatian, Greek, Irish, Norwegian, Polish, and Swedish Americans, have claimed that a representative of their nationality predated Columbus's landing in the New World. Columbus's own ethnic origin has also been disputed, and it has, for example, been argued that he was of Jewish origin. Furthermore, Columbus was seen as an American symbol without any particular ethnic connotations until the 1890s, when the process began through which he became an Italian American.[13]

For the Swedish Americans, the Viking journeys to settlements in what they called Vinland on the North American continent in the eleventh century provided an excellent opportunity to lay the grounds for a myth of foundation. The cultural leadership did its best to promote and prove that the Vikings had indeed been the first Europeans in America, thus giving the Swedes (as well as other Scandinavians) a special birthright in America. This was an attempt not only to bring the Swedish immigrants up to the same level as the New England colonists, whom the Swedish immigrant cultural leadership clearly perceived as a core group of the American Republic, but also to go beyond the colonial history and claim the right of discovery for the Scandinavians. They were, as Arnold Barton has pointed out, helped by a growing interest in the Vinland voyages in American society, partly prompted by the publication of the medieval texts concerning the Viking journeys in the 1830s.[14]

Enander was one of the main proponents of these ideas, and they came to the fore very clearly in his first significant historical work. Spurred by the American centennial in 1876, Enander published a series of articles in his newspaper, *Hemlandet,* that presented American history to the newspaper's Swedish readership.[15] The articles were also printed in a book called *Förenta Staternas historia utarbetad för den svenska befolkningen i Amerika* (The History of the United States, Written for the Swedish Population in America), brought out by Enander's own publishing house between 1874 and 1877.[16] Even though American colonial history in its entirety is presented in Enander's book, a fifth of the book deals with the Viking journeys to North America as well as a background of Scandinavia at the time. In this section, Enander claims that the "Norsemen" not only discovered America but also founded colonies there "with which Greenland and Iceland maintained contacts until 1347."[17] Enander realized that his strong emphasis on the "life and culture of the Norsemen" was open to criticism but defended his decision by saying that his intended audience, "a Swedish-American public," ought to be aware of the "child of Norse culture" who "had been planted on American soil more than five centuries before Columbus landed there." His main intention in writing the book was, he declared in the preface, to ensure that the memory of "our heroic distant past never would fade among those Scandinavian descendants who inhabit American soil."[18]

Enander's view of the full scope of Swedish-American history was well formulated in a 1890 speech given in Chicago. The occasion was a celebration of what was called "Our Forefathers Day," an attempt to establish a Swedish-American "national day" of celebration, in which Enander was a driving force.[19] As Beijbom has pointed out, a celebration like "Our Forefathers Day" provided Swedish Americans with both an opportunity to stake out their historical claims in the American Republic and a way of asserting the contemporary cultural work in Swedish America.[20] An editorial comment in *Hemlandet* from 1890 also underscored this dual dimension of "Our Forefathers Day," as the paper commented that the celebration was not only intended to remember the old but that "the rich inheritance, given to us by our fathers," was a valuable "treasure," worth preserving for "our nationality" and "for the benefit and advantage of our adopted fatherland."[21]

In his speech, called "A Dream" (En dröm), Enander outlined his view of the Viking presence in North America. According to Enander, the Viking settlements in North America lasted longer than just a few years. In fact, they continued to thrive, and Enander maintained that, despite various hardships, Viking and Norse settlements existed on the North American continent for at least two centuries. By 1121, he claimed, there were prosperous Norse farming communities in North America, a large village, and a sizable population where the inhabitants were dressed in similar costumes to what "we still today can see in the memory-rich Dalarna, parts of the beautiful Södermanland, in Norway's valleys or on Iceland."[22] That same year, Christianity came to America, as a bishop from Iceland, whom Enander referred to as "America's first ordained bishop," visited the community and decided to erect a baptismal building.[23] Eventually, however, the Viking settlements in America went under, and the memories of these settlements faded in Europe. It was only in Iceland that the memories of the Viking journeys lingered and provided Columbus, who visited the island in 1477, the information he needed for his journey to America. According to Enander, the Vikings thus both directly and indirectly discovered America.[24]

The Columbian Exposition, which opened in 1892 in Chicago, provided Enander with another opportunity to reiterate his claim for the Viking "discovery" of America. In that year, his book published by the ABC, *Nordmännen i Amerika,* presented his case for a Viking presence in America.[25] The book gives a detailed description of the arrival of the Vikings and the subsequent settlements, taking issue with "Anglo-American" scholars who have disputed these facts. In the conclusion, Enander laments the fact that his views have not been accepted and attributes this to the strong influence of the Italians in the United States and to the pope, who had declared "that the saint-like Columbus, inspired by the Holy Ghost and protected by the Virgin Mary," was the first European to reach America, which had resulted in a situation where it was "considered High Treason" to voice dissenting opinions. However, concludes Enander, the "historic truth" lives on, and long after the speeches about Columbus have been forgotten, the fact will remain "that the Norsemen discovered America and founded lasting colonies there 500 years before Columbus saw the light of day."[26] The book was reviewed favorably in *Augustana,* which called it "thorough" and "correct," recommending it for general reading.[27]

It is interesting to note that Enander was not only arguing the case for the early Viking presence, which in his view could be seen as "Swedish," but also placing the issue in a contemporary context. Enander's attacks on the Italian Americans should be seen as one way in which the Swedish Americans were trying to establish superiority over another immigrant group in America, with whom the Swedish Americans had to compete for economic and political influence. Enander's anti-Catholicism is not surprising, given both the strong anti-Catholic feelings in the Augustana Synod and in the United States in general at the time.[28]

Another example of framing the issue of the Viking landings in North America in contemporary terms comes from the Swedish-American educator J. S. Carlson, also associated with the Augustana Synod and an active participant in Swedish-American cultural life around the turn of the century. Born in Sweden but educated at Augustana and Gustavus Adolphus colleges, he became professor of Scandinavian languages at the University of Minnesota in the 1880s.[29] In 1908, a year after leaving his professorship at Minnesota, Carlson published a booklet called *Amerikas siste svensk* (America's Last

Swede), based on a speech he had delivered on this topic in Minneapolis. In it, Carlson looks into the future, invoking the image of the last Swede in America, whom he defines as the last Swedish American interested in preserving a sense of Swedishness in this country. The last Swede in America reflects on the long and glorious history of his compatriots in the New World and on a history that spans almost a millennium, from the time of the arrival of the Vikings up to the present Swedish immigrants.

Like Enander before him, Carlson also uses the Vikings as an opportunity to comment on contemporary matters. Indeed, it might be difficult to decide which was more important to Carlson, to try to set the historical record straight or to show the superiority of the Swedish immigrant group. Carlson claims that as the "Nordic dragon ships set sail for the west" and landed in America, "the first white, a Nordic Viking, stepped on the shores of America; and the first foreign language to reach the ears of the Indians was the language of the North." He thunders: "Mark this, you smug Briton, you proud son of England, you who have never been first at anything, except pilfering that which others have discovered. . . [T]he birthright to the discovery of America is not yours; you cannot get it even by bribing the Italian, because he himself has borrowed it. The birthright to the discovery of America belongs to the North and to no-one else." Carlson goes one step further than Enander in that he not only attacks the Italians but also criticizes the English, as he perceived the movement to Americanize immigrants in America as essentially the same as imposing English customs and values on the immigrant community.[30] To him, the Vikings thus became not only a part of a myth of foundation or a dimension of inter-ethnic strife with Italian Americans but also a way of resisting the perceived assimilatory forces from American society at large.

The Viking tradition in America has remained strong up until the present time. The controversy over the so-called rune stone in Alexandria, Minnesota, which was discovered in 1898 and was claimed to have been erected in 1362 by Vikings on a mission from the king of Sweden and Norway, is another example of the longevity of the Viking heritage. Although it was immediately declared to be a forgery by prominent American and European scholars at the time and by subsequent generations of scholars, it has continued to have a great appeal to generations of Swedish and Scandinavian Americans, suggesting that the Vikings are still an important element in Swedish- and Scandinavian-American identities.[31]

Colonial America

Establishing a connection to the American colonial period was one important way of claiming an American past. Joshua Fishman and Vladimir Nahirny speak of groups that sought to create "a bilateral line of descent" to both the American colonial past and to their own homeland, a process that, for example, meant discovering their respective ancestors "among the contemporaries of John Smith, George Washington and Abraham Lincoln."[32]

To the Swedes, the most important aspect of their colonial history was the New Sweden colony on the Delaware River, which Sweden maintained between 1638 and 1654 and which left a rather small imprint on subsequent American history. The opportunity to put the New Sweden colony to use as a means of establishing an early presence in the New World was not lost on the nineteenth-century Swedish immigrants in America. Although links between the Swedes on the Delaware in the mid-seventeenth century and the Swedish Americans some two centuries later were virtually nonexistent, nineteenth-century Swedes in America did their best to portray the New Sweden colonists as their forerunners, and all the virtues that could be associated with the colonists could then, by implication, be carried over to the immigrants in the nineteenth century. In this view, Swedish colonists had been on American soil, showing the beginnings of an organized Swedish-American society, a mere eighteen years after the landing of the *Mayflower*.

One of the earliest instances of the colony's use in the construction of a Swedish-American history was a major celebration of the 250th anniversary of the colony's founding, held in September 1888 in Minneapolis.[33] It is telling that the celebrations took place in Minneapolis, a rapidly growing center for nineteenth-century Swedish Americans, and not at the original site in Delaware. The celebration included a parade, which attracted some 15,000 persons, as well as a number of prominent speakers from different segments of the Swedish-American community, religious and secular alike, and was characterized as the most grandiose Swedish-American celebration to date.[34]

One of the main thrusts of the celebration was to establish the fact that the Swedes had been a colonial people in America. Hans Mattson, one of the best-known Swedes in Minnesota who had served as a colonel in the Union army in the Civil War and as secretary for the Minnesota State Board of Immigration, phrased it well in his speech, stating that a few colonial peoples—the English, the Dutch, the Swedes, the Scotch, and the French—had settled the New World and had all contributed to its growth. "History" had, however, been "partial" in favor of the English, leaving the other peoples "forgotten or ignored," making it urgent to remedy this historical error by letting the Swedes assume their rightful place in American history.[35]

The Augustana Synod was also represented at this celebration. In the parade that preceded the speeches, the synod delegation marched in the second division, and the invocation at the meeting was given by Hasselquist, president of the college and seminary in Rock Island. Other speakers included such well-known Augustana Synod representatives as Enander and Carl A. Swensson, president of Bethany College. In his speech, Enander emphasized two legacies of the New Sweden colony—one religious and one political. He maintained that the Swedish colonists had led a life "completely governed by Christianity" and that they had also proved instrumental in bringing Christianity to the Indians in the area. From a political point of view, the Swedish immigrants had brought a commitment to "freedom" to America. Most notably, Enander maintained, there was personal freedom—and absence from slavery—in the colony, showing that the Swedes "were ahead of their times" on this important issue, which would render them "eternal honor."[36]

Both Enander and Swensson tried to establish a connection between the New Sweden colony and the Swedish-American community of the late nineteenth century. Enander maintained that since the establishment of the colony, Swedish immigration to the United States "has never completely stopped,"[37] and Swensson made a connection between the past and the present by calling the present celebration a "wedding occasion" in which "the first two hundred and fifty years of Swedish-American history" had "been united with bonds of love and memory to the common history of the American nation."[38] This connection also meant that parallels between the New Sweden colonists and their compatriots of 250 years later could be drawn. Both groups were deeply religious, and both were committed to the ideals of freedom. For example, just as the Swedish colonists abhorred slavery, Enander exclaimed, the nineteenth-century Swedish immigrants answered the call to defend the cause of freedom in the Civil War in which "thousands" of Swedes "bled and died heroic deaths."[39]

New Sweden's centrality to the Swedish-American history emerging in the Augustana Synod can also be seen in the cultural and literary publications *Ungdomsvännen* and *Prärieblomman*. In *Ungdomsvännen*, the New Sweden colony was the topic for a series of no less than nineteen articles published between 1901 and 1903 called The Swedes on the Delaware. The

Putting the Past to Use

author of these articles was Anders Schön, editor of *Prärieblomman,* close collaborator with Enander, and clearly anchored within the Augustana sphere in Swedish America.[40] In these articles, a very positive account of the colony is given, emphasizing the colony's good contacts with the Indians, the spread of Christianity to the Indian community, and the colony's general peaceful, religious, and politically stable development.[41] *Prärieblomman* also dealt with the topic several times, including biographical articles about Governor Johan Printz and his wife, the latter subtitled "A Profile of a Woman from Seventeenth Century Swedish America."[42]

Enander's role in connection with the New Sweden colony was vital. In his Swedish-language history of the United States discussed above, the New Sweden colony is featured prominently in the section dealing with the thirteen colonies. It receives almost twice as much attention as what Enander gives to the history of Pennsylvania, and, excepting a fairly lengthy treatment of the Massachusetts colonies, the New Sweden colony is the first one discussed, preceding, for example, Pennsylvania, Maryland, and Virginia.[43] Enander describes the life of the New Sweden colony in very positive terms, emphasizing the friendly relations with the Indians and the Christian and politically stable nature of life in New Sweden,[44] themes that would be repeated many times during the years to come.

The attempts to create a longer historical continuity between the seventeenth-century Swedes on the Delaware and the nineteenth-century Swedes in the Midwest was an important part of the 1888 anniversary celebrations and continued into the twentieth century. For example, Norelius, the official Augustana historiographer, explicitly included the Delaware colony in his conception of Swedish-American history in an article in *Prärieblomman* from 1900, in which he wrote that Swedish immigrants were sometimes called "greenhorns and aliens"—a characterization that was incorrect since the Swedes could "point back to 1638 and answer that the first New England colonists came to this country only 18 years before the first Swedish colonists."[45] It is also interesting to note that in 1914 and 1915, the Augustana Synod actually discussed purchasing the property at the site of landing in Delaware in order to erect a monument, a project which, however, came to naught as the price asked was considered too high.[46]

Another example of placing the Delaware colony in a longer Swedish-American historical tradition comes from 1906 when the recently founded organization Svensk-Amerikanska Historiska Sällskapet (The Swedish-American Historical Society) had its first annual meeting in Chicago. Although not exclusively a group based on the Augustana Synod, a number of leading persons from the synod were active members in the society. Present at the meeting in 1905 when the organization was founded were, for example, Schön, Pastor L. G. Abrahamsson, and Gustav Andreen. The first president of the group was, significantly enough, Enander.[47] In his address at the meeting in 1906, Secretary Schön extended Swedish-American history to include not only the era of the nineteenth-century immigrants but also their compatriots from the seventeenth century. He noted that the society met on the day marking the 268th anniversary of the Swedish landing in Delaware and said that one of the main tasks for Swedish Americans was to better learn their history and themselves, a history that had already begun during America's "era of colonization" itself.[48] Another important task for this newly founded society was, according to Schön, to erect memorials at "important Swedish-American sites," defined not only as such nineteenth-century pioneer settlements as Pine Lake, Wisconsin, and Bishop Hill, Illinois, but also, by chronological and geographical extension, Delaware.[49]

MYTHS OF IDEOLOGICAL GIFTS:
SWEDISH CONTRIBUTIONS TO AMERICA

Swedish Americans also engaged in writing a history in which the ways in which Swedes and Swedish Americans were perceived as having contributed ideas to foundations of American society played a prominent role. In these "myths of ideological gifts," as Øverland calls them, a fundamental Swedish contribution to the American Republic was personal and political freedom.

In a speech in Philadelphia during the centennial celebrations in 1876, Enander noted that "every attempt to make the 4th of July an exclusively Anglo-American holiday, when the deeds of the English puritans and the descendants of the cavaliers are honored, is an ignorance of justice, of history's witness."[50] Enander instead maintained that the American freedom and independence honored on the 4th had their roots in Sweden. It was a theme to which he returned frequently, but it receives its fullest expression in a manuscript entitled "Sweden's Role in World History," which, despite its title, deals with Sweden's influence only on United States history. From internal evidence, one can conclude that the speech was presented to a meeting of Swedish Americans (possibly at Augustana College) some time shortly before 1891.

In what way had Sweden contributed to American freedom, according to Enander?[51] In the very opening sentence of the manuscript, Enander states that "during the ice-gray antiquity," there lived a people in "a country close to the Polar Star" that was untouched by foreign foes as well as by the "shameful chains of domestic slavery." This is, according to Enander, the country from which much of the political and constitutional freedoms in the world in general and in the United States in particular stem, since, as he puts it, "the American tree of freedom found one of its deepest roots in this by us all so beloved country, long before the Star Spangled Banner flew over a free people" in the United States.

This freedom was spread throughout the world via the Vikings, who "following the decrees and judgement of a higher Divinity punishing and paving way for a new society." First it reached Normandy, where in 911, when the Viking chief Rollo asked his men who their king and lord was, the answer given, according to Enander, was "the very opening words of the Declaration of Independence of the United States—865 years before their inclusion in the letter of rupture between our adopted country and England," namely, "We have no master or king, we are all equals." Following 1066, it was transplanted to England and eventually arrived in America, where this "spirit of freedom" grew stronger than in any other country and "laid the foundations to the empire of which we are citizens today."

It was also the Vikings who, through their conquests and settlements on the European continent, spread "self-governance and a society built on just laws." The Viking influence was most noticeable on the political and constitutional development in England. Following the Viking attacks in 753, all of England eventually came under the Nordic rule of King Canute. His government was "wise and just" and brought "the judicial system and army in excellent order." "Never before," Enander states, "had such a spirit of freedom and self-governance reigned in the country and the Anglo-Saxons and the Viking descendants gradually melted into one people." Yet another Nordic influence was introduced in England after 1066 and the victory of the Norman king William the Conqueror at the Battle of Hastings. In this way, a new nationality emerged in England—the English—consisting of the Anglo-Saxons, the Viking descendants, and the Normans, all profoundly shaped by the Nordic heritage.

This heritage of political independence and legality can be clearly seen when King John Without Land lost large parts of the realm and became indebted to the pope. At this point, Enander writes, "the Norman descendants in the country could no longer stand the shame and dishonor brought upon the country, and their old love for freedom and independence, which could stand abuse from neither King nor Pope, came into the fore." They "seized power" and forced "the godless and cowardly King" to issue the Magna Carta in 1215. The constitutional and political liberties in England can, according to Enander, be traced to this point, and he concludes that "the seed of freedom planted by Viking descendants and Normans thus bore rich fruit" and that "the people of England [were] fostered to freedom and self-governance through laws which originally had been formulated by descendants from the original home of freedom—from the Far North."

When the "restless spirit of freedom" no longer could thrive properly in an English society "characterized by oppression and violence against dissidents," a westward emigration began, and "thousands upon thousands" sought refuge in America to "live like a free people under their own laws." In this way, "the spirit of freedom and self-governance which once resided in the Viking halls, decorated with shields, and in the Normans' impressive castles, now lived quietly in the low block-houses and the dug-outs of the untamed American forests," assuring that the American political and legal system bore the imprints of the Nordic heritage.

But freedom and equality were brought not only indirectly to the United States through the Vikings and Normans. The New Sweden colony is once again assigned an important role as it exercised a "considerable and beneficial influence on [its] neighbors." At a time when the English colonists "had begun to blacken the conscience for reason of greed" with that "awful institution of slavery," Enander writes, the freedom of the individual in America was defended only by "the freedom-loving yeomen from Sweden" and by a few Germans. The Swedish colony also provided freedom and protection for people of various religious persuasions, while the prisons in the English colonies were full of "sighs and lamentations from the victims of religious intolerance and superstition."

The freedom of religion associated with the New Sweden colony was a theme that also featured prominently in Enander's 1890 speech "A Dream" and in other contemporary accounts of the colony.[52] In 1906, for example, Schön argued that the Swedish colonists came to America not in pursuit of freedom but rather to "transplant that freedom which they and their fathers had won themselves" in Sweden. They did not seek to inflict their religious beliefs on other early Americans, immigrants and natives alike, as had the Puritans at Plymouth Rock, who had come to America seeking freedom but who were "spiritually narrow-minded" in imposing their religion on others.[53]

It is interesting to note that Enander also claims that independence and self-government came through the Viking and Norman heritage. The Swedish nineteenth-century immigrants had contributed just as significantly to the growth of American society. Here, he speaks of the Swedish settlers in "the Far West," where previously unused land has been "tamed by the Swedish-American plow" and where significant settlements have been founded. These settlements constitute the advance of civilization and ordered society, which will continue to grow to become the cities and states of the future. In this way, Enander and his fellow Swedes, although they formed a relatively small part of the American people, "will follow in the foot-steps of the first colonists" and continue to add the highly beneficial elements of freedom, self-governance, and an orderly society to the American Republic.[54]

Swedes and the American Revolution

The American Revolution became the logical fulfillment of these ideas of personal, political, and religious freedom, and as noted above, Enander argued that the spirit of the Declaration of Independence had already existed among the Vikings in Normandy in the tenth century. In addition to providing an ideological foundation for the Declaration, Swedish Americans were also said to have been of great significance in its actual adoption in Philadelphia in July 1776.

Again, Enander played an important role, and in his Philadelphia speech in 1876 he maintained that it was not only Englishmen and their descendants who stood behind "the heroic actions" in Philadelphia a century earlier but also colonists of Swedish, German, and Dutch ancestry. This was particularly true for "the Swedish Americans at the time," who, through their representative, Pennsylvania delegate "noble Johan Morton," cast the deciding vote in favor of the adoption of the first clause of the Declaration of Independence in Philadelphia in July 1776, thus placing that state on the affirmative side and "determining the future of the fatherland."[55] Morton's role was emphasized by other Swedish-American authors as well. In a recitation at Augustana College's fiftieth anniversary celebrations in 1910 by E. W. Olson, an editor at the ABC and a leading literary figure within the synod, Morton is described as someone who "sat in council with the wise." His decisive vote in the Pennsylvania delegation in favor of the Declaration led Olson to conclude: "When half the chamber cowered to declare / For liberty it took a Swede to dare."[56]

A final example of the Swedish role in the adoption of the Declaration of Independence comes from the poem "Ett fosterländskt minne" (A

Patriotic Memory) by Augustana pastor and poet Ludvig Holmes, written in 1896. After having conjured up the scene of the vote and Morton's decisive role, Holmes writes, "John Morton was Swedish, and the vote he gave was Swedish, / because it put an end to the oppression." The poem ends with a small Swedish boy running to ask his Swedish father to ring the bell when the vote is final. In the last stanza of the poem, the boy tells his father in "pure Swedish": "Now ring father! Now ring father! It is done! / America has taken leave from England!"[57]

The fact that there had been Swedish participants in the Revolutionary War was also important to Enander. He maintained that during the War of Independence, "Swedish-American troops" were in the forefront at the Battle of Trenton, and their outstanding performance caused George Washington to reflect: "If only all my troops were such heroes as these descendants of Swedes, to whom no undertaking is too difficult, no obstacle insurmountable or no duty too heavy."[58] And in his 1910 oration, E. W. Olson asserted that Swedes had played an active part in the War of Independence, claiming that "[b]eneath this standard, borne by Washington, with Fersen and with Stedingk we marched on."[59]

Swedish officers like Axel von Fersen and Curt von Stedingk participated in the French expeditionary force during the Revolutionary War. John Morton, of course, also took part in the events in Philadelphia in the summer of 1776 and cast an important vote within the Pennsylvania delegation. It is also clear that Morton was of Swedish background, as an ancestor, Mårten Mårtensson, born in Sweden circa 1645, had emigrated to the New Sweden colony as a child.[60] The significance of Morton, Fersen, and Stedingk for the construction of Swedish-American homemaking myths is not this nor so much their authenticity as Swedes but rather the ways in which that Enander and others appropriated them, and in that way established ideological links between themselves and central events in and aspects of the history of their adopted country. A conception of Swedish-American history developed, and, as the editor of *Ungdomsvännen* wrote in 1916, anyone browsing the annals of Swedish America, from the Vikings via New Sweden to the present time, would have to conclude that rather than being aliens in their new homeland, "America belongs to the Swede!"[61]

CULTURE HEROES

The emphasis on the contributions by significant Swedish Americans to American history or by Swedes to world history was another characteristic of the creation of a Swedish-American history. Willi Paul Adams has called attention to what he terms the "culture-heroes" of different ethnic groups. They were not only important to the group itself but were also widely recognized by American society at large. "With or without their approval," Adams continues, "they are claimed by the group and held up to society at large as proof of its collective ability, its contribution to building America, and so forth."[62]

An examination of specific culture heroes in the Augustana Synod shows that two persons were particularly important: Swedish-born nineteenth-century engineer John Ericsson and King Gustavus Adolphus.

John Ericsson

John Ericsson came to America in 1839. He had been a successful engineer who, before his arrival in the United States, had worked on the construction of canals in Sweden and on building locomotives in Great Britain. During the Civil War, his services were enlisted by the North. He designed a ship, the *Monitor*, which was put into battle against the Confederate *Merrimac* at the battle of Hampton Roads in 1862, where it helped prevent the destruction of the Union fleet. His ties to organized Swedish America were weak. It was instead the Swedish-American leadership who, in the manner suggested by Willi Paul Adams, claimed him as a symbol of the group, arguing that a Swede in a very significant way had contributed to the outcome of the Civil War. In 1926, following a decade-long fund-raising campaign, a commemorative statue of Ericsson was erected near the Lincoln Memorial in Washington, D.C., and was unveiled in a ceremony in the presence of the Swedish crown prince and President Coolidge, during which the president spoke in highly congratulatory terms of both Ericsson and Swedish Americans in general.[63] Moreover, the symbol of Ericsson was exploited politically, at least in Illinois, where in the mid-1890s a Swedish-American Republican League was formed, using Ericsson as a symbol. This organization sought to ensure that the traditional Swedish support for the Republican Party would continue, at a time when Swedish voters had begun to be attracted by populist and Democratic political ideas.[64]

Ericsson was also a major figure within the Augustana Swedish-American cultural sphere and a common historical topic in *Prärieblomman* and *Ungdomsvännen*. In one article by Ernst Zetterstrand in *Prärieblomman* in 1904, Ericsson was labeled "a typical Swedish American,"[65] and the calendar also included several other articles on Ericsson and/or the battle of

Hampton Roads.⁶⁶ *Ungdomsvännen* carried a serialized biography of Ericsson in 1903, published an account of the battle of Hampton Roads in 1911, and described the construction of the *Monitor* in 1912.⁶⁷ In 1893, *Augustana* reprinted a speech by Augustana minister C. A. Blomgren, which talked about "great memories" providing inspiration to the Swedish Americans. One such memory dealt with the defense of the American Union and the abolition of slavery, in both of which, Blomgren maintains, Ericsson was of crucial importance. Blomgren also draws a parallel between Ericsson's role for the United States and that of Gustavus Adolphus and Axel Oxenstierna for seventeenth-century Europe, stating that "[a] son of Svea" emerged to save the United States, "like Gustavus Adolphus and Oxenstierna came forth and saved Europe," concluding that "in the Pantheon of America . . . his picture will be placed among the foremost, and the jubilations of the people will be mixed with the waves of the Atlantic and the Pacific in a song of praise of the greatest Swede in the New World."⁶⁸

At Augustana College, the life of Ericsson was celebrated several times. The 100th anniversary of Ericsson's birth was celebrated on 24 July 1903. President Andreen spoke about "[t]he life and significance of John Ericsson for us Swedes and for our native country," Swedish folk songs were sung, and twenty-four young girls performed a flag exercise.⁶⁹ When the fiftieth anniversary of the battle of Hampton Roads was marked in March 1912, *Augustana* commented that it was an important date for the United States in general and for "us Swedish Americans in particular" and that it was "appropriate for us Swedes to honor a man whose life lends credit to Swedes wherever they live and work."⁷⁰ The 1906 article in the Augustana student newspaper about "Patriotism at Augustana," already referred to in chapter 4, promoted a specific Swedish-American patriotism at the school and held up Ericsson as an example of this, who in the author's opinion was "a poor Swede [and] a poor American [but] a splendid Swedish American!"⁷¹

Gustavus Adolphus

The Swedish king Gustavus Adolphus occupied a special position at Augustana College, and throughout the years a number of celebrations in his memory took place. In his person, the Augustana Swedish Americans could combine both the religious and ethnic elements of their identity as they celebrated him both as a Lutheran and as a Swede. In fact, in several instances the Gustavus Adolphus celebration was called a Reformation festivity. The death date of the king was 6 November, and most of the celebrations at

Augustana were held as close as possible to that date. This emphasis on Gustavus Adolphus was also paralleled in Sweden during the late nineteenth century, especially in conjunction with the 250th anniversary of the king's death in 1882. The king's significance for maintaining Lutheranism in Sweden and for defending Protestantism in Europe was emphasized by contemporary historians, as was the king's and Sweden's function as a Germanic barrier against Russia.[72]

In 1891, the Gustavus Adolphus celebration was held on 5 November. Enander, who had recently assumed the professorship of Swedish, spoke on his view of Gustavus Adolphus in world history, outlining the king's intervention in the Thirty Years' War, his role as a man of education (the university in Tartu in Estonia was founded during Gustavus Adolphus's reign), and his interest in America's position in the development of civilization, where "a home for all poor and freedom loving persons" was eventually created (plans for the New Sweden colony were made during his reign). Enander concluded that the king's life was an example of the life of a true Christian.[73]

Two years later, the day was celebrated on 6 November, and *Augustana* reminded its readers that this date was of importance "to us as Swedes and Lutherans." The celebration took place in the afternoon with speeches about Gustavus Adolphus in both Swedish and English, and in the evening a "successful" concert was held.[74] In 1901, a Reformation festival was held in November in conjunction with the visit of Bishop von Schéele. References to Gustavus Adolphus do not seem to have been specifically included in the program; still, the focus on the Reformation was sure to bring the king's name to mind. The celebration in 1902 included a speech in Swedish by seminary professor Nils Forsander on "the first and the most important Swedish Christian heroes," who, according to Forsander, were Ansgar and Gustavus Adolphus.[75]

In 1907, it had been 275 years since the king had fallen at the battle of Lützen, and preparations were underway at Augustana for a commemoration. Enander, who by now was both aging and physically weak, had heard of the plans for the festivity and sent President Andreen several memorial medallions coined in Sweden for the occasion; he asked to be notified of the program for the celebration.[76] Held in the Augustana chapel, the program marked the anniversary of a king who had died for "faith and freedom of thought," as the report in *Augustana* put it. As in 1901, Forsander spoke in Swedish on the topic "Our Most Glorious Memory," and I. M. Anderson addressed the topic "Gustavus Adolphus. Why Honor Him?" in English.[77]

Putting the Past to Use

The following year, Professor Oscar Montelius, a leading Swedish archaeologist who was visiting the campus, spoke on the topic of Sweden during the Viking Age on 6 November, "Gustavus Adolphus Day" as *Augustana* now called it.[78]

The ethnic and religious aspects of celebrating Gustavus Adolphus were expressed in 1915. *Augustana* argued for the continued celebration of the memory of the king and stated that by remembering him, Swedish Americans would combine a pride in their "ancestral faith" with "the glorious history, language, and literature" of their ancestral country.[79] The celebration at Augustana College, which *Augustana* called "a commemoration of our ancestry," also combined religion with ethnicity, as hymns were sung and G. N. Swan spoke on Tegnér and *Fritiofs saga*.[80]

Even when formal celebrations did not take place, comments and articles about Gustavus Adolphus were often published in Augustana publications during the month of November. In 1900, for example, Swan presented the king to readers of *Augustana,* concluding that every Swede in Sweden was familiar with the life of the king through the public schools and that it ought to be a "happy duty" *(kär plikt)* for the Swedish-American youth to read about him as well. "Who can read about his life without feeling proud to be Swedish?" he asks.[81] A 1909 editorial comment in *Augustana* maintained that the 6th of November was a day that should be celebrated, preferably with the same patriotism that American holidays were marked. The paper linked Gustavus Adolphus and Lincoln by suggesting that the king fought for the same principles as the president, namely political freedom and freedom of thought.[82] In its comment in 1913, *Augustana* emphasized the fact that the power of the pope had diminished as a result of Gustavus Adolphus's actions, adding that it ought to be of great interest to the Swedish people that the king's memory was still highly regarded by Swedish Americans.[83]

The significance of the Gustavus Adolphus celebrations is also shown in a booklet of "dialogues and monologues" for youth groups in the Augustana Synod, published by Augustana pastor and author C. W. Andeer in 1904. In a dialogue concerning the reasons why Swedish Americans ought to celebrate the king, Person A asks why he as an American should celebrate a Swedish king. The answer given by Person B is that Gustavus Adolphus is celebrated because of his historical significance in defending freedom of religion and the Protestant cause during the Thirty Years' War. Moreover, in a vein similar to the editorial comment in *Augustana* from 1909, Person B also links Gustavus Adolphus and his grandfather, sixteenth-century king Gustav

Vasa, to prominent American historical persons by saying Gustav Vasa had fought for political freedom for Sweden in the same way Washington and Lincoln had done in the United States. Gustavus Adolphus, however, had gone even further in espousing the cause of religious freedom, which made him even more worthy of celebrations.[84]

By November 1915, *Augustana* could happily conclude that "Gustavus Adolphus days" were celebrated more and more throughout the Augustana Synod, including in its congregations and in its youth groups. These celebrations contributed toward both the preservation of a "great national memory" in Swedish America and an appreciation of "what we as a people have in common." The two most important elements in this Swedish-American commonality that, according to *Augustana,* served to "hold us together as a people" were "our ancestral faith," to which Gustavus Adolphus had dedicated his life, and "the glorious history, literature, and language of our ancestral country."[85]

John Ericsson represented a Swede who had played an important part in American history, while Gustavus Adolphus's significance rested with his role as a defender of Lutheran religion. By celebrating the lives of these individuals, the ethnic and religious elements of the synod's identity were combined. It also meant that the Augustana Swedish Americans appropriated the positive characteristics ascribed to two individuals with no immediate connections to the synod, thus making Ericsson and Gustavus Adolphus a part of their Swedish-American identity.

FOUNDERS DAY AND THE GOLDEN ANNIVERSARY

Celebrations that focused more specifically on the history of the ethnic group itself provide yet another way of examining the growth of a sense of history among the Swedish Americans. At Augustana, a commemoration of what was called Founders Day took place during a few years at the beginning of the first decade of the twentieth century, and in 1910 the synod observed its fiftieth anniversary in a weeklong celebration. Both Founders Day and the fiftieth anniversary of 1910 provided the Augustana Swedish Americans with opportunities to reflect on their characteristics and history in America.

Founders Day

In March 1901, the student association Svenska Vitterhetssällskapet at Augustana College suggested that a "Swedish Day" should be observed at the school. It was argued that it was "only fair that we . . . have a Swedish day of such nature," as Washington's birthday was celebrated on 22 February. It was also suggested that 1 May would be an appropriate date for such a day.[86] The matter was discussed by the board of directors, and in May 1901 it was announced that the student proposal had been granted.[87] When the first celebration was observed the following year, it was called Founders Day to honor the founders of the synod, college, and seminary and was, according to President Andreen, to be marked every 27 April henceforth. This would be an opportunity, said Andreen, to "build our own traditions, to celebrate the arrival of spring in a dignified manner, and to not forget the most important ingredient from the May celebrations in Sweden, the white student cap."[88] Andreen asserted that this day would be Swedish in nature, regardless of the language used, as the founders of the school and synod were Swedish, and would help fulfill "the mission God has given us as a Swedish-American people in the New World."[89]

The first Founders Day events took place at the end of April 1902 and lasted from a Thursday evening until Sunday afternoon. The main focus of this celebration was on the history of the Augustana Synod and on the early founding fathers and included visitors, singing, speeches by synod leaders, and a trip "by street car" to the graves of former presidents Hasselquist and Olsson at Riverside Cemetery in Moline. Several hundred persons were in attendance.[90]

The main speech was delivered by Norelius, one of the founding fathers from 1860 who was often called the patriarch of the Augustana Synod, and dealt with the events that led up to the founding of the Augustana Synod. In Norelius's estimation, the decision to break with the Synod of Northern Illinois in 1860 and, among other things, to establish the Augustana seminary was a "declaration of independence" that was necessary to "save the faith and the creed and to make the Swedish-American cultural development *[den svensk-amerikanska odlingen]*" possible.[91] A festive poem was then read by Holmes, which, according to Carl Sundbeck, who attended the celebration, was equal to the poetry of Johan Olof Wallin.[92]

As a member of the Patriotic Student Association (Fosterländska studentförbundet) in Uppsala, Sundbeck also met with a delegation of Augustana students who sent a greeting to Sweden in poetic form. In it, the old homeland is assured that the Swedish Americans, even those "born and raised under the Star Spangled Banner," still use the Swedish language, still love the music of the north, and still have not "sold" their "inheritance" and "childhood faith" for the "gold of a foreign land."[93]

A week after this celebration, *Augustana* echoed opinions similar to those of Norelius, emphasizing the "independent men" who formed the synod and suggesting that their motives were to preserve "their religious faith, their language and their ancestral way of thinking." This was a feeling shared by other Swedes in America, *Augustana* continued, and it did not take them long to understand that "here in America [it] was possible to maintain all of their ancestral good and still be just as good American citizens" because it was not in their "nature" to "without further ado shed what over the trial of centuries had been judged to be of inestimable value."[94]

Founders Day was celebrated in 1903 and 1904 in a similar manner as in 1902.[95] After those years, no sources mention continued celebrations. Apparently, the day never achieved the status of a Swedish-American national day, as some had hoped.

The Golden Anniversary

In June 1910, the Augustana Synod commemorated its fiftieth anniversary with a grand celebration in Rock Island. In 1905, a committee had been appointed to plan these observances, commemorating the history of both the synod and Augustana College and Theological Seminary.[96] This "golden anniversary" became, in Conrad Bergendoff's words, "the greatest event in Augustana history,"[97] providing opportunities to look back and ponder the accomplishments of the past half century as well as to look ahead to the future. The celebrations began on 5 June, lasted for a full ten days, and are well documented in *Minnen från jubelfesten*. During the first five days, the semi-centennial of Augustana College and Theological Seminary was commemorated, including the commencement exercises for the classes of 1910 for both institutions, whereas the second part of the program was devoted to the Augustana Synod.

The events were directed toward both an American and a Swedish audience, as the list of official participants in and the greetings at both the college and synodical anniversary celebrations demonstrate. As noted in chapter 2, the audience naturally enough included representatives from the Augustana Synod in general but also other American Lutheran denominations and non–Swedish-American colleges and universities (primarily in Illinois). Governor Adolph Eberhart of Minnesota, who was of Swedish descent, was also in attendance.

The rapprochement between official Sweden and the Augustana Synod resulted in three Swedish delegates: Henrik Schück, professor of literature and *rector magnificus* at Uppsala University, representing Uppsala and Lund universities; Bishop von Schéele representing the Church of Sweden; and the Reverend Per Pehrsson of the Swedish pastoral association. In addition, telegrams and greetings were received from more than fifty other individuals and organizations in Sweden. Greetings from both President Taft and King Gustav V further illustrate the dual emphasis in the Golden Anniversary and the official nature of the event.[98]

Many speeches were held during the weeklong celebration, focusing on what had been achieved during the past five decades, and in them two themes characteristic of the synod's purpose emerged. In his presidential report to the synod, held at the synodical annual meeting at the same time, Norelius looked back on the denomination's history, something he was uniquely qualified to do, since he was one of the few persons who had been present at the denomination's founding in 1860 and who was still alive. He spoke of the growth of the synod, its institutions, and its influence throughout Swedish America. He concluded that the Augustana Synod was the Swedish-American denomination that best "had preserved the faith of our fathers and their special Swedish culture and language,"[99] thus emphasizing the synod's dual religious and ethnic significance. The ethnic emphasis represented a change of opinion for Norelius, as he had been one of the advocates for the movement to prepare for the disappearance of Swedish five decades earlier.

In one of the main addresses at the synod jubilee, Pastor J. A. Krantz spoke on the topic of "the mission of the Augustana Synod," a talk that can serve as an illustration of the synod's dual mission. According to Krantz, the synod's most important tasks were religious, namely to "reestablish and cherish a true and confessional Lutheran Christianity," to "be a true evangelical free church," and to "gather our Swedish people in [the church's] bosom."[100]

However, Pastor Krantz also stated that another important task for the synod was to "preserve the Swedish language and cherish Swedish culture" in America. The Swedish culture to be maintained by the Augustana Synod would also, according to Krantz, represent "the noblest, purest and most useful dimensions" of the ancestral traditions brought to America by the Swedish immigrants, and the main vehicle for its preservation was the language.[101] Krantz's argument thus not only showed the significance of the ancestral culture for the synod but also reflected the general tendency to emphasize certain, suitable dimensions of the Swedish cultural baggage available to the Augustana Swedish Americans.

What was celebrated during Founders Day and at the Golden Anniversary in Rock Island during the first decade of the twentieth century? Clearly, the emphasis was on what had been achieved since the founding of the synod in 1860, focusing on the denomination's religious heritage. However, the ethnic element also played an important role. The student association that initially proposed the idea of Founders Day spoke of celebrating a "Swedish day," explicitly likening it to such an American celebration as Washington's birthday. The greeting from the Augustana students to their compatriots in Uppsala with their assurances that their heritage had not been sold for the gold of a foreign land also underscores this interpretation, and in 1910 Pastor Krantz explicitly spoke of maintaining the Swedish culture and language as one of the main tasks of the Augustana Synod. The dual emphasis on the synod's religious and ethnic identity had thus developed fully by the Golden Anniversary in 1910.

History was a significant element in the creation of a Swedish-American identity in the Augustana Synod. It was used by the cultural leadership of the immigrant group as a means to gain legitimacy, acceptance, and status in the United States. It established the Augustana Swedes as good and loyal Americans while it maintained and promoted their ethnic pasts. A specific Swedish-American history was established, beginning with the Viking journeys to America and ending with the Swedish immigrants of the nineteenth and twentieth centuries. A central part of the history-making in Swedish America in general and the Augustana Synod in particular involved the creation of different homemaking myths, through which certain individuals and events from Swedish, Swedish-American, and American history were given special prominence and a new meaning as they became a part of the Swedish-American tradition that emerged within the synod. The establishment of an early presence in America, the highlighting of significant Swedish and Swedish-American contributions to the American Republic, and the emphasis on certain positive character traits from Swedish and Swedish-American history became particularly important in this process. Certain individuals became especially prominent, assuming the role of cultural heroes.

Swedish Americans were not alone in creating homemaking myths. Many of the aspects of Swedish-American history were also common among Norwegian Americans, in particular in the writings of newspaper editor and educator Rasmus Bjørn Anderson. Anderson devoted much of his life as an educator and newspaperman to advancing the cause of the Viking discovery of America, predating the Swedish efforts under Enander. In 1874 he published the book *America Not Discovered by Columbus,* in which he argued not only that the Vikings has been the first Europeans in the New World but also that the Viking spirit of freedom via the English Magna Carta had found its way into the American Declaration of Independence. It is likely that Enander was aware of Anderson's ideas and was influenced by them as he developed his conception of Swedish-American history.[102]

As noted in chapter 2, Swedish America was a culturally and socially divided community. History can be both divisive and unifying, and shaping a Swedish-American history and choosing the cultural heroes was thus a potential source of cultural conflict within the community, just as had been the case with regard to the kind of literature that was deemed appropriate to read. Although relatively little research has been done on these questions, the discussion of the erection of the Linnaeus statue in Chicago in 1891 provides one example of the cultural divisions over history in Swedish America.

As Eric Johannesson has shown,[103] a number of statues with ethnic connotations had been erected in Chicago in the late nineteenth century, including sculptures of Friedrich von Schiller, Johann Wolfgang von Goethe, Giuseppe Garibaldi, and Tadeusz Kościuszko. In 1882, Enander proposed erecting a statue of King Gustavus Adolphus in 1882, which created strong differences of opinion between the city's religious (primarily Augustana) and secular Swedish groups. The secular and liberal-leaning Swedish Americans in Chicago opposed the idea, as Gustavus Adolphus was seen as too closely associated with religion. In addition, it was argued, it was impossible to raise a statue of a king in the American Republic. In 1886, the project was once more brought up, but this time the person chosen to honor was Carolus Linnaeus, the eighteenth-century Swedish botanist, and as Johannesson notes, Linnaeus became a compromise candidate, behind whom both the secular and religious factions of the Swedish-American community could unite. Following a five-year fund-raising campaign headed by Enander, the statue was finally unveiled in May 1891 in Chicago's Lincoln Park, with several thousand Swedish Americans present. Interestingly, the program at the unveiling followed the pattern from the ceremony from the Schiller statue inauguration in 1886, and contemporary newspaper accounts claimed between 20,000 and 50,000 Swedish Americans attended the ceremony in Lincoln Park.

As also noted in chapter 2, the cultural struggles within the Swedish-American community could be overcome. This can be seen in the conception of a Swedish-American history, where some historical symbols were less controversial than others, and most factions within the community seem to have embraced both the Vikings and the New Sweden colonists. Religion did play an important part and obviously played a central role for the Augustana Synod, which became especially clear in the fiftieth anniversary celebrations in 1910. Gustavus Adolphus was also a particularly important cultural hero for the Augustana Swedes. The discussion of the Linnaeus statue shows, though, that when the need for the Chicago Swedes to contribute a statue of their own to the growing collection of ethnic statuary in the capital of Swedish America was strong enough, the incentive for reaching a compromise over more contentious dimensions of history overcame otherwise deep-seated religious and cultural differences.

Moreover, it is also clear that Augustana's version of what constituted a Swedish-American culture in general and a Swedish-American history in particular was becoming embraced by wider parts of the Swedish-American community by the turn of the century. When the first Swedish-American historical organization, Svensk-amerikanska historiska sällskapet (The Swedish-American Historical Society), was established in 1905, the initiative came from Enander, and the Augustana representatives played an important role in the organization. Not surprisingly, Enander became its first president, and influential Augustana persons such as Andreen, Schön, and C. W. Foss (professor of history at Augustana College) served as board members.

It is noticeable, though, that the board members also included prominent representatives from other parts of Swedish America, such as David Nyvall, president of the Mission Covenant North Park College; C. G. Lagergren, dean of the Swedish Baptist Seminary; C. G. Wallenius, the head of the Swedish Methodist Seminary in Evanston, Illinois; and Charles Johansen, editor of the New York–based cultural magazine *Valkyrian*.[104] An analysis of the contributions to the society's five yearbooks, which were published intermittently between 1905 and 1917, and Gunnar Thander's study of how Swedish-American history was conceived of in the pages of *Valkyrian* shows strong parallels to the patterns in the Augustana Synod discussed above, with a commonality of views and opinions of prominent Swedish contributions to American life and with homemaking myths from the Vikings to John Ericsson.[105]

8

Epilogue: Being Swedish American in the Augustana Synod

What did it mean to be Swedish American in the Augustana Synod around the turn of the century? This concluding chapter will provide a general discussion of the nature of the Swedish-American identity that developed in the Augustana Synod as well as a discussion of how a Swedish-American identity was created in the Augustana Synod, what it consisted of, and why it came into being.

The construction of a Swedish-American identity in the Augustana Synod was not unique. Other immigrant and ethnic groups in the United States were also engaged in similar processes. Indeed, the nineteenth century in both Europe and America was characterized by the growth of national feelings and traditions that were, in the words of Eric Hobsbawm, being "invented." Although different in nature, the nation-building processes in Sweden and the United States in the late nineteenth century provided the framework within which the ethnic identity of the Augustana Synod was created. The developments in the Augustana Synod are thus an example of this larger process, providing an illustration of how one particular group fashioned an answer to the question of who they were.

The significance of ethnicity varied greatly among Swedish immigrants and their children in late-nineteenth- and early-twentieth-century America. To some, it meant nothing or very little, while the opposite was true of a small group of cultural activists or ethnic leaders who formulated a sense of Swedishness. Thus, there arose a range of possible identifications, varying from a weaker ethnic awareness to a fully developed ethnic identity. This study has concentrated on the more developed identity on the group and institutional level, in that the ethnic identity of the Augustana Synod and its leadership has been the focus of analysis.

This study has also argued that the nature of ethnic identities can vary from an everyday level, often rooted in the daily lives of members of the ethnic community, up to what has been called an elite level. This elite level has formed the basis for the discussion of the ethnic identity in the Augustana Synod. Moreover, this ethnic identity was seen as something new and specific to the American context in which the members of the ethnic community lived. It was constructed or invented through a gradual selection process, consisting of cultural elements from both Old and New World experiences. This duality meant that the new ethnic identity that emerged in America, was, literally, Swedish American.

As we have seen, the Swedish-American community was divided along several fault lines. Religion, social status, and cultural and political opinions were important characteristics that further subdivided the Swedish-American group, and at times quite a keen competition for influence in the community took place between these groups. Although not exclusively concerned with the issue of ethnic identity, these many Swedish-American organizations were important in the creation of a Swedish-American identity. Given the split nature of the Swedish-American community, different versions of a Swedish-American identity were advocated that sometimes opposed each other, so it is possible to speak of a struggle for cultural hegemony in Swedish America.

However, Swedish America was not characterized only by division. At times the community—or at least parts of it—was also able to unite. Public manifestations such as the 1888 New Sweden Jubilee in Minneapolis, the campaign for the Linnaeus statue in Chicago, and the 1893 Columbian Exposition show that differences within the community could be overcome when the group was presenting itself to the larger American community.

All this said, the Augustana Synod was the leading organization in Swedish America. The synod's membership was between a fifth and a third of all persons of Swedish descent in the United States during the period of my investigation, but the synod clearly also reached beyond its membership proper in terms of influence in Swedish America, as many nonmembers also availed themselves of the synod's services. Based on the number of Swedish Americans who belonged to one of the many Swedish-American organizations that existed over time, the synod's dominance was even greater, and in 1920, 60 percent of all members in a Swedish-American organization

Epilogue

belonged to the Augustana Synod. By the turn of the century, its network of congregations, educational and benevolent institutions, publishing house and publications, and bookstores spanned the entire American continent, making it possible to speak of an Augustana sphere of influence in Swedish America in which a Swedish-American identity was both created and maintained.

HOW WAS AN IDENTITY CREATED?

In examining the nature and characteristics of the Swedish-American identity in the Augustana Synod, it is first important to assess how a Swedish-American identity was created in the Augustana Synod. There was obviously an important temporal dimension to the development of a Swedish-American identity in the synod, and a definite turning point occurred during the last decade of the nineteenth century. During the early years of the synod's history, there seems to have been relatively small concern with the preservation of the contents of a sense of Swedishness among the Augustana Synod. Instead, a great deal of importance was placed on the "Americanization" of the Swedish immigrants, a discussion that was largely couched in terms of the use and role of the Swedish and English languages. As we have seen, such influential synod leaders as Erland Carlsson, Eric Norelius, and T. N. Hasselquist spoke about the futility of preserving the Swedish language in America and instead underscored the necessity of learning English.

This attitude was also reflected in the emphasis on the English language at Augustana College, the constitution of which from the very beginning called for one of the three professorships to be filled by an English-speaking instructor. From the late 1880s on, Swedish was used only rarely as the language of instruction in the college, and as a result of a series of curricular reforms beginning in the mid-1880s, it even became possible to graduate from Augustana without having studied the Swedish language at all. In addition, the curriculum had already in 1869 been organized along American lines with four student classes, and the addition of the different vocational programs of study at the college, such as the "commercial school," which primarily attracted students from the immediate vicinity of non-Swedish background, also shows how important the American context was at Augustana during the early years.

From around 1890, however, a noticeable change with regard to the position of Swedish in the Augustana Synod can be observed. At Augustana College, official pronouncements from the college leadership, statements in the college catalogs, and comments from visitors and observers of the contemporary Swedish-American scene all emphasized the importance of Swedish at Augustana at this time. In 1891, the professorship of Swedish and Christianity was separated into two positions, and the first instructor to teach exclusively Swedish in the college was, significantly enough, Johan Enander, one of the leading Swedish-American cultural activists. The college actively sought to hire well-qualified teachers of Swedish during the following years.

Moreover, from 1902 the college catalogs singled out Swedish as a subject of particular importance and encouraged all students of Swedish parentage to enroll in the courses. There was a substantial interest among students in studying Swedish as well as in engaging in Swedish-related extracurricular activities. Several Swedish literary societies were started at the school during the years around the turn of the century, including Svenska Vitterhetssällskapet from 1896, Tegnér-förbundet from 1901, and Iduna from 1902. The discussions in the Phrenokosmian Society, which had been established in 1860, also showed a greater interest in topics relating to the college's ethnic background from around 1890. Swedish- and Swedish-American–related celebrations began to be observed, and several visitors from Sweden were received on the campus.

Further examples of an emphasis on the synod's interest in its ethnic background can be found among its publishing activities. Although the great majority of the publications at the ABC up until 1915 were in Swedish, those publications that dealt with topics relating to Swedish or Swedish-American culture began appearing in earnest precisely during the latter part of the 1890s. *Prärieblomman* and *Ungdomsvännen,* ABC's leading cultural periodicals, first appeared under ABC imprint in 1900, and during the following two decades they were followed by a number of books of prose and poetry by Swedish-American authors such as C. W. Andeer, Vilhelm Berger, Jakob Bonggren, Ludvig Holmes, C. A. Lönnqvist, Anna Olsson, and Johan Person.

The emphasis on Swedish conditions at the ABC at this time can also be seen in a content analysis of two of the leading primers at the ABC, *Församlingsskolans läsebok* and *Tredje läseboken* from 1891 and 1917. The latter book put much greater weight on both Swedish and Swedish-American topics than the former, evidence for a very noticeable change of emphasis over a sixteen-year period. In addition, Swedish literature also began to be published at the ABC after the turn of the century, including *Ur svenska sången* (1901), *Fritiofs saga* (1914), and *Fänrik Ståls sägner* (1915).

Epilogue

The years around 1890 thus appear to be something of a watershed for the significance of a Swedish ethnicity both at Augustana College and in the denomination at large. Prior to that time, Swedishness seems to have played a relatively small role, at least judging from official pronouncements and from the activities at Augustana College. The situation was quite different after 1890, when both the Swedish and Swedish-American nature of the Augustana Synod was underscored. A growing sense of ethnicity was expressed in what has been called a Swedish-American cultural tradition that was being constructed or invented, providing the foundations for the synod's Swedish-American identity. Although there were some parallels to the ways in which Swedish nationalism of the 1890s was formulated, the emergence of the Swedish-American tradition in the Augustana Synod is better understood within its American context, especially in light of the generational change and the varying significance of religion and ethnicity in the Augustana Synod.

Two phases can be discerned in the synod's early history that help to explain this development. The first phase was the period from 1860 to about 1890, when relatively little significance was attached to the denomination's ethnicity. Two main explanations can be given for this. As has been shown in chapter 2, the period 1860–90 was a phase of rapid growth and institution-building. The synod grew quickly from its original thirty-six midwestern congregations with a few thousand members in 1860 to close to eight hundred congregations with over 175,000 members and a number of educational and benevolent institutions spanning the entire American continent in the mid-1890s. This period of institution-building created tensions within the synod, as the relative independence of individual congregations and regional conferences resulted in decentralizing tendencies. It was not until 1894 that a synodical constitution was adopted, creating a lasting balance between the central, regional, and local elements in the synod. The synod was also challenged from the outside—for example, through the conflict with the followers of what became the Mission Covenant Church in the 1870s and also with secular, more urban-based groups in the 1870s and 1880s. Much of the work of the Augustana Synod during this first period was thus focused on building and sustaining the denomination as well as on meeting challenges from the outside. Maintaining a Lutheran faith among Swedish immigrants in America was paramount to the synod, which also meant that the religious dimension of the synod became central during this first phase, helping to explain the relative indifference the denomination seems to have shown for its ethnicity.

Epilogue

A second explanation deals with the generational composition of the Augustana Synod. Although the synod statistics do not include any specific information on the birthplace of its members, it seems evident that the Augustana Synod was dominated by Swedish-born members during the 1860s, 1870s, and 1880s. The immigration of Swedes on a large scale began in earnest after the Civil War, which means that at least two decades would have had to pass before an American-born generation would become dominant. The analysis of the student body at Augustana College confirms this assumption. The dominance of Swedish-born individuals provides the second explanation for the lack of interest in the synod's ethnicity during this first phase of the institution's history. These Augustana Swedes—born in Sweden, of rural background, and with roots in the Swedish religious revival movement of the mid-nineteenth century—were grounded in Swedish circumstances where a sense of national Swedish identity was weak. In leaving for America, they sought emancipation from the Swedish economic, social, and even religious conditions rather than the opportunity to express national feelings. Once in America, characterized by great ethnic, religious, and cultural variety, the Augustana Synod provided these Swedes with mostly a religious continuity, which was, however, expressed in familiar Swedish forms, particularly in terms of the language. During this first phase of the synod's history, then, the sense of Swedish ethnicity was an unreflected upon or taken-for-granted part of the synod's religious identity, a fact that further helps to explain the weak position of the denomination's ethnic background during this time.

The second phase of the denomination's history lasted between circa 1890 to 1915. By this time, the synod was well established as the dominant force in Swedish America, and although there were still distinct religious and ideological differences between the Augustana Synod and other Swedish-American groups, conflicts of the kind noticeable in the 1870s and 1880s seem to have been fewer.

Moreover, the synod was dominated by the children and the grandchildren of the Swedish immigrants during the second phase, groups that had different national and ethnic needs than did their parents and grandparents. At Augustana College, the American-born students were rapidly becoming a majority after 1890, something that also seems to have been true for the synod as a whole. The analysis of the student body at Augustana College also shows that the Augustana Swedish Americans were leaving the farms and entering white-collar professions and that the majority of them remained within the Augustana sphere of Swedish America upon graduation.

As we have seen, it was during this second phase that the synod's ethnic identity began to be emphasized and to co-exist with its religious identity. Thus, a window of opportunity was opened, and it became possible to formulate a sense of Swedishness within the Augustana Synod. Given the significance of generational change for the character of ethnic identities, it can further be argued that, as the American-born generations of Swedish Americans in the Augustana Synod with no personal experience of Sweden and with limited knowledge of the Swedish language or Swedish cultural traditions in general became dominant, the nature of their ethnic identity changed. It became an ethnic ideology, which was something that had to be learned. This reflected upon and actively formulated ethnicity of the second phase was thus radically different from the unreflected upon and taken-for-granted sense of Swedish identity presumed during the first period of the synod's history, and we can thus say that the Augustana Synod went from being Swedish to being Swedish American.

WHAT DID THE IDENTITY CONSIST OF?

The second question deals with what the Swedish-American identity consisted of. The analysis of the ethnic identity in the Augustana Synod has been based on a variety of materials and sources, including Augustana College with its curriculum, student organizations, and general cultural activities; the ABC and its publishing profile; and the construction of a specific Swedish-American history within the synod.

Augustana's Swedish-American identity consisted of both Swedish and Swedish-American elements, and it expressed itself, often in a highly idealized and romantic manner, in a classroom at Augustana College, at a Swedish-American celebration on campus, or in a publication from the ABC. The sense of self drew on selected cultural elements from a Swedish and Swedish-American—and to a lesser extent American—repertoire of "high culture," such as literature, history, and religion. It emphasized great Swedish and Swedish-American accomplishments and underscored such traits as freedom, bravery, and religiosity thought to be characteristic of both Swedes and Swedish Americans.

The turning point with regard to the significance given to ethnicity in the Augustana Synod around 1890 also meant that the nature of the ethnicity changed. Prior to that time, the sense of Swedishness at Augustana College, as expressed through the authors studied in the Swedish classes or discussed in the literary societies, to a large degree mirrored the contemporary literary

Epilogue

selections in the Swedish secondary schools. Relatively little attention was paid to specific Swedish-American cultural conditions, which also confirms this pattern.

As we have seen, the advent of the second phase meant an affirmation of ethnicity within the Augustana Synod. As the American-born generations began to dominate the synod, their Swedishness was no longer taken for granted but had to be learned or constructed. What I have called a Swedish-American cultural tradition began to emerge, consisting of both Swedish and Swedish-American cultural elements. The selection of Swedish literature and history continued to reflect an idealized, romantic, and patriotic view of the Swedish past. At Augustana College, for example, Swedish history was most often represented by King Gustavus Adolphus, and the Swedish authors most frequently studied and discussed were drawn from the romanticism of the nineteenth century, with Johan Ludvig Runeberg and Esaias Tegnér by far the two most popular authors. The Swedish literary selections at the ABC also showed an emphasis on romanticism and critically established authors of the nineteenth century.

A fairly careful selection process was also at work within the Augustana Synod with regard to those cultural elements from Sweden that were included in the synod's view of Swedish culture. Although the synod's ethnic identity was being affirmed and given possibilities to develop in its own right, religious concerns still set clear boundaries for the cultural expressions in the Augustana Synod. We have seen how a particular view of literature and culture was encouraged. Augustana exercised its role as a gatekeeper in such ways as engaging in debate over the selection of poems for Enander's anthology of Swedish poetry *Ur svenska sången* (where we have found a specific "Augustana point of view"); objecting to the importation of certain popular Swedish fiction *(smutslitteratur)* to Swedish America; and carefully examining, rejecting, or sending back for rewriting some of the manuscripts it received for consideration. The absence of a number of authors of popular fiction at the ABC who were frequently read in both Sweden and elsewhere in Swedish America and August Strindberg's weak position in the Augustana Synod's view of Swedish literature are also illustrative of how the synod acted as gatekeeper.

Furthermore, it must be strongly underscored that the contents of this ethnic identity that emanated from Sweden took on a meaning that was specific to its new American context. The Swedish cultural symbols that were included in Augustana College's version of a Swedish-American identity, such as *Fritiofs saga, Fänrik Ståls sägner,* or Gustavus Adolphus, were all given a new significance in their American context. Even though Augustana College's Swedish curriculum and general view of Swedish culture to a large degree echoed cultural patterns in Sweden as they were expressed, for example, in the Swedish secondary schools, the meaning of *Fritiofs saga* or the achievements of Gustavus Adolphus in Swedish America around 1900 were given a Swedish-American significance. The authors, literary works, or historical persons that made up the Swedish-American tradition were shaped by the American and Swedish-American context in which these cultural elements functioned and by the needs they fulfilled in the Augustana community.

The kings Gustavus Adolphus and Charles XII were both prominent parts of the Swedish national movement associated with the 1890s, symbolizing Sweden's era of greatness and successes in the European political theater. At Augustana, however, it was Gustavus Adolphus who dominated the stage in numerous contexts during the first two decades of the twentieth century. He became a perfect symbol for the Augustana Synod as he embodied both the religious and ethnic dimensions of the denomination. The emphasis on independence and freedom discerned in the writings of Runeberg and Tegnér also provided an opportunity to assign such characteristics to members of the Augustana Swedish-American community, qualities that could also be communicated to the larger Swedish-American and American communities.

In addition to the cultural elements drawn from the national Swedish cultural repertoire, the Swedish-American identity of the second phase also meant a strong awareness of a specific Swedish-American culture that was emerging within the Augustana Synod. The Augustana Swedish Americans now began to see themselves as different from the homeland Swedes, with their own culture and history. From 1903, the Augustana College catalogs stated that one of the missions of the school was to be an "exponent of Swedish-American culture," and President Andreen spoke of the importance of the Swedish-American colleges in making "thoroughly dedicated" Swedish Americans out of their students. As we have seen, many aspects of Swedish-American culture were also discussed in the college literary societies or celebrated on the campus during the first two decades of the twentieth century.

Several of the Swedish-American authors whose fiction or poetry were published by the ABC after the turn of the century also specifically dealt with the nature of this new Swedish-American identity. In his *Svensk-amerikanska studier* from 1912, Person argues that the Swedish Americans were becoming a separate "people," which was "neither Swedish, nor American . . . but a combination of both." In the works of Andeer, moreover, Swedish-American life is portrayed in highly positive terms, especially within the sphere of the Augustana Synod. Andeer also contrasts Swedish Americans and Swedish-American culture against conditions in Sweden, a comparison which is favorable to Swedish America. The two leading cultural periodicals published by the ABC, *Ungdomsvännen* and *Prärieblomman,* also became important vehicles in promoting Swedish-American culture and identity.

The comparison of the ABC's primers *Församlingsskolans läsebok* from 1891 and *Tredje läseboken* from 1917 also illustrates the shift in emphasis from Swedish to Swedish American in Augustana's sense of Swedish ethnicity. In the first book, the national or ethnic elements deal almost exclusively either with national Swedish conditions, such as Swedish history or literature, or with cultural aspects of the immigrants' adopted homeland, such as selections of American poetry in Swedish translation. Twenty-six years later, when *Tredje läseboken* appeared, the Augustana Synod's Swedish-American identity was fully developed, and a large part of the book is devoted to accounts of the lives and times of Swedes in America, from the New Sweden colony up until what was then the present time.

This sense of a specific Swedish-American identity also included the construction and celebration of a specific Swedish-American history. We have seen how a concern for recording and writing the history of the Swedes in America in general and of the Augustana Synod in particular developed from an early date. The historical consciousness among the Augustana Swedes also manifested itself in the creation of special celebrations of the synod's history. Founders Day was established in 1902 to commemorate the founders of the synod, and the fiftieth anniversary celebration in 1910 also became an opportunity to look back at half a century of work in the new land and to mark the achievements of the synod.

Moreover, we have also seen how the attempts to write a Swedish-American history focused not only on the nineteenth and twentieth centuries. Enander's historical writings provide a particularly good example of the tendency to establish, in Orm Øverland's words, Swedish-American "homemaking myths," in which the establishment of an early presence in America became particularly important. Here, the New Sweden colony from the seventeenth century was of central significance. Although no connections existed between the colony and the Swedish immigrants of some two hundred years later, the latter still sought to establish a historical continuity between the colony and themselves, providing them with an opportunity to become a "colonial people" in an attempt to place themselves on the same level as the seventeenth-century New England colonists. Moreover, the many positive characteristics that existed in the New Sweden colony, such as freedom, religiosity, and hard work, were also characteristics that by extension were applied to the Swedish immigrants of the late nineteenth and early twentieth centuries.

In addition to the New Sweden colony, the life and achievements of John Ericsson were important in Augustana's conception of a Swedish-American history, and he and his accomplishments were praised and celebrated throughout the Augustana Synod. Given Ericsson's role in the construction of the *Monitor,* he became, in the words of Willi Paul Adams, an excellent "culture hero" for the Augustana Synod. Although his connections to organized Swedish America were weak, the Swedish-American ethnic leadership still appropriated him, making him into one of their own. The achievements of Ericsson and his contributions to the American Republic became those of other Swedish immigrants of the nineteenth and twentieth centuries, as Ericsson was, in the words of Ernst Zetterstrand in a 1904 article about him in *Prärieblomman,* a "typical Swedish American."

Additional elements in the creation of a Swedish-American history included other such Swedish contributions to the growth of the American Republic and participation in the Revolutionary War and at the signing of the Declaration of Independence in 1776. The Vikings were also important in the conception of Swedish-American history. Although no direct Viking impact on the history of the United States could be found, the case for the Viking landing on the North America continent had to do with establishing that the true "discoverers" of America were Scandinavians, not Italians or Spaniards. To some Augustana authors, such as Enander and E. W. Olson, this history of a Swedish presence in North America extending back almost a millennium gave the Swedes a special status or birthright in America, making it possible for Olson to claim that "America belongs to the Swede!"

The cultural elements in the Swedish-American identity of the Augustana Synod were thus based on selective parts of both the Swedish and Swedish-American past and cultural traditions. An idealized and romantic Swedish Americanism was created, emphasizing famous persons, Swedish and Swedish-American accomplishments and achievements, and enviable and lofty character traits, supposedly typical of both Swedes and Swedish Americans.

Thus, readers of *Ungdomsvännen* would be exposed to fiction and poetry by notable Swedish writers such as Runeberg and Tegnér as well as stories and poetry by Swedish-American authors like Andeer or Holmes. They would marvel at the achievements of Gustavus Adolphus and his defense of the Lutheran religion during the Thirty Years' War, at the establishment of a Swedish colony on the Delaware River in 1638, and at John Ericsson's genius during the Civil War. In this way, a separate Swedish-American canon evolved with its own history, literature, heroes, and heroines.

Although a systematic examination of the cultural expressions of other parts of Swedish America is outside the focus of this study, some evidence suggests that the Augustana version of a Swedish-American identity became the preeminent one in the cultural struggle in the Swedish-American community, and other factions of the community seem to have accepted at least some parts of the Augustana Swedish-American identity. This is not surprising, given the dominant position the synod had in Swedish America in terms of the number of members and synod institutions. The need to establish an early presence in America seems to have transcended the ideological divisions of the Swedish-American community, and we have seen that the 250th anniversary celebration of the New Sweden colony in 1888 also managed to bring together large parts of the Swedish-American community. The same can be said of the significance attached to the Vikings. Still, as the example of the Linnaeus statue in Chicago shows, historical symbols could be contested, and in order to maintain a united Swedish-American community, compromises had to be made.

WHY DID THE IDENTITY DEVELOP?

Finally, some answers to the question of why this Augustana version of a Swedish-American identity developed will be offered. Obviously, the generational shift was of great significance. The Swedish-born generation, with religious rather than ethnic priorities, was succeeded by American-born Swedish Americans to whom ethnicity was more important. To them, the development of the ethnic identity became a strategy for interacting with the American society. As we have seen, Augustana's Swedish-American identity placed emphasis on such positive traits as religiosity, freedom, and independence, characteristics that were also central in the American Republic. In addition, the Swedish-American identity underscored how both Swedes and Swedish Americans had contributed significantly to the development of the American nation.

This conception of what it meant to be Swedish American also placed the group in the American racial and ethnic hierarchies at the time, and like other European immigrants, the Swedes too had to come to terms with what it meant to be white in mid- to late-nineteenth-century America. The notion that American origins were to be found in a specific Anglo-Saxon political and social tradition and that the United States belonged to an Anglo-Saxon "race" developed from circa 1840 and proved very important for the Swedes. The racial discourse became a way of excluding some groups, such as the Irish, from membership in the Anglo-Saxon group, and the attempts to link the Swedish Americans with Anglo-Saxon origins was clearly a strategy to position the group as closely as possible to what was perceived as American origins and core values. The construction of a Swedish-American history, ranging from the Vikings, to the colonial Swedish experience of the seventeenth century and Swedish contributions to the establishment of the American Republic, and to John Ericsson's significant contributions to the victory of the Union in the Civil War, are examples of how the Augustana Swedish Americans sought to portray the group as especially appropriate for becoming Americans.

It is also possible to see the ethnic identity as one element in the competition between Swedish Americans and other ethnic groups for resources, influence, and a place in the American social fabric. The growing nativist sentiments around the turn of the century most likely also provided an important impetus for the Swedish Americans to use their ethnicity as a way of emphasizing their proximity to mainstream America and of distancing themselves culturally from the new immigrants from southern and eastern Europe. It became one way of establishing superiority over other groups, and as we have seen, Enander's case for the Viking discovery of America was explicitly cast in terms of the contemporary American ethnic situation with a noticeable anti-Catholicism, as he suggested that Italian Catholics and the pope had sought to prevent the recognition of the Viking claim as the first Europeans in the New World.

Another way of looking at this question has to do with the nature of American nationalism and as a part of the ongoing nation-building process in nineteenth-century America. The American conception of nationalism allowed for a "voluntary pluralism" for most European groups, including the Swedish Americans. As long as the members of an ethnic group loyally adhered to the abstract political philosophies that formed the basis for the United States, the American national idea allowed for the maintenance and creation of the groups' ancestral cultures. It was thus possible for the Swedish immigrants and their children to affirm and even develop their ethnic identities and express support for Swedish and Swedish-American cultural symbols while at the same time remaining loyal Americans.

In fact, it can be argued that the creation of ethnic identities, be they German-American, Italian-American, Norwegian-American, or Swedish-American, was a logical consequence of American nationalism. Other groups also developed conceptions of ethnicity, emphasizing traits similar to the Swedish Americans'. The relative lack of emphasis on ethnicity in the conception of American nationalism thus provided an opportunity for those European-American ethnic groups who chose to do so to use their respective ethnic identities as building blocks in the construction of their American national identity. Looked at from this perspective, the Swedish immigrants and their children living in turn of the century America were, by becoming Swedish Americans, also becoming Americans.

Notes

Bibliography

Index

Notes

1. SETTING THE STAGE: ETHNICITY AND IDENTITY IN SWEDISH AMERICA

1. E. Olson [1910?], 5.
2. Ibid., 4.
3. Beijbom 1980, 257.
4. *Augustana,* 28 November 1901.
5. Barton 1978, 3.
6. Ibid.; Beijbom 1980.
7. Norelius 1891 and 1916; C. Peterson 1898; Olson, Schön, and Engberg 1908.
8. See Saveth 1948, chap. 8.
9. For more detailed and systematic overviews of academic research on Swedish migration to North America, see Barton 1978; Ostergren 1986; Norman and Runblom 1988b; Anderson and Blanck 1991, introduction; and Blanck 1996.
10. Stephenson 1932.
11. Ander 1931; Lindquist 1953; Bergendoff 1969.
12. Kälvemark 1971; Westin 1932; Nelson 1943.
13. Thistlethwaite 1960, 32–60.
14. Runblom and Norman 1976. Examples of individual studies from the period include Beijbom 1971; S. Lindmark 1971; Ljungmark 1971; Tedebrand 1972; Norman 1974; Ostergren 1988; and Nordstrom 1978.
15. Anderson and Blanck 1991, 2001; Beijbom 1986, 1990a, 1993; Björk 2000; Lovoll 1985, 1993; B. Svensson 1994; Thander 1996; Williams 1991; Wendelius 1990. See also the special issue of *Swedish-American Historical Quarterly* 43 (July 1992).
16. Barton 1984, 1994.
17. Beijbom 1990a, chap. 6; Beijbom 1988.
18. Hasselmo 1974.
19. Erickson 1996; Nordahl 1994; Anderson et al. 1995; Swanson 1996.
20. Attebery 2000, 2003; B. Svensson 1994; Williams 1991.
21. Yinger 1994, 3.
22. Isaacs 1975; Conzen et al. 1992, 4; Patterson 1975; Yancey, Erickson, and Juliani 1976; Fischer 1986; A. Smith 1984a, 1984b.
23. McKay and Lewins 1978, 413–22.
24. A. Smith 1991, 20–21.

25. Yinger 1994, 3–5.
26. Thomas and Znaniecki 1985, 239–55.
27. See, e.g., Bodnar 1985, 120–30 for an overview of the role of ethnic fraternal organizations.
28. Breton 1964.
29. Kantowicz 1977, 184.
30. Conzen 1976, 225–28.
31. Abramson 1980; T. Smith 1978; Marty 1972.
32. Handlin 1951.
33. Vecoli 1964.
34. Gerber 1989, 118.
35. Gjerde 1997, 59–60.
36. Øverland 2000, 193. Cf. also Glazer 1954, 163–65.
37. Sollors 1986, 1989.
38. Conzen et al. 1992, 5.
39. Hroch 1981; Hobsbawm 1990; A. Smith 1992; Yinger 1994, 13; Hobsbawm 1983, 1–4.
40. Jansson 1985, 65–71; Jansson 1990, 344.
41. Furuland 1991b, 72.
42. Björck 1946, 38–69; Elvander 1961, 341–50, 419–24; Jansson 1994, 32–33. Cf. also various contributions in Medelius and Rentzhog 1991.
43. Connor 1990, 93–95.
44. C. Peterson 1898, 448.
45. J. Person 1912, 114–15.
46. Ibid., 116.
47. Lipset 1963.
48. Zelinsky 1988, 17, 223.
49. Berovitch 1978, 161.
50. Glazer 1997, 99.
51. Higham 1988, 344; Zelinksy 1988, chaps. 2 and 3; Kammen 1991, chap. 5; Karsten 1978, chap. 5; Fuchs 1990, 4–5.
52. Gleason 1980, 32.
53. Fuchs 1990, 5.
54. Hasselmo 1974, 38–9; Gjerde 1997.
55. Kivisto and Blanck 1990; Hansen 1938.
56. Appel 1961; Lazowitz and Rowitz 1964.
57. Fishman and Nahirny 1965, 321.
58. Ibid. 1966, 350.
59. Hobsbawm 1990, esp. chaps. 2 and 4; Appleby, Hunt, and Jacob 1994, chap. 3; A. Smith 1984b.
60. Chapman, McDonald, and Tonkin 1989, 4–5.
61. Hobsbawm 1983, 12.
62. Barth 1969, 15.
63. Sollors 1986, 28.

64. Glazer and Moynihan 1975, 8.
65. Conzen 1991, 10–11.
66. Ibid., 11–12.
67. Higham 1980, 642.
68. Greene 1987, 4–16, quotation from p. 4.
69. Conzen et al. 1992, 16; Breton 1992, 13–14.
70. Williams 1991, 209; Greene 1987, 76–80.
71. Johannesson 1991b.
72. Conzen 1985, 134.
73. Gerber 1989, 119; Breton 1992, 13.
74. Hasselmo 1974, 37–38.
75. Beijbom 1990a, 146–49, 153–55.

2. COMING TO AMERICA: THE ESTABLISHMENT OF THE AUGUSTANA SYNOD

1. Berger 1933, 8.
2. The following figures for the number of Swedes in the United States are based on the U.S. Federal Censuses. The 1920 census contains a useful summary for the years 1850–1920 (Bureau of the Census, hereafter *Census,* 1920, vol. 2). The figures for number of Swedes emigrating from Sweden are based on the official Swedish emigration statistics as reported in Barton 1994, 343–45.
3. Norman 1974, 211–32; Ostergren 1988.
4. *Census* 1870, 1880.
5. Anderson and Blanck 1991, 1–2.
6. S. Lindmark 1971, 37.
7. C. Peterson 1898, 411ff.; Skarstedt 1917, 133.
8. Benson and Hedin 1938, 142.
9. Granquist 1994; Stephenson 1932; K. Olsson 1962.
10. For these statistics, see *Referat* 1921, Religious Bodies 1926, 1291, and S. Lindmark 1971, 243. The titles for the minutes of the Augustana Synod vary somewhat over the years. For the sake of consistency, the short reference form of *Referat* plus the year will be used to refer Augustana Synod Minutes. The minutes 1860–78 were reprinted and published by the Augustana Book Concern in 1917. All references from those years are quoted from this reprint edition. The places and dates of publication include: Chicago, 1860–1872; Red Wing, Minn., 1873; Rock Island, 1874; Moline, Ill., 1875; Chicago, 1876; Red Wing, 1877; Chicago, 1878–79; Moline, 1880–83; and Rock Island, 1884–1921.
11. Beijbom 1990b, 63.
12. Ibid.
13. Nordahl 1994, 48–56.
14. Beijbom 1990b, 63.
15. Björk 2000.
16. Arden 1963; H. Söderström 1973; Stephenson 1932.
17. *Referat* 1860, 26–27.

18. H. Söderström 1973, 25–30.
19. Arden 1963, 44–58; Stephenson 1932, 178–95; H. Söderström 1973, 47–55.
20. For the following, see Arden 1963, 51–58; Stephenson 1932, 184–95; and H. Söderström 1973, 61–66.
21. H. Söderström 1973, 72–76.
22. *Hemlandet,* 22 August 1860; Blanck 1983, 12–16.
23. Arden 1963, 135–42.
24. Quoted in Arden 1963, 138. Cf. also H. Söderström 1973, 99–100.
25. Jenswold 1985.
26. Norman and Runblom 1988a, 270–71.
27. This paragraph is based on Gustafsson 1966, chap. 8. Cf. also Sanders 1995, chaps. 1 and 2 for a more recent discussion of the revival; Stephenson 1932, chaps. 2, 3, and 10; and Eklund 1995. H. Söderström 1973, 15–21, discusses the precise position of the early Augustana leaders in the revival.
28. Sanders 1992, 193.
29. Andrén 1973, 116.
30. Erling 1992, 34–36.
31. Runeby 1969, 273–74, 262–63.
32. See the statistical sections in *Referat* 1871, 1881, 1891, 1901, 1911, and 1921.
33. *Minnesskrift* 1910, 480.
34. Stephenson 1932, chap. 22.
35. O. Olson 1956, 48. Cf. also Mattson 1941, 267–300.
36. *Referat* 1917, 284–89. Cf. also *Minnesskrift* 1910, 230–90.
37. This section is based on Hasselmo 1974, 63–72; *Minnesskrift* 1910, 293–318, 437–74; and E. Olson 1910.
38. See the statistical sections in *Referat* 1921.
39. Bergendoff 1973, 238.
40. Legreid 1993, 78.
41. Ostergren 1988, 221–22.
42. A. Olson 1990, 306.
43. The following figures are based on 1910 Augustana Synod Statistics (*Referat* 1911) and *Census* 1910.
44. Augustana Synod Statistics, *Referat* 1881.
45. Carlsson 1976, 125–48.
46. Bergendoff 1973, 238.
47. "Vår kyrkas kallelse med afseende på de skaror landsmän som, särskilt i de större städerna, stå utanför henne," *Augustana,* 13 March 1902.
48. C. W. Andeer, "Årets stora folkvandring," *Augustana,* 16 July 1903.
49. *Augustana,* 16 May 1912.
50. Ibid., 13 August 1914. Cf. also 2 August 1918 for similar attitudes.
51. *Census* 1910.
52. Barton 1994, 332–34, quotation from p. 333; Beijbom 1990b, 48–49. Cf. Bodnar 1985, 142, for the same point among other ethnic groups.
53. K. Olsson 1963, 108–9.

54. Ibid. 1962, 175–303; P. Anderson 1994, 6–11.
55. *Referat* 1874, 14.
56. Quoted in Ander 1931, 166.
57. P. Anderson 1994, 8; Arden 1963, chap. 9.
58. H. Söderström 1973, 149; Erling 1996, 64–65.
59. *Referat* 1892, 19–20; Stephenson 1932, 318.
60. Barton 1994, 334.
61. *Referat* 1910, 32–33, quotation from p. 32.
62. *Minnen* 1911, 101–41, 234–58.
63. Erickson 1996, 74–131; Beijbom 1971, 288–332; Williams 1991, 96, 107; Nyberg 1978; Wendelius 1990, 32–55; Nordahl 1994, 114–55.
64. Blanck 1988, 1991; Williams 1991, 167; Erickson 1996, 124–31.
65. Barton 1993, 89–90, quotation from p. 90.
66. Runeby 1969, 265; letter from af Wingård to Esbjörn, 8 March 1849, printed in Westin 1932, 37–38.
67. Stephenson 1932, 214–18, 223–39; Erling 1992, 46–48.
68. *Augustana*, 14 April 1892.
69. Barton 1994, 96–97.
70. *Augustana*, 14 and 22 June 1893.
71. Ibid., 25 May 1893.
72. Ibid., 20 June 1893.
73. Ibid., 5 December 1901.
74. Von Schéele 1894, 3–6.
75. Ibid., 151–52, quotation from p. 152. Cf. also von Schéele's very positive speech at the celebrations in Rock Island in *Augustana*, 22 June 1893.
76. Carlsson 1984, 241.
77. Ibid., 245.
78. Blanck 1995, 273–79.
79. Bergendoff 1980, 74, 14–15.
80. Albrecht 1950, 23–25; *Catalog* 1880–81.
81. Yale University to Andreen, 31 May 1898, ACL, GAP.
82. Wilstadius 1961, 163, states that Andreen was in Uppsala to "study Scandinavian Languages"; letter from Andreen to Noreen, 18 September 1899, UUB, ANC.
83. Letter from Andreen to "a friend" in Rock Island, 6 June 1900, reprinted in "Stor och glädjande nyhet," *Augustana*, 2 August 1900; Andreen 1900.
84. Letter from Andreen to Noreen, 8 July 1903, UUB, ANC; and letter from Andreen to Schück, Rock Island, 27 January 1910, ACL, GAP.
85. For the following, see "Till den svenska allmänheten" (1901) in ACL, GAP.
86. *Augustana*, 19 and 23 March 1903; *Vårt Land*, 23 March 1903; *Aftonbladet*, 23 March 1903; letter from Andreen to Noreen, 28 January 1903, UUB, ANC.
87. *Referat* 1910, 64–65.
88. "Bref från Sverige," *Augustana*, 6 November 1902.

89. *Minnen* 1911, 111–41.
90. Ibid., 115.
91. Pehrsson 1912.
92. Cf. Arden 1963, 15–16.
93. Norman and Runblom 1988a, 76–79, 89–90.

3. SCHOOLING THE SWEDISH AMERICANS: EDUCATION IN THE AUGUSTANA SYNOD

1. Stolarik 1995, 18.
2. Seller 1981, 5.
3. Bodnar 1985, 189–97. See also Anderson et al. 1995; Beck 1939; Cremin 1984, 383–85; Olneck and Lazerson 1980; and Weiss 1982.
4. Bodnar 1985, 196. See also Christianson 1995.
5. T. Smith 1969, 525.
6. P. Person 1941, appendix.
7. Stephenson 1932, 335.
8. *Minnesskrift* 1910, 483–84.
9. *Referat* 1891, 41–42.
10. Ibid. 1873, 17.
11. Nordgren 1935, 276. In 1906, a formal curriculum for these schools was adopted. *Referat* 1906, 147–48. The proposal was presented in 1902. *Referat* 1902, 103–17. Cf. also Arden 1963, 106–7.
12. Ulrich 1980.
13. *Referat* 1890, 22–24.
14. Ibid., 1860, 5, 24–25.
15. For the following overview, see Bergendoff 1969.
16. For enrollment figures, see *Minnesskrift* 1910, 485; and *Catalog* 1910–11, 144, and 1920–21, 191.
17. *Referat* 1864, 11. The synod minutes refer to the "college" for the first time in 1865. *Referat* 1865, 25.
18. Ibid. 1870, 33.
19. The constitution is found in *Referat* 1869, 35–38.
20. *Catalog* 1883–84, 36; Bergendoff 1969, 56.
21. *Referat* 1869, 35–36, quotation from p. 35.
22. Ibid. 1887, 30.
23. Bergendoff 1969, 70–71.
24. *Referat* 1890, 25, and 1891, 41. Cf. also *Catalog* 1892–93, 7.
25. Bergendoff 1969, 100.
26. *Minnesskrift* 1910, 483.
27. The following is based on *Referat* 1860, 24–25. Cf. also Bergendoff 1969, 20.
28. *Referat* 1860, 24.
29. Ibid.
30. Ibid. 1863, 22.
31. Ibid. 1865, 24.

32. *Catalog* 1875–76, 8.
33. Ibid. 1883–84, 28–33, 36.
34. Ibid. 1884–85, 20–21.
35. *Referat* 1889, 45.
36. *Catalog* 1890–91, 9–17.
37. Ibid. 1895–96, 26–28.
38. Ibid. 1900–1901, 28–34.
39. Ibid. 1902–03, 17.
40. Ibid., 19.
41. Ibid., 17.
42. Ibid. 1916–17, 21.
43. Pettersson 1992.
44. Ander 1931, 75.
45. The following is based on Florin and Johansson 1993, 81–86.
46. Bergendoff 1969, 102, 118.
47. *Minnen* 1911, 115.
48. Rudolph 1962, chap. 14.
49. *Catalog* 1902–03, 10.
50. Quoted in Arden 1960, 69.
51. Printed in Westin 1932, 137.
52. Arden 1960, chap. 5.
53. Cf. Arden 1960, 192–96.
54. *Referat* 1872, 15.
55. *Augustana,* 12 November 1891.
56. See *Referat* 1892, 50–59, for the constitution. Quotation from p. 50. The constitution was adopted in 1893. *Referat* 1893, 42. Cf. also Mattson 1941, 148.
57. *Augustana,* 24 January 1901.
58. *Referat* 1903, 10.
59. Ibid. 1914, 18.
60. Here quoted from *Catalog* 1902–03, 10.
61. Ibid. 1909–10, 13.
62. *Referat* 1892, 58. Also reprinted in Mattson 1941, 161. One representative example of the struggle against alcohol is the article series "Nykterhet och reform" in *Augustana,* 17 and 24 October and 1 November 1895.
63. *Referat* 1911, 40; *Augustana,* 13 April 1911, 18 January 1912, 17 April and 8 May 1913. See also "Om dans och teaterbesök," *Ungdomsvännen* 1906, 69.
64. E.g. *Catalog* 1892–93, 45. Cf. also Bergendoff 1969, 124.
65. *Catalog* 1909–10, 104.
66. Bergendoff 1969, 123–24.
67. Arden 1963, 94.
68. *Referat* 1860, 24.
69. O. Olson 1935, 111.
70. Augustana Student Database. See chap. 4 for explanation of the database.
71. Beck 1939, 288.

72. As quoted in Norelius 1900, 266–72.
73. O. Olsson, "Välkomsthälsning till vår kunskaps- och bildningstörstande ungdom," *Augustana,* 25 August 1892.
74. "Hvad kunna vi vänta af våra blifvande affärsmän," *Augustana,* 18 August 1892.
75. *Augustana,* 31 October 1901.
76. Ibid., 24 October 1901.
77. Bergendoff 1969, 53–54, 80, 101.
78. *Referat* 1898, 27.
79. Bergendoff 1992, 3.
80. L. Carlson 1941, 45.
81. K. Olsson 1963, 110–12.
82. Ibid. 1962, 514.
83. O. Olson 1935, 109.
84. Nothstein 1945, 209–10.
85. Ibid. 1944, 18.
86. Eric Norelius in *The Missionary,* 24 May 1860, reprinted in Ander and Nordstrom 1942, 127.
87. Quoted in Nothstein 1945, 210.
88. *Referat* 1868, 35; 1869, 29; 1875, 44.
89. Ibid. 1867, 24; 1865, 35.
90. Ander 1931, 229.
91. *Catalog* 1884–85, 22.
92. Minutes, 8 September 1884, BdDir, ACL.
93. *Catalog* 1887–88, 34; 1889–90, 33.
94. Ibid. 1893–94, 31.
95. Ibid. 1902–03, 27; 1905–06, 25; 1908–09, 29.
96. "Engelsk-amerikansk eller svensk-amerikansk," *Hemlandet,* 13 February 1890.
97. "Är det välbetänkt?" *Hemlandet,* 20 March 1890.
98. "Anspråken stiga," *Hemlandet,* 20 March 1890. George Stephenson has suggested that the author of this article was Johan Enander. Stephenson 1932, 308.
99. *Referat* 1890, 35.
100. "Om svenska språket vid vårt läroverk," *Augustana,* 1 December 1893.
101. Minutes, 13 December 1898, BdDir, ACL.
102. Stephenson 1932, 381.
103. C. A. Hultkrans, "Om vartannat," *Ungdomsvännen* 1899, 43.
104. Olof Olsson, "Också ett tack på tacksägelsedagen," *Augustana,* 7 December 1899.
105. Marcus Skarstedt diary, 25 October 1908, ESC, SSIRC.
106. Ibid., 25 October 1908, 18 February 1909.
107. Bergendoff 1969, 77.
108. *Referat* 1896, 24.
109. Cf. Blanck 1982, 300–301.

110. *Catalog* 1888–89, 1894–95.
111. Ibid. 1894–95, 81–92. It should, however, be noted that not all students began their studies in the college in their freshman year. Of the thirty graduating seniors in 1897–98, eleven were not enrolled as freshmen in 1894–95 but entered mostly as sophomores, and no information is available as to which track of study they were in.
112. Swensson 1891, 19–20.
113. *Augustana,* 9 January 1902.
114. Ibid., 20 November 1902.
115. Ibid., 17 September 1903.
116. Ibid., 26 October 1905.
117. *Referat* 1903, 25.
118. *Catalog* 1902–03, 18.
119. Ibid. 1903–04, 10. This wording appeared in all catalogs until 1929–30.
120. *Aftonbladet,* 23 March 1903.
121. *Augustana,* 7 June 1910.
122. Bergendoff 1980, 24.
123. *Augustana,* 19 March 1891.
124. Ibid., 21 November 1901.
125. Ibid.
126. Ibid., 30 May 1901.
127. Barton 1994, 120.
128. C. Peterson 1898, 71–73.
129. *Augustana,* 17 September 1903.
130. Ibid., 9 August 1906.
131. *Augustana Observer,* August 1903.
132. K. G. William Dahl to parents, 27 September 1903. Printed in Dahl n.d.
133. Hasselmo 1974, 44–45; 1978, 227.

4. A SWEDISH-AMERICAN TRADITION AT AUGUSTANA COLLEGE

1. *Catalog* 1874–75, 1875–76, 1881–82.
2. Minutes, 2 October 1882, 20 March 1883, BdDir, ACL.
3. Minutes, 14 June 1877, BdDir, ACL; Bergendoff 1969, 55. In 1879, Esbjörn was granted $150 by Augustana's board of directors for his first year of study at the University of Pennsylvania. Minutes, 6 June 1879, BdDir, ACL.
4. Minutes, 1 April 1890, BdDir, ACL.
5. *Referat* 1890, 39, 42.
6. Minutes, 25 June, 15 July 1890, BdDir, ACL.
7. Ibid., 28 June, 18 August 1893; letters from J. A. Enander to G. N. Swan, 26 July, 21 August 1893; Swan to Enander, 21 August 1893; Enander to Swan, 2 September 1893, GNS, SSIRC.
8. Minutes, 1 May 1894, BdDir, ACL; Bergendoff 1980, 45.
9. Letter from J. S. Carlson to G. N. Swan, Minneapolis, 24 April 1923, GNS, SSIRC.

10. Minutes, 21 April, 2 December 1897, 29 March 1898, BdDir, ACL; *Referat* 1897, 81–82.

11. Minutes, 13 March 1901, BdDir, ACL.

12. Ibid., 14 May, 9 July 1901, 4 April 1902; *Referat* 1901, 20–21.

13. For the following, see Blanck 1994, vii–xv; and Andreen 1931, 214–21.

14. *Augustana,* 6 November 1902.

15. Barton 1994, 64.

16. For the following discussion, see *Catalog* 1870–71, 1916–17.

17. Ibid. 1883–84, 28–32.

18. For the use of these textbooks, see, for example, *Catalog* 1883–84, 28–32; 1885–86, 22–23; 1893–94, 31; and 1894–95, 31.

19. See, for example, ibid. 1884–85, 19; 1891–92, 26–27; 1893–94, 31; 1894–95, 20; 1898–99, 23, 34; 1901–02, 19.

20. Ibid. 1885–86, 22.

21. Ibid. 1886–87, 27–28.

22. Ibid. 1891–92, 26–29.

23. Ibid., 52.

24. Ibid. 1894–95, 31.

25. Ibid. 1895–96, 20–21; 1896–97, 20.

26. Ibid. 1898–99, 23.

27. Ibid. 1902–03, 40–41.

28. Ibid. 1906–07, 41–42.

29. Ibid. 1910–11, 44–45.

30. Letter from Jules Mauritzson to Gustav Andreen, December 1912, GAP, ACL.

31. *Catalog* 1916–17, 48–49.

32. Tarschys 1955, 150–51, 155–56, 265; Hillman 1952, 13–22.

33. Tarschys 1955, 281.

34. Ibid., 171–72, 276; Lewan 1972; Martinsson 1989, 156–63.

35. Tarschys 1955, 262.

36. Brink 1992, 250–51, 255–57.

37. Widén 1950, 64.

38. Andeer 1904a, 10.

39. Brink 1988, 10.

40. *Masterpieces* 1906, 1908.

41. Tegnér 1914; Runeberg 1915.

42. B. Svensson 1994, 147.

43. Brink 1992, 249–64.

44. Tarschys 1955, 163; Brink 1992, 258–59.

45. Williams 1995, 216.

46. For Tegnér, see Lönnroth and Delblanc 1988a, 287–307; and for Runeberg, see ibid. 1988b, 113–39.

47. For the 1890s, see Lönnroth and Delblanc 1989, 69–113.

48. Ibid. 1988b, 295–300.

49. For Runeberg and nationalism, see ibid., 130–35; for Tegnér and nationalism, see ibid., 1988a, 287–307.
50. Tarschys 1955, 262ff.
51. Minutes, 2 April 1902, BdDir, ACL; *Augustana,* 21 November 1901.
52. Barton 1994, 140–46; Beijbom 1990a, 221–30.
53. Sundbeck 1904b, 145.
54. Ibid. 1904a, 16.
55. *Augustana,* 10 November 1904.
56. Ibid., 8 May 1902.
57. Ibid., 21 May 1903.
58. C. P. Peterson, "Svensk-amerikanens roll i nationens drama," *Ungdomsvännen* 1904, 168–69.
59. *Augustana,* 12 May 1904.
60. Ibid., 14 May 1891, 11 February 1904, 16 February 1905.
61. Ibid., 29 March 1900; letters from Jules Mauritzson to G. N. Swan, 2 February 1911, 27 October 1914, GNS, SSIRC.
62. *Catalog* 1881.
63. All the subsequent information about topics of discussion in the society comes from the minutes of the Phrenokosmian Society in PS, ACL. Information for the period 1860–77 is also based on the Record Book of Program Topics in PS, ACL.
64. Minutes, Tegnér: 26 January 1877 ("Svea"), 28 February 1879 ("Svea"), 2 May 1879 ("Kungarne på Salamis"), 24 September 1880 ("Det eviga"), 27 January 1882 ("Kungarne på Salamis"), 17 February 1882 ("Det eviga"), 6 September 1884 *(Fritiofs saga),* 13 March 1885 ("Det eviga"), 18 January 1887 *(Fritiofs saga),* PS, ACL. *Fänrik Ståls sägner* by Runeberg was discussed on 14 January 1879, 24 September 1880, 26 November 1886, and 25 February 1887.
65. Minutes, 24 March 1882, PS, ACL.
66. Ibid., 3 October 1879 (Gustav Vasa), 3 December 1880 (Gustavus Adolphus).
67. Ibid., 13 March 1896 (Geijer), 8 October 1897 (Wallin), 27 November 1891, 28 October 1892 (Kellgren), 6 October 1891 (Lenngren), 19 March 1897 (Gustavian era), 28 October 1898 (Stagnelius).
68. Ibid., 10 April 1891.
69. Ibid., 1 November 1889 (Engelbrekt Engelbrektsson), 16 October 1896 (the Middle Ages), 6 November 1896 (Gustavus Adolphus).
70. Ibid., 19 February 1892 (nature in Swedish provinces), 15 November 1895 (meeting of Swedish provinces), 28 November 1890 (Swedish provincial dialects).
71. Although the information in the catalogs is uneven, American history is mentioned already in 1876–77. *Catalog* 1876–77, 15. In 1884–85, both American history and geography were studied, and in addition to textbooks in American history, the 1892–93 catalog also includes a textbook on the U.S. Constitution. *Catalog* 1884–85, 23; 1892–93, 31. By 1909–10, there were several courses on both U.S. history, politics, and literature. *Catalog* 1909–10, 24–43.

72. *Augustana,* 27 October 1892.

73. Minutes, 13 February 1880 (Washington, Lafayette), 12 February 1897 (Lincoln), 23 October 1896 (Columbus or Washington), PS, ACL.

74. Ibid., 6 March 1896 (Civil War), 29 January 1897 (Revolutionary War).

75. Ibid., 9 October 1896 (Longfellow), 4 November 1898 (American humor), 3 March 1891, 20 October 1893 (Shakespeare).

76. Ibid., 25 October 1895 (political parties), 25 September 1896 (free silver).

77. Ibid., 1 March 1878.

78. Ibid., 15 March 1897.

79. Ibid., 10 March 1893 (Swedes in Minnesota), 13 October 1893 (reasons for Swedish emigration), 22 January 1897 (Delaware), 7 April 1897 (emigrants), 13 May 1892 (John Ericsson).

80. Ibid., 8 May 1896 (Swedish-American youth), 28 January 1898 (Swedish-American literature), 1 April 1898 (Swedish-American duties).

81. For additional information, see *Catalog* 1909–10, 106–7.

82. Ibid. 1902–03, 105.

83. Minutes, 8 April 1905, SV, ACL.

84. Oscar Montan, "Svenska Vitterhetssällskapets historik," *Julrunan* 1911, 24.

85. *Augustana,* 7 June 1900.

86. F. E. Sard, "När Svenska Vitterhetssällskapet bildades," *Julrunan* 1905, 23–24; Oscar Montan, "Svenska Vitterhetssällskapets historik," *Julrunan* 1911, 23–24.

87. Minutes, Runeberg: 29 January 1902, 10 March 1909; Tegnér: 6 May 1908, 22 October 1914, SV, ACL.

88. *Runan*: 28 March 1903, 28 January 1905, 3 February 1909, SV, ACL.

89. Minutes, 28 March 1903 (Levertin), 12 October 1902 (Wahlenberg), 10 February 1906 (Rydberg), 15 November 1902 (Hallström), 28 March 1903 (Forsslund), 12 November 1904 (Wallin), 2 March 1910 (Malmström), SV, ACL.

90. *Runan*: 13 December 1902 (Stiernhielm), no date (Topelius), 10 February 1906 (Oscar II), 28 April 1905 and 3 November 1906 (Sigurd), SV, ACL.

91. Minutes, Heidenstam: 15 February, 1 March, 26 October, 8 November, 4 December 1911; Strindberg: 2 November, 2 December 1912, 27 January, 10 March, 13 April, 6 October, 3 November, 11 December 1913; 22 January 1914, SV, ACL.

92. Ibid., Jerusalem: 12 February and 11 March 1914; *Fritiofs saga:* 22 October, 12 November 1914.

93. *Runan*: 11 October 1902, 14 February 1903, SV, ACL.

94. Ibid., 15 November 1902.

95. Ibid., 28 March 1903.

96. Ibid., 10 February 1906.

97. *Augustana,* 9 May 1901.

98. Minutes, 11 March 1903, 6 May 1903, SV, ACL. Cf. minutes, 8 April, 12 November, 10 December 1904; 8 April, 28 June 1905; 10 February 1906.

99. Minutes, 10 March, 3 October 1906.

100. *Runan:* 3 November 1906, SV, ACL.

101. Minutes, 10 December 1904, 28 January and 18 February 1905, 12 November 1908, SV, ACL.
102. *Runan*: 28 March 1903, 9 December 1905, SV, ACL.
103. For the following, see *Julrunan* 1905, 1911, and 1912.
104. *Augustana*, 21 December 1905.
105. Anna Olsson, "Babetistera," *Julrunan* 1905; K. G. William Dahl, "Nelly och Pete," *Julrunan* 1911.
106. Christopher Carlson, "Minnen och bilder från Augustana-synodens möte i Stanton," *Julrunan* 1905; Edor [pseud.], "När kyrkan 'restes' i Saron. Bilder från nybyggarlifvet," *Julrunan* 1912.
107. S. M. Hill, "'Vår' litteratur," *Julrunan* 1905, 11–12.
108. S. G. Youngert, "Amerika och Svensk-Amerikanerna," *Julrunan* 1905, 21.
109. E. W. Olson, "Nya banor," *Julrunan* 1912, 12.
110. *Catalog* 1871–1914; RF, ACL.
111. *Korsbaneret* 1881–1915; Bergendoff 1980; *Who Is Who* 1923.
112. Augustana Student Database.
113. *Census* 1910, vol. 1.
114. Ibid.
115. The main sources for the classification scheme have been Norman 1974, excursus 2, and Thernstrom 1973, appendix B. The occupations have been grouped in the following manner:

I: major proprietors, landowners, higher officials, managers, professionals
II: petty proprietors, master artisans, clerks, lower officials, semiprofessionals
III: farmers
IV: craftsmen, artisans, skilled and semiskilled labor
V: unskilled labor, domestic service, agricultural labor

For comparative purposes, group I corresponds to the American "high white collar," group II to "low white collar," group IV to "skilled workers," and group V to "unskilled workers." The farmers constitute a problem in this classification, as the occupational notations suggested that almost all were free-holding farmers both in Sweden and the United States. It has been argued that in the rural Swedish context, such a category of farmers should be classified in a fairly "high" group (Jansson 1982, 55–59.) This may well be the case, and it could be argued that groups II and III should change places in this scheme. Still, to conform with existing Swedish and American practices, I will leave the scheme as it is.

116. Carlsson 1984.
117. *Augustana*, 18 July 1918.
118. Ibid.
119. For the following, see *Augustana Observer*, February 1906.
120. *Runan*: January 1919, SV, ACL.
121. "Den svensk-amerikanska kulturen," *Vårt Land*, 23 March 1903; "Svensk-Amerika och dess kulturella arbete," *Aftonbladet*, 23 March 1903.

122. Letter from Gustav Andreen to C. A. Swensson, New Haven, Conn., 30 December 1897, GAP, ACL.

5. READING, WRITING, AND IDENTITY FORMATION IN SWEDISH AMERICA

1. Berger 1916, 46–55, quotation from p. 46.
2. Øverland 1996, ix.
3. Sollors 1998, 7. See many contributions in Sollors 1998 and Øverland 2001 as well as Gulliksen 2004.
4. B. Peterson 1991, 58. Cf. also 3–5 for similar arguments.
5. Martellone 1998; Conolly-Smith 1998; Majewski 1998; Yin 2000.
6. Williams 1991, 209–14. Cf. also Keillor 1992 and Westerberg 1995 for discussions of reading practices among Norwegian and Swedish Americans.
7. B. Anderson 1991, chaps. 3 and 5.
8. Stockenström 1978, 263–65.
9. Hasselmo 1974, 63–71; Jarvi 1991.
10. Wendelius 1990.
11. Williams 1991, chap. 2.
12. Johansson 1973, 1987; S. Svensson 1983, 19–21; D. Lindmark 2004.
13. Svedjedal 1990, 30–31.
14. Bennich-Björkman and Furuland 1988, 269–76.
15. Furuland 1991b. Cf. also Tarschys 1955, 156.
16. Fishman 1966, 42–43.
17. Park 1922, 359; Björk 1987, chap. 1; S. Lindmark 1971, 219–21.
18. Beijbom 1986, 174.
19. Björk 2000; Scott 1991, 195–206.
20. Cf. Beijbom 1986, 175–76; Williams 1991, 32–33.
21. Williams 1991, 29–34.
22. Beijbom 1971, 288–332.
23. A. Söderström 1910.
24. Beijbom 1986, 174.
25. Björk 1987, 62, 37.
26. For circulation figures, see Björk 1987, 61–63, and S. Lindmark 1971, 330–33.
27. Circulation statistics are based on *N. W. Ayer* 1910; Beijbom 1986, 174; and Fishman 1966, 52–60.
28. Wendelius 1990, 28–30; Beijbom 1971, 187.
29. Landelius 1951, 224. This article is one of the few overviews of the Swedish language bookstores in the United States.
30. Wendelius 1990, 29.
31. Landelius 1951, 216–17.
32. Williams 1991, 34.
33. Furuland 1996; Larsson and Tedenmyr 1988, 18.
34. Svedjedal 1993, 208–13.
35. "Stort slag för Sverige i Amerika," *Veckojournalen,* 8 September 1912.

36. Svedjedal 1993, 205, 213.
37. Hasselmo 1974, 64.
38. E. Olson 1910.
39. Barton 1988, 6.
40. *Svenska Socialisten,* 27 February 1913.
41. Larsson and Tedenmyr 1988, 248, and 236–37 for the Covenant church, 255–56 for the Methodists, and 95–98 for the Baptists. See also Stephenson 1932, 246–92, for a discussion of publishing activities among the non-Augustana denominations.
42. Larsson and Tedenmyr 1988, 269.
43. Ibid., 275.
44. Ibid., 234–58.
45. Lönnroth and Delblanc 1988b, 20–24, 279. Cf. also Furuland 1972.
46. Bjursten 1898 was issued as number 119.
47. Larsson and Tedenmyr 1988, 128. It is unclear if more than these three titles were published in this series.
48. Dalkullan's series was called Populära detektivromaner (Popular Detective Stories). Larsson and Tedenmyr 1988, 155.
49. *Engberg* 1876.
50. The compilation is based on the information provided in E. Olson 1910.
51. Jarvi 1991, 260.
52. *Förteckning; Katalog . . . Relling* 1878; *Katalog . . . Österholm* (1890–91?).
53. Wendelius 1990, 28–29.
54. *Förlags-katalog* 1912.
55. Stockenström 1978, 256.
56. See Kussak 1982, 21–25, for a discussion of how literature and fiction were viewed among the revival groups.
57. Pleijel 1967, 40.
58. Stockenström 1978, 264.
59. For Åberg, see *Svenskt litteraturlexikon* 1970, 636; for Thomasson, see Furuland 1962, 147–57.
60. *Svenskt litteraturlexikon* 1970, 167 (Flygare-Carlén), 229 (Hedenstierna), and 496 (Schwarz).
61. Westerberg 1977, 87–90.
62. Linnström 1961; *Svensk Bok-Katalog* 1866–75, 1876–85, 1886–95, and 1896–1900; Furuland 1962, 148–49.
63. Furuland 1962, 148–49.
64. Johannesson 1980, 122. Cf. also Svedjedal 1994 for a discussion of the popularity of several of the noted female authors.
65. Berg 1969, 124–25. See also Lundevall 1953, 176–77.
66. Johannesson 1980, 159.
67. Lyons 1987, 90–92.
68. J. Adams 1987, 163.
69. *Dalkullan* 1910, n.p.
70. Furuland 1990, 105ff.

71. Schersten 1933, 55.
72. Williams 1991, 119–20. Cf. also Wendelius 1990, 97, for similar results from *Rockford-Posten.*
73. *Referat* 1889, 25–26.
74. E. Olson 1910, 4–5.
75. Nystrom 1962, 10.
76. Ibid., 14.
77. Ibid., 14–28; *Augustana Book Concern* 1914, 35–41.
78. E. Olson 1910, 75–116; 10 May, 27 June, 11 October 1911; 30 January 1912; 1 July 1913; 7 July, 6 October 1914; 26 June, 21 August 1917, ABCMin, AFP.
79. Williams 1991, 34–36.
80. Larsson and Tedenmyr 1988, 230–94.
81. Nystrom 1962, 96–100.
82. Svedjedal 1993, 213.
83. "Vitterhet" in *Förlags-katalog* 1912.
84. *Förlags-katalog* 1912, 180, 188.
85. Enander 1892a and 1901. Cf. also *Förlags-katalog* 1912, 29, 59.
86. ABC database, described later in the chapter. It should, however, also be noted that *Eterneller och vårblommor* first appeared at Hemlandet Publishing Company in Chicago (judging from the preface, probably in 1888), at which time Enander was editor of *Hemlandet.* In 1891, Engberg-Holmberg bought "half the share" of *Eterneller,* and some time "later" it was sold to the ABC where it first appeared in 1892 (E. Olson 1910, 157.) Still, a copy of the book with the Engberg-Holmberg imprint from 1894 exists in the Uppsala University Library, a fact that illustrates the difficulties in establishing the exact bibliographic provenance for Swedish-American imprints.
87. Enander 1892a.
88. "Historiska anmärkningar," following the selection of poems in Enander 1892a.
89. *Förlags-katalog* 1912. Strindberg is noted on p. 189.
90. Larsson and Tedenmyr 1988, 128.
91. Hasselmo 1974, 63–65.
92. The publication profiles of the Mission Covenant Book Concern and the Baptist Publication Society are based on Larsson and Tedenmyr 1988.
93. *Augustana,* 4 June 1908.
94. 14 July 1908, ABCMin, AFP; letter to C. J. Bengtson from the Augustana Book Concern, 14 July 1908, CJB, ELCA.
95. *Referat* 1884, 20.
96. Ibid., 18.
97. *Augustana,* 12 January 1893.
98. Ibid., 4 June 1908.
99. Ibid., 17 November 1910.
100. "En beaktansvärd varning," ibid., 25 April 1912.
101. "Smutslitteratur," *Svenska Journalen,* 17 January 1913. It is interesting to note

the parallel to the discussion in Sweden a few years earlier about the dangers of popular and inexpensive fiction, which came to be symbolized by the stories about the detective Nick Carter. Cf. Boëthius 1989.

102. For statements of Bonnier and Åkerlund, see "Svensk smutslitteratur till Amerika?," *Svenska Dagbladet*, 23 January 1913. For information about Åhlén & Åkerlund and *Julstämning*, see "Stort slag för Sverige i Amerika," *Veckojournalen*, 8 September 1912.

103. For the following, see "Svensk smutslitteratur till Amerika," *Augustana*, 20 February 1913.

104. 11 April 1916, ABCMin, AFP.
105. 2 February, 27 June 1916, ibid.
106. *God Jul* 1916.
107. Williams 1991, 178–82, 185–86.
108. 12 April 1899, ABCMin, AFP.
109. 10 and 11 July 1900, ibid.
110. 15 May 1901, ibid.
111. Bonggren 1902.
112. *Förlags-katalog* 1912.
113. 14 August 1901, ABCMin, AFP.
114. Lönnroth and Delblanc 1988b, 165.
115. 12 April 1899, ABCMin, AFP.
116. Enander 1901, 3–4.
117. *Fosterlandet*, 4 December 1901. An identical review was published on the same date in *Svenska Tribunen*, another Chicago newspaper.
118. *Hemlandet*, 4 December 1901.
119. *Svenska Amerikanaren*, 3 December 1901.
120. "Något om en viss kritik," *Svenska Kuriren*, 10 December 1901.
121. *Svenska Kuriren*, 17 December 1901.
122. *Augustana*, 7 November 1901.
123. Ibid., 12 December 1901.
124. *Fosterlandet*, 25 December 1901. This article was also printed simultaneously in *Svenska Tribunen*.
125. Johan Enander, "En liten vidräkning," in *Augustana*, 9 January 1902.
126. Enander 1901, 5.
127. Williams 1991, 167.
128. *Referat* 1894, 63.
129. Ibid. 1907, 55; 14 July 1908, ABCMin, AFP.
130. 20 April 1909, ABCMin, AFP.
131. 19 April 1910, ibid.

6. THE AUGUSTANA BOOK CONCERN AS A SOURCE FOR SWEDISH-AMERICAN IDENTITY

1. *Referat* 1901, 8–10.
2. *Minnesskrift* 1910, 391–410.

3. Andersson 1986, 15–22, and Brink 1992, chap. 7, include useful discussions of the role of canons and schoolbooks in Sweden. See also Elson 1964 and Tingsten 1969 for further discussions of both American and Swedish conditions.

4. B. Svensson 1994, 32–33.

5. Total copies printed for those authors where national origin was established: 257,785. Of those identified, 42,250 copies were of Swedish origin and 179,835 copies German.

6. Hamrin 1979, 74.

7. Kussak 1982, 158. See also chap. 4, 94–141. A similar situation has been noted regarding the reading habits among those in a youth temperance lodge in Sweden 1909–20, which of course emphasized abstinence of alcohol but also good morals, honesty, and industriousness (Rydbeck 1995, 220–23.)

8. See Doderer 1973–82, 4 vols. The authors are: Frida von Kornoff, vol. 2, 270; Margarete Lenk, vol. 4, 369–70; Sophie von Niebelschütz, vol. 4, 427–28; Karl Gustav Nierirtz, vol. 2, 555–57; Christoph von Schmid, vol. 3, 290–92; and Ottile Wildermuth, vol. 3, 804–7.

9. Mählqvist 1977, 59–61. See also Klingberg 1973, 81–82.

10. *Evangeliska* 1906, 55.

11. *Svensk Bok-Katalog* 1866–75, 1876–85, 1886–95, 1896–1900, 1901–05, 1906–10, 1911–15, 1916–20. The time periods in question are for Lenk 1901–20, Fries 1866–1919, and Rüdiger 1906–15.

12. Pirated editions of Swedish books were not uncommon in Swedish America, and it was not until 1911 that a copyright treaty was signed between Sweden and the United States. Williams 1991, 36.

13. Fries 1904 (ABC), 1908 (EFS). Cf. also Stein 1893 (ABC) and 1911 (EFS).

14. *Förlags-katalog* 1912, 40, 44.

15. See Åhlén 1942, vol. 1, 260 (Grytzell), 393–94 (Karlsson), and 517–18 (Lybecker), and vol. 2, 886 (Wiedemann). Cf. also Nordlinder 1991, 63–64; and Kussak 1982, 206–7.

16. See Nordlinder 1991 for an analysis of the *Kunstmärchen* in Swedish Christmas magazines. Eva Nordlinder has also helped in the identification of unsigned contributions to *Vid Juletid*.

17. Bates 1980, 13–18.

18. Cf., e.g., Hanna Frosterus Segerstråle, "Den lille studentens 'julgåfva,'" and "Var barmhärtig," *Vid Jesu krubba* 1907, and "Frihet," *Guds vägar* 1908.

19. "Tvenne olika julaftnar," *Vid Jesu krubba* 1908.

20. *Referat* 1889, 25.

21. Ibid. 1890, 25.

22. Bersell 1898 (hereafter abbreviated FL 1898), 4.

23. Bersell 1897, 4.

24. *Katalog . . . Augustana* 1920, 53.

25. *Läsebok* 1878 (hereafter abbreviated LfF). For further information about the book and its history, see Furuland 1991b.

26. Furuland 1991b, 66–73.

27. Ibid., 72.

28. "Förord" in Bersell 1890 (hereafter abbreviated FL 1890), 3.

29. Ibid., 3. The original Swedish reads: "lämpadt efter våra, svensk-amerikanska förhållanden," "har en ren, sedlig prägel," "positivt kristliga."

30. *Katalog . . . Lutheran* 1900, 49.

31. E.g., *Augustana*, 6 November 1890 and 5 February 1891.

32. In my comparisons between the two books, I will use the 8th edition of *Läsebok för folkskolan* (LfF) printed in Stockholm in 1878. As the 9th edition appeared in 1890, it was the 8th edition that was available as the work with *Församlingsskolans läsebok* (FL) was underway in Swedish America. LfF 1878 runs 629 pages, whereas FL 1890 is 384 pages long.

33. E.g., "Hvem gjorde skyn," FL 1890, 209–11, is identical to "Guds Godhet," LfF 1878, 1–2, and "Under höbärgnien," FL 1890, 248–49, is identical to "I Husaby (Under Höbergningen)," LfF 1878, 36.

34. "Karl den store," FL 1890, 323–24, was also published as "Carl den store," LfF 1878, 530–31; "Korstågen," FL 1890, 325–29 is an edited version of "Det första korståget," LfF 1878, 531–32; and "Esaias Tegnér," FL 1890, 372–76 is an edited version of "Esaias Tegnér," LfF 1878, 415–19.

35. LfF 1878, 419.

36. Ibid., 360–61, 362–67.

37. Ibid., 336–39, 340–43, 343–46. It should be noted that the entry on George Washington relates the legend of young George and the cherry tree, although in the Swedish-American version it has become a pear tree.

38. Ibid., 378–81.

39. Ibid., 372.

40. Ibid., Nos. 218 and 219.

41. Elson 1964, 188–206.

42. Karsten 1978, chap. 5.

43. Ibid., 98–101.

44. Hilen 1947, chap. 4.

45. O. Olsson 1896, 13–14.

46. Mauritzson 1917 (hereafter abbreviated TL 1917).

47. 31 July 1916, ABCMin, AFP.

48. Ibid., 4 October 1916.

49. Ibid., 10 April 1917.

50. Hammer and Wallgren 1915 (hereafter abbreviated FL 1915); Hammer and Wallgren 1916 (hereafter abbreviated AL 1916).

51. The following items appear in both TL 1917 and AL 1916: "Skyddängelns röst," "Nu blir det vår," "När bina vaknade," "Vad vinden gjorde," "Sommarens första ros," "En farlig räv," "Gammelgäddan i vassviken," "Sagor om björn och räv," "En tam björn," "Kom hör min vackra visa," "Det är Vilhelm," "Mors varghistoria," "Den underbara gröten," "Vita blomster," and "Haren." The following items appear in both TL 1917 and FL 1915: "Snöklockans sång" and "Tores julgran."

52. Nordlinder 1991, 31, 55.

53. TL 1917, 275–91.
54. Edqvist 1915, 145–181.
55. TL 1917, 282–83.
56. Ibid., 286.
57. The following is based on ibid., 289–90.
58. The following is based on ibid., 292–303.
59. Ibid., 300.
60. "Våra fäder deltaga i inbördeskriget" and "Nybyggarliv," ibid., 303–8.
61. "Augustana-synodens stiftande," "Ett studentupptåg," and "En morgon vid diakonianstalten," ibid., 308–26.
62. "Julen i 'Bethlehem'" and "Fjärde juli på prärien," ibid., 326–36.
63. Hvenekilde 1992, 584–86.
64. Johannesson 1991b; Williams 1991, 42–48.
65. Holmes 1896, 1904, 1911.
66. Johanesson 1991b, 96, 109.
67. Andeer 1904b, 1911, 1914.
68. Bonggren 1902.
69. Lönnqvist 1907, 1916.
70. A. Olsson 1905, 1917.
71. 28 January, 6 October 1914, ABCMin, AFP.
72. Linder 1914.
73. *Augustana,* 10 December, 26 December 1914.
74. B. Svensson 1994, 25.
75. 25 April 1900, 15 May 1901, ABCMin, AFP.
76. B. Svensson 1994, 42–43.
77. Ibid., 32–33.
78. Ibid., 36–40, chap. 3.
79. Ibid., chap. 5.
80. 25 October 1899, ABCMin, AFP.
81. 29 January 1913, ibid.
82. 23 April 1918, ibid.
83. 8 October 1918, ibid.
84. "Ett ord till Ungdomsvännens prenumeranter," *Ungdomsvännen* 1918, 268.
85. Ibid. 1911, table of contents.
86. 1 July 1913, ABCMin, AFP.
87. 6 October 1914, ibid.
88. 27 June 1916, ibid.
89. B. Svensson 1994, 42–44.
90. 31 October 1917, ABCMin, AFP.
91. "Ett ord till Ungdomsvännens prenumeranter," *Ungdomsvännen* 1918, 268.
92. Norelius 1891.
93. 19 January 1909, 19 April, 19 July 1910, 24 April, 29 May 1913, ABCMin, AFP.
94. Norelius 1900.

95. *Augustana Synod . . . History* 1910; *Minnesskrift* 1910; *Minnen* 1911.
96. Enander 1892b.
97. 11 November 1903, ABCMin, AFP.
98. Sundbeck 1904b.
99. Barton 1994, 142.
100. Ibid., 142–46.
101. J. Person 1912; Berger 1916.
102. On Person, see Björk 1993; and on Berger, see Beijbom 1981, 64–81.
103. Berger 1912.
104. Letters from Vilhelm Berger to G. N. Swan, 1 December 1910, 20 April, 12 September 1911, GNS, SSIRC.
105. Holmes 1896, 11–12.
106. Linder 1914, 288.
107. Ludvig Holmes, "En hälsning till det gamla landet," *Ungdomsvännen* 1903, 20.
108. Alfred Bergin, "Hafva vi som svenskar några gemensamma lifsintressen?" *Ungdomsvännen* 1913, 86. Cf. also Vilhelm Berger, "Vår tidningspress," *Ungdomsvännen* 1913, 274, for similar sentiments.
109. J. Person 1912, 9–10. Cf. also B. Svensson 1994, 109–10 for a discussion in *Prärieblomman* of how Swedish America's unique characteristics were misunderstood in Sweden.
110. J. Person 1912, 5.
111. Sundbeck 1904b, 59–62.
112. Ibid., 17.
113. E-n, "Den svensk-amerikanska litteraturens framtid," *Ungdomsvännen* 1905, 88.
114. David Nyvall, "Bort med bindestrecket?" *God Jul* 1916 (n.p.), quotation from the last line.
115. See, for example, "Olika falla ödets lotter," "Ett löst problem," "Mörker-ljus," and "En faktor i samhället" in Andeer 1904b.
116. "Svensk-amerikanen," in Andeer 1904b.
117. Olof Olsson, "Något om sann svensk-amerikansk patriotism," *Ungdomsvännen* 1903, 201–3.
118. *Ungdomsvännen*: 1900, Declaration of Independence, 208–10; 1904, George Washington, 53; 1909, American presidential elections, 118–21; 1914, American national anthem, 277.
119. Cf. Williams 1995, 214–17.
120. Cf. Erickson 1996, 126–28.
121. Williams 1991, 64–81, 97–101, 167.
122. Ibid., 185–87.
123. *Augustana,* 27 November 1902. Cf. also the positive review in 25 September 1902.
124. Thander 1996, 26–27.
125. Ibid., 115.

126. Ibid., 156.
127. 26 January 1910, ABCMin, AFP.

7. PUTTING THE PAST TO USE: THE CREATION OF A SWEDISH-AMERICAN HISTORY

1. Conzen 1995, 49.
2. Bodnar 1992, 43.
3. Breton 1992, 7–8.
4. Øverland 2000, 19–21.
5. *Referat* 1867, 9.
6. Ibid. 1869, 20; Norelius 1900, 1916.
7. Swan 1915, 40–41.
8. Skarstedt 1897, 51–53.
9. Beijbom 1980, 264.
10. Schön 1910, 372. For comments on Enander in Swedish America, see, e.g., Beijbom 1980, 263–70; and Barton 1994, 64–67.
11. Beijbom 1980, 276–77.
12. Kammen 1991, 218. Cf. also Davies 1955.
13. Øverland 2000, 63–76.
14. Barton 2002, 62–65; Falnes 1937.
15. Beijbom 1980, 264–65.
16. Enander 1874–77.
17. Ibid., 50.
18. Ibid., preface.
19. *Våra förfäders dag* 1, no. 1 (6 September 1890): 1.
20. Beijbom 1980, 268.
21. *Hemlandet*, 4 September 1890.
22. Enander 1892c, 19.
23. Ibid., 20–21.
24. Ibid., 22.
25. Enander 1892b.
26. Ibid., 65–66.
27. *Augustana*, 8 June 1893.
28. Ibid., 7 April, 23 June, 15 December 1892, 29 June 1893.
29. Kastrup 1975, 413.
30. J. Carlson 1908, 12.
31. Barton 2002, 73–74.
32. Fishman and Nahirny 1966, 350.
33. Blanck 1988, 5–20.
34. A. Söderström 1899, 320.
35. Mattson 1888, 4–5.
36. Ibid., 26–27.
37. Ibid., 25.
38. Ibid., 37.

39. Ibid., 28.
40. B. Svensson 1994, 34–36.
41. "Svenskarna i Delaware," *Ungdomsvännen* 1901–03.
42. Amandus Johnson, "Johan Printz. Nya Sveriges guvernör 1643–1653," *Prärieblomman* 1912; Anders Schön, "Fru Anna på Printzhof. En kvinnoprofil från 1600-talets Svensk-Amerika," *Prärieblomman* 1903.
43. Enander 1874–77.
44. Ibid., 27–32.
45. Eric Norelius, "Den första svenska invandringen till Förenta Staterna," *Prärieblomman* 1900, 37.
46. *Referat* 1914, 163; 1915, 171.
47. Swan 1915, 45–46.
48. *Year-Book* 1905–07, 32, 36.
49. Ibid., 44.
50. Enander 1892c, 261.
51. The following paragraphs are based on GLA, RSBU: Sveriges roll.
52. Enander 1892c, 22–23.
53. *Year-book* 1905–07, 36–37.
54. GLA, RSBU: Sveriges roll.
55. Enander 1892c, 24.
56. E. Olson 1947, 184.
57. Holmes 1896, 42–43.
58. Enander 1892c, 24–25.
59. E. Olson 1947, 184.
60. Craig 1996, 2–3.
61. E. W. Olson, "Några bindestreck mellan Sverige och Amerika," *Ungdomsvännen* 1916, 113–15, quotation from p. 115.
62. W. Adams 1985, 153.
63. *Proceedings* 1926; Norman and Runblom 1988b, 208–9.
64. *Proceedings* 1896–97.
65. Ernst A. Zetterstrand, "John Ericsson. En karekteristik af den store uppfinnaren," *Prärieblomman* 1904, 49.
66. See the following in *Prärieblomman:* Hjalmar Edgren, "Sjöstriden på Hampton Roads 1862," 1902; Jakob Bonggren, "John Ericsson," 1913; E. W. Olson, "John Ericsson March," 1907; and Wilhelm Reslow, "Monitor," 1905.
67. See the following in *Ungdomsvännen:* "John Erickson," 1903, 264; "Sjöstriden på Hampton Roads," 1911, 241–44; and "Huru Ericssons Monitor kom till," 1912, 89–93.
68. *Augustana,* 10 October 1895.
69. Ibid., 30 July 1903.
70. Ibid., 14 March 1912.
71. *Augustana Observer,* February 1906.
72. Oredsson 1992, 100–105.
73. *Augustana,* 5 November, 12 November 1891.

74. Ibid., 16 November 1893.
75. Ibid., 6 November 1902.
76. Letters from Johan Enander to Gustav Andreen, 18 and 27 October 1907, GAP, ACL.
77. *Augustana,* 14 November 1907.
78. Ibid., 19 November 1908.
79. Ibid., 4 November 1915.
80. Ibid., 11 November 1915. Cf. also letter from Jules Mauritzson to G. N. Swan, 16 October 1915, GNS, SSIRC.
81. *Augustana,* 8 November 1900.
82. Ibid., 4 November 1909.
83. Ibid., 30 October 1913.
84. Andeer 1904a, 39–41.
85. *Augustana,* 4 November 1915.
86. Augustana College Faculty Minutes, 8 February 1901, CFC, ACL. Cf. also *Augustana,* 7 March 1901.
87. *Augustana,* 30 May 1901.
88. Ibid., 27 February 1902.
89. Ibid.
90. "Grundläggarnes dag vid Augustana College och Teologiska Seminarium," ibid., 1 May 1902.
91. Ibid., 21 April 1902.
92. Ludvig Holmes, "Festdikt," in Holmes 1904, 304–12; Sundbeck 1904a, 159.
93. Sundbeck 1904a, 163–64.
94. *Augustana,* 8 May 1902.
95. Ibid., 30 April 1903 and 5 May 1904, report on celebrations in 1903 and 1904.
96. Bergendoff 1969, 120.
97. Ibid., 121.
98. *Minnen* 1911, 5–8.
99. *Referat* 1910, 32.
100. *Minnen* 1911, 187–93.
101. Ibid., 194–95.
102. Hustvedt 1966; Øverland 2000, 63, 155.
103. Johannesson 1991a, 269–75.
104. *Year-book* 1905–07, 59.
105. Thander 1996, 190–211.

Bibliography

UNPUBLISHED PRIMARY SOURCES

Sweden

Göteborg

"Sveriges roll i världshistorien," ms. by Johan Enander, n.d. (Sveriges roll), Collection of Riksföreningen för svenskhetens bevarande i utlandet (RSBU), Provincial Archives of Göteborg (Göteborgs landsarkiv, GLA).

Uppsala

Adolf Noreen Collection (ANC), Uppsala University Library (Uppsala universitetsbibliotek, UUB).

United States

Chicago, Illinois

C. J. Bengtson Collection (CJB), Archives of the Evangelical Lutheran Church in America (ELCA).

Rock Island, Illinois

Augustana College, Swenson Swedish Immigration Research Center (SSIRC)
    Ernst Skarstedt Collection (ESC).
    G. N. Swan Collection (GNS).
Augustana College and Theological Seminary, Augustana College Library, Special Collections (ACL)
    Gustav Andreen Papers (GAP).
    Board of Directors (BdDir).
    College Faculty and Committees (CFC).
    Phrenokosmian Society (PS).
    Registration Forms (uncataloged) (RF).
    Svenska Vitterhetssällskapet (SV).

Minneapolis, Minnesota

Augustana Book Concern Collection (uncataloged), Board of Directors, Minutes (ABCMin), Archives of the Augsburg Fortress Publishing House (AFP).

PUBLISHED PRIMARY SOURCES

Aftonbladet [newspaper] (Stockholm), 1903.
Åhlén, Bengt, ed. *Svenskt författarlexikon 1900–1940. Biobibliografisk handbok till Sveriges moderna litteratur*, 2 vols. (Stockholm, 1942).
Andeer, C. W. *Dialoger och monologer för ungdomsföreningar* (Rock Island, 1904a).
———. *I brytningstid. Skisser från det svensk-amerikanska folklifvet* (Rock Island, 1904b).
———. *Augustanafolk. Bilder och karaktärer ur vårt kyrkliga arbete* (Rock Island, 1911).
———. *Augustanafolk. Andra samlingen. Flera Bilder och karaktärer ur vårt kyrkliga arbete* (Rock Island, 1914).
Ander, O. Fritiof, and Oscar Nordstrom, eds. *The American Origin of the Augustana Synod* (Rock Island, 1942).
Augustana [periodical] (Rock Island), 1891–1918.
Augustana Book Concern 1889–1914 samt Augustanasynodens tidigare förlagsverksamhet: festskrift med anledning af verksamhetens 25-årsjubileum (Rock Island, 1914).
Augustana Observer [periodical] (Rock Island), 1903–16.
The Augustana Synod. A Brief Review of Its History, 1860–1910 (Rock Island, 1910).
Augustana Synod Minutes. *Protokoll hållet vid Skandinaviska Ev. Lutherska Augustana Synodens årsmöte* (Chicago, 1860–72; Red Wing, Minn., 1873; Rock Island, 1874; Moline, Ill., 1875; Chicago, 1876; Red Wing, 1877; Chicago, 1878–79; Moline, 1880–83).
———. *Officiellt referat öfwer förhandlingarna wid Skandinaviska Ev. Lutherska Augustana Synodens årsmöte* (Rock Island, 1884–90).
———. *Referat öfwer förhandlingarna wid Skandinaviska Evangelisk Lutherska Augustana Synodens årsmöte* (Rock Island, 1891–94).
———. *Referat öfwer förhandlingarna wid Evangelisk Lutherska Augustana Synodens årsmöte* (Rock Island, 1895–1900).
———. *Referat öfver förhandlingarna vid Augustana Synodens årsmöte* (Rock Island, 1901–05).
———. *Referat af förhandlingarna vid Augustana Synodens årsmöte* (Rock Island, 1906–11).
———. *Augustana-synodens referat årsmöte* (Rock Island, 1912–19).
———. *Minutes of the Annual Convention of the Evangelical Lutheran Augustana Synod in North America* (Rock Island, 1920–21).
Bergendoff, Conrad. *The Augustana Ministerium* (Rock Island, 1980).
Berger, Vilhelm. *Vårt språk* (Rock Island, 1912).
———. *Svensk-amerikanska mediationer* (Rock Island, 1916).
Bersell, A. O., ed. *Församlingsskolans läsebok* (Rock Island, 1890).
———, ed. *Barnens andra bok för skolan och hemmet* (Rock Island, 1897).
———, ed. *Församlingsskolans läsebok* (Rock Island, 1898).
Bjursten, Herman. *Två flammor* (Minneapolis, 1898).
Bonggren, Jakob. *Sånger och sagor* (Rock Island, 1902).

Bureau of the Census. *Ninth Census of the United States 1870* (Washington, D.C., 1872).

———. *Tenth Census of the United States 1880* (Washington, D.C., 1883).

———. *Thirteenth Census of the United States 1910* (Washington, D.C., 1912).

———. *Fourteenth Census of the United States 1920*, vol. 2, *Population* (Washington, D.C., 1922).

———. *Religious Bodies: 1926* (Washington, D.C. 1929).

Carlson, J. S. *Amerikas siste svensk* (Minneapolis, 1908).

Catalog of Augustana College and Theological Seminary (Rock Island, 1860–1917).

Dahl, K. G. William. *Letters Home from the Prairie Priest,* trans. Rev. Earl Helge Byleen (privately printed, n.d.). Available at Augustana College Library, Special Collections.

Dalkullan. Almanack och Kalender för 1910 (Chicago, 1910).

Edqvist, Märta. "Svenskarna i Nya Sverige." In *Bilder ur fädernas kyrka för barn och ungdom* (Stockholm, 1915).

Enander, Johan Alfred. *Förenta Staternas historia utarbetad för den svenska befolkningen i Amerika* (Chicago, 1874–77).

———, ed. *Eterneller och vårblommor. Deklamationsstycken och Dialoger för Föreningar och Sällskap samt för läsning i hemmet* (Rock Island, 1892a).

———. *Nordmännen i Amerika eller Amerikas upptäckt. Historisk afhandling med anledning af Columbiafesterna i Chicago 1892–1893* (Rock Island, 1892b).

———. *Valda Skrifter, I* (Rock Island, 1892c).

———, ed. *Ur svenska sången under det nittonde seklet samt blad ur den svenska sångens historia. Poetisk läsebok för de svensk-amerikanska hemmen, ungdomsföreningarna och litterära sällskapen* (Rock Island, 1901).

Engberg, Holmberg & Lindells Bokförteckning (Chicago, n.d. [1876?]).

The Engberg-Holmberg Publishing Company's Bokförteckning N:o 5 (Chicago, n.d.).

Evangeliska Fosterlandsstiftelsens 50-åriga verksamhet 1856–1906. En minnesskrift (Stockholm, 1906).

Förlags-katalog från Augustana Book Concern (Rock Island, 1912).

Förteckning å böcker som finnas i Nya Svenska Bokhandlen i St. Paul (St. Paul, Minn., n.d.).

Fosterlandet [newspaper] (Chicago), 1901.

Fries, Nikolaus. *Vid fyrelden* (Rock Island, 1904).

———. *Vid fyrbåken* (Stockholm, 1908).

God Jul [periodical] (Rock Island), 1916.

Guds vägar. Berättelser för ungdom av M. L. m.fl. (Rock Island, 1908).

Hammer, Bertil, and Anders Wallgren, eds. *Första läseboken,* 15th ed. (Stockholm, 1915).

———, eds. *Andra läseboken,* 11th ed. (Stockholm 1916).

Hemlandet [newspaper] (Chicago), 1860–1917.

[Holmes, Ludvig]. *Dikter af Ludvig* (Rock Island, 1896).

———. *Nya dikter av Ludvig* (Rock Island, 1904).

———. *Ludvigs dikter. 1:a bandet.* (Rock Island, 1911).
Julrunan [periodical], 1905, 1911, 1912.
Katalog från Augustana Book Concern (Rock Island, 1920).
Katalog från Lutheran Augustana Book Concern. 1900 (Rock Island, 1900).
Katalog öfver Böcker och Musikalier som finnas i A. Österholm & Co.'s bokhandel. No. 13 State Street, N.Y, N.Y. (New York, n.d. (1890/91?).
Katalog öfver den svenska afdelningen af I. T. Relling & Co.'s Boklager 226 Milwaukee Avenue, Chicago (Chicago, 1878).
Korsbaneret [periodical], 1881–1915.
Larsson, Gunilla, and Eva Tedenmyr, eds. *Svenskt tryck i Nordamerika. Katalog över Tell G. Dahllöfs samling* (Stockholm, 1988).
Läsebok för folkskolan, 8th ed. (Stockholm, 1878).
Linder, Oliver. *I Västerled. Stycken på vers och prosa* (Rock Island, 1914).
Linnström, Hjalmar, ed. *Svenskt boklexikon åren 1830–1865,* vols. 1–2 (Uppsala, 1961).
[Lönnqvist, C. A.]. *Dikter af Teofilus* (Rock Island, 1907).
———. *Vildros. Ett nytt knippe dikter* (Rock Island 1916).
Magnusson, Hulda, ed. *Första läseboken för skolan och hemmet* (Rock Island, 1908).
———. *Andra läseboken för skolan och hemmet* (Rock Island, 1910).
Masterpieces from Swedish Literature, vols. 1–2 (Rock Island, 1906–08).
Mattson, Hans, ed. *250th Anniversary of the First Swedish Settlement in America, September 14, 1888* (Minneapolis, 1888).
Mauritzson, Jules, ed. *Tredje läseboken för skolan och hemmet* (Rock Island, 1917).
Minnen från jubelfesten. Program, predikningar och tal vid Augustana Colleges och Augustana-synodens Femtio-års-jubileum den 5–15 juni 1910 (Rock Island, 1911).
Minnesskrift med anledning af Augustana-synodens femtioåriga tillvaro. Historisk översikt af hvad som uträttats under åren 1860–1910 (Rock Island, 1910).
N. W. Ayer and Son's American Newspaper Annual and Directory (Philadelphia, 1910).
Norelius, Eric. *De svenska lutherska församlingarnas och svenskarnes historia i Amerika,* 2 vols. (Rock Island, 1891 and 1916).
———. *T. N. Hasselquist, lefnadsteckning af E. Norelius* (Rock Island, 1900).
Nothstein, Ira O., ed. *Selected Documents Dealing with the Organization of the First Congregations and the First Conferences of the Augustana Synod* (Rock Island, 1944).
Olson, Ernst W. *En bokhandelshistoria* (Chicago, 1910).
——— [E. Döbbelju, pseud.]. *Charley Washington. Studentkomedi* (Rock Island, n.d. [1910?]).
Olsson, Anna. *Från solsidan* (Rock Island, 1905).
———. *En prärieunges funderingar* (Rock Island, 1917).
Olsson, Olof. *A Pilgrim Story from Augustana College* (Rock Island, 1896).
Pehrsson, Per. *Råd och anvisningar till utvandrare* (Stockholm, 1912).
Person, Johan. *Svensk-amerikanska studier* (Rock Island, 1912).

Peterson, C. F. *Sverige i Amerika. Kulturhistoriska och biografiska teckningar* (Chicago, 1898).
Prärieblomman [periodical] (Chicago), 1899, and (Rock Island), 1900–1912.
Proceedings at the Unveiling of the Statue of John Ericsson in Potomac Park, Washington, D.C. (Washington, D.C., 1926).
Proceedings of the Conventions of the Swedish-American Republican League of Illinois 1896–1897 (n.p., n.d. [Chicago 1897?]).
Runeberg, Johan Ludvig. *Fänriks ståls sägner,* edited by A. Louis Elmquist (Rock Island, 1915).
Skarstedt, Ernst. *Våra pennfäktare* (San Francisco, 1897).
———. *Svensk-amerikanska folket: helg och söcken* (Stockholm, 1917).
Stein, Armin. *August Herman Franke. En lifsbild från den tyska pietismens tid* (Rock Island, 1893).
———. *August Herman Franke. En lifsbild från den tyska pietismens tid* (Stockholm, 1911).
Sundbeck, Carl. *Svensk-Amerika lefve! Några tal hållna i Amerika* (Stockholm, 1904a).
———. *Svensk-amerikanerna. Deras materiella och andliga sträfvanden* (Rock Island, 1904b).
Svenska Amerikanaren [newspaper] (Chicago), 1901.
Svenska Dagbladet [newspaper] (Stockholm), 1913.
Svenska Journalen [newspaper] (Rockford), 1913.
Svenska Kuriren [newspaper] (Chicago), 1901.
Svenska Socialisten [newspaper] (Chicago), 1913.
Svenska Tribunen [newspaper] (Chicago), 1901.
Svensk Bok-Katalog för åren 1866–1875 (Stockholm, 1878).
Svensk Bok-Katalog för åren 1876–1885 (Stockholm, 1890).
Svensk Bok-Katalog för åren 1886–1895 (Stockholm, 1900).
Svensk Bok-Katalog för åren 1896–1900 (Stockholm, 1904).
Svensk Bok-Katalog för åren 1901–1905 (Stockholm, 1908).
Svensk Bok-Katalog för åren 1906–1910 (Stockholm, 1913).
Svensk Bok-Katalog för åren 1911–1915 (Stockholm, 1919).
Svensk Bok-Katalog för åren 1916–1920 (Stockholm, 1923).
Svensk Katalog från C. Rasmussens Bokhandel (Minneapolis, 1907).
Svenskt litteraturlexikon (Lund, 1970).
Swensson, Carl A. *I Sverige. Minnen och bilder från mina fäders land* (Stockholm, 1891).
Tegnér, Esaias. *Fritiofs saga,* edited by Andrew A. Stomberg (Rock Island, 1914).
Ungdomsvännen [periodical] 1899, (St. Paul, Minn.), 1900–1918, (Rock Island).
Våra förfäders dag [periodical] (Chicago), 1890.
Vårt Land [newspaper] (Stockholm), 1903.
Veckojournalen [periodical] (Stockholm), 1912.
Vickner, E. J. *A Brief Swedish Grammar* (Rock Island, 1917).
Vid Jesu krubba (Rock Island, 1907).

Vid Juletid [periodical] (Rock Island), 1896–1910.
Westin, Gunnar, ed. *Emigranterna och kyrkan. Brev till och från svenskar i Amerika, 1849–1892* (Stockholm, 1932).
Who Is Who among the Alumni? (Rock Island, 1923).
Wilstadius, Paul. *Smålands nation i Uppsala. Biografiska och genealogiska anteckningar, II 1845–1950* (Uppsala, 1961).
Year-Book of the Swedish-American Historical Society 1905–1907/Svensk-Amerikanska Historiska Sällskapets Årsbok (Chicago, 1907).

SECONDARY SOURCES

Abramson, Harold J. "Religion." In *Harvard Encyclopedia of American Ethnic Groups,* edited by Stephan Thernstrom (Cambridge, Mass., 1980).
Adams, J. R. R. *The Printed Word and the Common Man: Popular Culture in Ulster 1700–1900* (Belfast, 1987).
Adams, Willi Paul. "Ethnic Leadership and the German-Americans." In *America and the Germans,* edited by Frank Trommler and Joseph McVeigh (Philadelphia, 1985).
Åkerman, Sune. "From Stockholm to San Francisco: The Development of the Historical Studies of External Migrations." *Annales Academiae Regiae Scientiarum Upsaliensis* 19 (1975).
Albrecht, Esther Andreen. *Gustav Andreen and the Growth of Augustana College and Theological Seminary* (Rock Island and Minneapolis, 1950).
American Quarterly 21 (Fall 1969).
Ander, O. Fritiof. *T. N. Hasselquist: The Career and Influence of a Swedish-American Clergyman, Journalist, and Educator* (Rock Island, 1931).
Anderson, Benedict. *Imagined Communities: Reflections on the Origin and Spread of Nationalism* (London, 1991).
Anderson, Philip J. "Paul Peter Waldenström and America. Influence and Presence in Historical Perspective." *Covenant Quarterly* 52 (November 1994).
———. "Education and Identity Formation among Swedish-American Mission Friends: The Case of Ansgar College, 1873–1884." In *Scandinavian Immigrants and Education in North America,* edited by Philip J. Anderson et al. (Chicago, 1995).
Anderson, Philip J., and Dag Blanck, eds. *Swedish-American Life in Chicago 1850–1930: Cultural and Urban Aspects of an Immigrant People* (Uppsala, 1991).
———, eds. *Swedes in the Twin Cities: Immigrant Life and Minnesota's Urban Frontier* (St. Paul, Minn., 2001).
Anderson, Philip J., et al., eds., *Scandinavian Immigrants and Education in North America* (Chicago, 1995).
Andersson, Inger. *Läsning och skriving. En analys av texter för den allmänna läs-och skrivundervisningen 1842–1982* (Umeå, 1986).
Andreen, Gustav. *Det svenska språket i Amerika* (Stockholm, 1900).
———. "Jules Mauritzson." *Korsbaneret* 52 (1931).
Andrén, Carl-Gustaf. *Kyrkokunskap* (Lund, 1973).

Appel, John. "Hansen's Third Generation Law." *Jewish Social Studies* 23 (January 1961).
Appleby, Joyce, Lynn Hunt, and Margaret Jacob. *Telling the Truth about History* (New York, 1994).
Arden, G. Everett. *The School of the Prophets: The Background and History of Augustana Theological Seminary 1860–1960* (Rock Island, 1960).
———. *Augustana Heritage: A History of the Augustana Lutheran Church* (Rock Island, 1963).
Attebery, Jennifer Eastman. "Claiming Ethnicity: Implicit and Explicit Expressions of Ethnicity among Swedish Americans." *American Studies in Scandinavia* 32 (Spring 2000).
———. "A Lonely Guy in Rocky Bar, Idaho: Imagining Swedish America From the Mines." *Swedish-American Historical Quarterly* 54 (July 2003).
Barth, Fredrik. "Introduction." In *Ethnic Groups and Boundaries: The Social Organization of Culture Difference* (Boston, 1969).
Barton, H. Arnold. "Clio and Swedish America: Historians, Organizations, Publications." In *Perspectives on Swedish Immigration,* edited by Nils Hasselmo (Chicago, 1978).
———. "The Life and Times of Swedish America." *Swedish-American Historical Quarterly* 35 (1984).
———. "Förord." In *Svenskt tryck i Nordamerika. Katalog över Tell G. Dahllöfs samling,* edited by Gunilla Larsson and Eva Tedenmyr (Stockholm, 1988).
———. "Cultural Interplay between Sweden and Swedish America." *Swedish-American Historical Quarterly* 43 (1992).
———. "Swedish Reactions to the Emigration Question around the Turn of the Century." *Swedish-American Historical Quarterly* 45 (April 1993).
———. *A Folk Divided: Homeland Swedes and Swedish Americans, 1840–1940* (Carbondale, Ill., 1994).
———. "Swedish Americans and the Viking Discovery of America." In *Interpreting the Promise of America: Essays in Honor of Odd Sverre Lovoll,* edited by Todd W. Nichol (Northfield, Minn., 2002).
Bates, Barbara Snedeker. "Denominational Periodicals: The Invisible Literature." *Phaedrus* 7 (Spring/Summer 1980).
Beck, Walter H. *Lutheran Elementary Schools in the United States* (St. Louis, 1939).
Beijbom, Ulf. *Swedes in Chicago: A Demographic and Social Study of the 1846–1888 Immigration* (Uppsala, 1971).
———. "The Historiography of Swedish America." *Swedish Pioneer Historical Quarterly* 31 (October 1980).
———. "Vilhelm Berger, en skildrare av emigranternas hundår." *Personhistorisk tidskrift* 77 (1981).
———. *Utvandrarna och Svensk-Amerika* (Växjö, 1986).
———. "Svensk etnicitet i Amerika och Australien. Några iakttagelser från den svenska utvandringens vanligaste respektive mest perifera mål 1846–1930." *Rig* 71 (1988).

———. *Svenskamerikanskt. Människor och förhållanden i Svensk-Amerika* (Växjö, 1990a).

———. "Swedish-American Organizational Life." In *Scandinavia Overseas: Patterns of Cultural Transformation in North America and Australia,* edited by Harald Runblom and Dag Blanck (Uppsala, 1990b).

———, ed. *Swedes in America: Intercultural and Interethnic Perspectives on Contemporary Research* (Växjö, 1993).

Bennich-Björkman, Bo, and Lars Furuland. "Vad folket sjöng och läste." In *Den svenska litteraturen. De liberala genombrotten 1830–1890,* edited by Lars Lönnroth and Sven Delblanc (Stockholm, 1988).

Benson, Adolph, and Naboth Hedin, eds. *Swedes in America 1638–1938* (New Haven, Conn., 1938).

Berg, Bodil. "Svedvi sockenbibliotek. En undersökning av bokbestånd, boklån och låntagare ned huvudvikten lagd på tiden 1886–1890." In *En bok om biblioteksforskning,* edited by Lars Furuland and Bengt Brundin (Uppsala, 1969).

Bergendoff, Conrad. "The Role of Augustana in the Transplanting of a Culture across the Atlantic." In *The Immigration of Ideas: Studies in the North Atlantic Community,* edited by J. Iverne Dowie and J. Thomas Tredway (Rock Island, 1968).

———. *Augustana . . . A Profession of Faith: A History of Augustana College 1860–1935* (Rock Island, 1969).

———. "Augustana in America and in Sweden." *Swedish Pioneer Historical Quarterly* 24 (October 1973).

———. "Fritiof Fryxell and Augustana." In *Earth Interpreters: F. M. Fryxell, Geology, and Augustana,* edited by David A. Schroeder and Richard C. Anderson (Rock Island, 1992).

Berger, Vilhelm. *Svensk-Amerika i målbrottet* (New York, 1933).

Berovitch, Sacvan. *The American Jeremiad* (Madison, Wisc., 1978).

Björck, Staffan. *Heidenstam och sekelskiftets Sverige. Studier i hans nationella och sociala författarskap* (Stockholm, 1946).

Björk, Ulf Jonas. "The Swedish-American Press: Three Newspapers and Their Communities." PhD diss., University of Washington, 1987.

———. "Making Swedish-America Visible: The Fiction and Essays of Johan Person." In *Out of Scandinavia,* edited by Poul Houe (Minneapolis, 1993).

———. "The Swedish-American Press as an Immigrant Institution." *Swedish-American Historical Quarterly* 51 (October 2000).

———. "*Svenska Amerikanska Posten:* An Immigrant Newspaper with American Accents." In *Swedes in the Twin Cities: Immigrant Life and Minnesota's Urban Frontier,* edited by Philip J. Anderson and Dag Blanck (St. Paul, Minn., 2001).

Blanck, Dag. "'A Language Does Not Die Easily': Swedish at Augustana College, 1860–1900." *Swedish-American Historical Quarterly* 33 (October 1982).

———. "Svensk eller amerikan. Till frågan om Augustana College och assimileringen av svenskar i USA 1860–1900." Unpublished seminar paper, Department of History, Uppsala University, 1983.

———. "History at Work: The 1888 New Sweden Jubilee." *Swedish-American Historical Quarterly* 39 (1988).

———. "The Swedish Americans and the 1893 Columbian Exposition." In *Swedish-American Life in Chicago 1850–1930: Cultural and Urban Aspects of an Immigrant People*, edited by Philip J. Anderson and Dag Blanck (Uppsala, 1991).

———. "Growing Up Swedish in America: The Construction of a Swedish Ethnic Consciousness in America." In *Out of Scandinavia*, edited by Poul Houe (Minneapolis, 1993).

———. "Introduction." In *Looking West: Three Essays on Swedish-American Life by Jules Mauritzson*, edited by Ann Boaden and Dag Blanck (Rock Island, 1994).

———. "North Stars and Vasa Orders: On the Relationship Between Sweden and Swedish America." *Swedish-American Historical Quarterly* 46 (July 1995).

———. "Five Decades of Transatlantic Research on Swedish Emigration to North America." In *Language Contact across the North Atlantic*, edited by P. Sture Ureland and Ian Clarkson (Tübingen, 1996).

Bodnar, John. *The Transplanted: A History of Immigrants in Urban America* (Bloomington, Ind., 1985).

———. *Remaking America: Public Memory, Commemoration, and Patriotism in the Twentieth Century* (Princeton, 1992).

Boëthius, Ulf. *När Nick Carter drevs på flykten: Kampen mot "smutslitteraturen" i Sverige 1908–1909* (Stockholm, 1989).

Breton, Raymond. "Institutional Completeness of Ethnic Communities and the Personal Relations of Immigrants." *American Journal of Sociology* 70 (September 1964).

———. "Collective Dimensions of the Cultural Transformation of Ethnic Communities and the Larger Society." In *Migration and the Transformation of Cultures*, edited by Jean Burnet et al. (Toronto, 1992).

Brink, Lars. "Vad läste studenterna vid college? En granskning av den litterära kanon vid Gustavus Adolphus College, 1890–1950." Unpublished seminar paper, Department of Literature, Uppsala University, 1988.

———. *Gymnasiets litterära kanon. Urval och värderingar i läromedel 1910–1945* (Uppsala, 1992).

Carlson, Leland H. *A History of North Park College* (Chicago, 1941).

Carlsson, Sten. "Chronology and Composition of Swedish Emigration to America." In *From Sweden to America: A History of the Migration*, edited by Harald Runblom and Hans Norman (Uppsala and Minneapolis, 1976).

———. "Augustana Lutheran Pastors in the Church of Sweden." *Swedish-American Historical Quarterly* 35 (July 1984).

Chapman, Malcolm, Mary McDonald, and Elizabeth Tonkin. "Introduction." In *History and Ethnicity*, edited by Malcolm Chapman, Mary McDonald, and Elizabeth Tonkin (London, 1989).

Christianson, J. R. "Shaping the Culture of an Immigrant College Town: Decorah, Iowa, 1850–1890." In *Scandinavian Immigrants and Education in North America*, edited by Philip J. Anderson et al. (Chicago, 1995).

Connor, Walker. "When Is a Nation?" *Ethnic and Racial Studies* 13 (January 1990).

Conolly-Smith, Peter. "'Ersatz-Drama' and Ethnic (Self)-Parody: Adolf Philipp and the Decline of New York's German-Language Stage, 1893–1918." In *Multilingual America: Transnationalism, Ethnicity, and the Languages of American Literature,* edited by Werner Sollors (New York, 1998).

Conzen, Kathleen Neils. *Immigrant Milwaukee, 1836–1860: Accommodation and Community in a Frontier City* (Cambridge, Mass., 1976).

———. "German-Americans and the Invention of Ethnicity." In *America and the Germans: An Assessment of a Three-Hundred-Year History,* vol. 1, edited by Frank Trommler and Joseph McVeigh (Philadelphia, 1985).

———. "Mainstream and Side Channels: The Localization of Immigrant Cultures." *Journal of American Ethnic History* 11 (Fall 1991).

———. "The Stories Immigrants Tell." *Swedish-American Historical Quarterly* 46 (January 1995).

Conzen, Kathleen Neils, et al. "The Invention of Ethnicity: A Perspective from the U.S.A." *Journal of American Ethnic History* 12 (Fall 1992).

Craig, Peter Stebbins. "Mårten Mårtensson and His Morton Family." *Swedish Colonial News* (Philadelphia) 1 (Spring 1996).

Cremin, Lawrence. *American Education: The National Experience 1783–1876* (New York, 1984).

Davies, Wallace Evan. *Patriotism on Parade: The Story of Veterans' and Hereditary Organizations in America 1783–1900* (Cambridge, Mass., 1955).

Doderer, Klaus, ed. *Lexikon der Kinder- und Jugendliteratur* (Weinheim and Basel, 1973–82).

Eklund, Emmett. "The Mosaic of Augustana's Swedish Lutheran Origins." *Swedish-American Historical Quarterly* 46 (July 1995).

Elson, Ruth. *Guardians of Tradition: American Schoolbooks of the Nineteenth Century* (Lincoln, Nebr., 1964).

Elvander, Nils. *Harald Hjärne och konservatismen. Konservativ idédebatt i Sverige 1865–1932* (Uppsala, 1961).

Erickson, Scott E. *David Nyvall and the Shape of an Immigrant Church: Ethnic, Denominational, and Educational Priorities among Swedes in America* (Uppsala, 1996).

Erling, Bernhard. "Augustana, Bishops, and the Church of Sweden." *Lutheran Forum* 26 (February 1992).

———. "The Augustana Synod and Sweden: Changes and Influences." In *American Religious Influences in Sweden,* edited by Scott E. Erickson (Uppsala, 1996).

Falnes, Oscar J. "New England Interest in Scandinavian Culture and the Norsemen." *New England Quarterly* 10 (June 1937).

Fischer, Michael M. J. "Ethnicity and the Post-Modern Arts of Memory." In *Writing Culture: The Poetics and Politics of Ethnography,* edited by James Clifford and George E. Marcus (Berkeley, Calif., 1986).

Fishman, Joshua. *Language Loyalty in the United States* (The Hague, 1966).

Fishman, Joshua, and Vladimir Nahirny. "American Immigrant Groups: Ethnic Identification and the Problem of Generations." *Sociological Review* 13 (1965).

———. "Ukrainian Language Maintenance Efforts in the United States." In *Language and Loyalty in the United States,* edited by Joshua Fishman (The Hague, 1966).

Florin, Christina, and Ulla Johansson. *"Där de härliga lagrarna gro . . ." Kultur, klass och kön i det svenska läroverket 1850–1914* (Stockholm, 1993).

Fuchs, Lawrence. *The American Kaleidoscope: Race, Ethnicity, and the Civil Culture* (Hanover, N.H., 1990).

Furuland, Lars. *Statarna i litteraturen. En studie i svenk dikt och samhällsdebatt* (Stockholm, 1962).

———. "Öresskrifter för folket." *Dagens Nyheter,* 2 September 1972.

———. "The Swedish-American Press as a Literary Institution of the Immigrants." In *Scandinavia Overseas: Patterns of Cultural Transformation in North America and Australia,* edited by Harald Runblom and Dag Blanck (Uppsala, 1990).

———. "From *Vermländingarne* to *Slavarna på Molokstorp:* Swedish-American Theater in Chicago." In *Swedish-American Life in Chicago 1850–1930: Cultural and Urban Aspects of an Immigrant People,* edited by Philip J. Anderson and Dag Blanck (Uppsala, 1991a).

———. "'Lyssna till den granens susning . . .' Om en läsebok som folkuppfostrare." In *Ljus över landet och andra litteratursociologiska uppsatser* (Hedemora and Uppsala, 1991b).

———. "Rättvikskullans sångbok i USA." *Rättvikskrus. Rättviks hembygsförenings årsskrift 1996* 16 (1996).

Gerber, David A. *The Making of an American Pluralism: Buffalo, New York 1825–1860* (Urbana, Ill., 1989).

Gjerde, Jon. *The Minds of the West: Ethnocultural Evolution in the Rural Middle West, 1830–1917* (Chapel Hill, N.C., 1997).

———. "Freedom and the Immigrant Myth." In *Norwegian-American Essays 2004,* edited by Orm Øverland (Oslo, 2005).

Glazer, Nathan. "Ethnic Groups in America: From National Culture to Ideology." In *Freedom and Control in Modern Society,* edited by Morroe Berger et al. (New York, 1954).

———. *We Are All Multiculturalists Now* (Cambridge, Mass., 1997).

Glazer, Nathan, and Daniel Patrick Moynihan, eds. *Ethnicity: Theory and Experience* (Cambridge, Mass., 1975).

Gleason, Philip. "American Identity and Americanization." In *Harvard Encyclopedia of American Ethnic Groups,* edited by Stephan Thernstrom (Cambridge, Mass., 1980).

Granquist, Mark. "Swedish- and Norwegian-American Religious Traditions, 1860–1920." *Lutheran Quarterly* 8 (Autumn 1994).

Greene, Victor. *For God and Country: The Rise of Polish and Lithuanian Ethnic Consciousness in America, 1860–1910* (Madison, Wisc., 1975).

———. *American Immigrant Leaders 1800–1910: Marginality and Identity* (Baltimore, Md., 1987).

Gulliksen, Øyvind. *Twofold Identities: Norwegian-American Contributions to Midwestern Literature* (New York, 2004).

Gustafsson, Bernt. *Svensk kyrkohistoria* (Stockholm, 1966).

Hamrin, Margareta. "A Study of Swedish Immigrant Children's Literature Published in the United States, 1850–1920." *Phaedrus* (Spring 1979).

Handlin, Oscar. *The Uprooted* (Boston, 1951).

Hansen, Marcus Lee. *The Problem of the Third Generation Immigrant* (Rock Island, 1938).

Harvey, Anne-Charlotte. "Performing Ethnicity: The Role of Swedish-American Theatre in the Twin Cities." In *Swedes in the Twin Cities: Immigrant Life and Minnesota's Urban Frontier,* edited by Philip J. Anderson and Dag Blanck (St. Paul, Minn., 2001).

Hasselmo, Nils. *Amerikasvenska. En bok om språkutvecklingen i Svensk-Amerika* (Stockholm, 1974).

———. "The Language Question." In *Perspectives on Swedish Immigration,* edited by Nils Hasselmo (Chicago, 1978).

Higham, John. "Leadership." In *Harvard Encyclopedia of American Ethnic Groups,* edited by Stephan Thernstrom (Cambridge, Mass., 1980).

———. *Strangers in the Land: Patterns of American Nativism, 1860–1925* (New Brunswick, N.J., 1988).

Hilen, Andrew. *Longfellow and Scandinavia: A Study of the Poet's Relationship with the Northern Languages and Literature* (New Haven, Conn., 1947).

Hill, S. M. "Nebraska-svenskarnas bildningsträfvanden. Ett litet stycke svenskamerikansk kulturhistoria." *Prärieblomman* 1907.

Hillman, Rolf. "Ur den svenska läsebokens historia." In *Till Nils Hänninger 27.5.1952,* edited by Nils Falck (Stockholm, 1952).

Hobsbawm, Eric. "Introduction: Inventing Traditions." In *The Invention of Tradition,* edited by Eric Hobsbawm and Terence Ranger (Cambridge, 1983).

———. *Nations and Nationalism since 1780: Programme, Myth, Reality* (Cambridge, 1990).

Hoglund, A. William. *Immigrants and Their Children in the United States: A Bibliography of Doctoral Dissertations, 1885–1982* (New York, 1986).

Hroch, Miroslav. *Social Preconditions of National Revival in Europe: A Comparative Analysis of the Social Composition of Patriotic Groups among the Smaller European Nations* (Cambridge, 1981).

Hustvedt, Lloyd. *Rasmus Bjørn Anderson: Pioneer Scholar* (Northfield, Minn., 1966).

Hvenekilde, Anne. "'Hvad gjør vi saa med arven?' En studie av abc-er og lesebøker utgitt til norsk morsmålsundervisning i Amerika." PhD diss., University of Oslo, 1992.

Isaacs, Harold. *Idols of the Tribe: Group Identity and Political Change* (New York, 1975).

Jacobson, Matthew Frye. *Whiteness of a Different Color: European Immigrants and the Alchemy of Race* (Cambridge, Mass., 1998).

Jansson, Torkel. *Samhällsförändring och sammanslutningsformer. Det frivilliga föreningsväsendets uppkomst och spridning i Husby-Rekarne från omkring 1850 till 1930* (Uppsala, 1982).

———. *Adertonhundratalets associationer. Forskning och problem kring ett sprängfyllt tomrum eller sammanslutningsprinciper och föreningsformer mellan två samhällsformationer c:a 1800–1870* (Uppsala, 1985).

———. "En historisk uppgörelse. När 1800-tals nationen avlöste 1600-talsstaten." *Historisk Tidskrift* 110, no. 3 (1990).

———. "Från stormakt till smånation. En väv av ekonomisk-politiska och sociokulturella trådar." In *Från stormakt till smånation. Sveriges plats i Europa från 1600-tal till 1900-tal,* edited by Stellan Dahlgren et al. (Stockholm, 1994).

Jarvi, Raymond. "The Rise and Fall of Engberg-Holmberg." In *Swedish-American Life in Chicago 1850–1930: Cultural and Urban Aspects of an Immigrant People,* edited by Philip J. Anderson and Dag Blanck (Uppsala, 1991).

Jenswold, John R. "The Rise and Fall of Pan-Scandinavianism in Urban America." In *Scandinavians and Other Immigrants in Urban America: The Proceedings of a Research Conference, October 26–27, 1984,* edited by Odd Lovoll (Northfield, Minn., 1985).

Johannesson, Eric. *Den läsande familjen. Familjetidskriften i Sverige 1850–1880* (Stockholm, 1980).

———. "The Flower King in the American Republic: The Linnaeus Statue in Chicago, 1891." In *Swedish-American Life in Chicago 1850–1930: Cultural and Urban Aspects of an Immigrant People,* edited by Philip J. Anderson and Dag Blanck (Uppsala, 1991a).

———. "Scholars, Pastors and Journalists: The Literary Canon of Swedish-America." In *Swedish Life in American Cities,* edited by Dag Blanck and Harald Runblom (Uppsala, 1991b).

Johansson, Egil. "Literacy Studies in Sweden: Some Examples." In *Literacy and Society in Historical Perspectives: A Conference Report,* edited by Egil Johansson (Umeå, 1973).

———. "Literacy Campaigns in Sweden." In *National Literacy Campaigns: Historical and Comparative Perspectives,* edited by Robert F. Arnove and Harvey J. Graff (New York, 1987).

Kälvemark, Ann-Sofie. *Reaktionen mot utvandringen. Emigrationsfrågan i svensk debatt och politik 1901–1904* (Uppsala, 1971).

Kammen, Michael. *Mystic Chords of Memory: The Transformation of Tradition in American Culture* (New York, 1991).

Kantowicz, Edward. "Polish Chicago: Survival Through Solidarity." In *The Ethnic Frontier: Essays in the History of Group Survival in Chicago and the Midwest,* edited by Melvin Holli and Peter d'A. Jones (Grand Rapids, Mich., 1977).

Karsten, Peter. *Patriot-Heroes in England and America: Political Symbolism and Changing Values over Three Centuries* (Madison, Wisc., 1978).

Kastrup, Allan. *The Swedish Heritage in America* (St. Paul, Minn., 1975).
Keillor, Steven J. "Rural Norwegian-American Reading Societies in the Late Nineteenth Century." *Norwegian-American Studies* 33 (1992).
Kivisto, Peter. "Overview: Thinking about Ethnicity." In *The Ethnic Enigma: The Salience of Ethnicity for European-Origin Groups*, edited by Peter Kivisto (Philadelphia, 1989).
Kivisto, Peter, and Dag Blanck, eds. *American Immigrants and Their Generations: Studies and Commentaries on the Hansen Thesis after Fifty Years* (Urbana, Ill., 1990).
Klingberg, Göte. *Das deutsche Kinder- und Jugendbuch im schwedischen Raum* (Weinheim and Basel, 1973).
Kussak, Åke. *Författaren som predikant. Ett frikyrkomsamfunds litterära verksamhet* (Stockholm, 1982).
Landelius, Otto Robert. "Några anteckningar till den svensk-amerikanska bokhandelns historia." *Bokhandlaren* 44, no. 33 (1951).
Lazowitz, Bernard, and Louis Rowitz. "The Three-Generation Hypothesis." *American Journal of Sociology* 69 (March 1964).
Legreid, Ann M. "'By the Oaks of Mamre': Swedish Lutheran Colonization on the Frontiers of Southwestern Iowa, 1870–1900." *Swedish-American Historical Quarterly* 44 (April 1993).
Lewan, Bengt. "Tegnér i skolan. Målsättningar i litteraturundervisningen 1840–1970." In *Vetenskapssociteten i Lund Årsbok 1972* (Lund, 1972).
Linder, Oliver. "Svensk-amerikanska litteraturen." In *Svenskarna i Amerika*, vol. 2, edited by Karl Hildebrand and Axel Fredenholm (Stockholm, 1925).
Lindmark, Daniel. *Reading, Writing, and Schooling: Swedish Practices of Education and Literacy, 1650–1880* (Umeå, 2004).
Lindmark, Sture. *Swedish America 1914–1932: Studies in Ethnicity with Emphasis on Illinois and Minnesota* (Stockholm, 1971).
Lindquist, Emory. *Smoky Valley People* (Lindsborg, Kans., 1953).
Lipset, Seymour Martin. *The First New Nation: The United States in Historical and Comparative Perspective* (New York, 1963).
Ljungmark, Lars. *For Sale—Minnesota: Organized Promotion of Scandinavian Immigration, 1866–1873* (Göteborg, 1971).
Lönnroth, Lars, and Sven Delblanc, eds. *Den svenska litteraturen. Vol 2. Upplysning och romantik* (Stockholm, 1988a).
———, eds. *Den svenska litteraturen. Vol 3. De liberala genombrotten 1830–1890* (Stockholm, 1988b).
———, eds. *Den svenska litteraturen. Vol 4. Den storsvenska generationen* (Stockholm, 1989).
Lovoll, Odd, ed. *Scandinavians and Other Immigrants in Urban America: The Proceedings of a Research Conference, October 26–27, 1984* (Northfield, Minn., 1985).
———, ed. *Nordics in America: The Future of Their Past* (Northfield, Minn., 1993).
Lundevall, Karl-Erik. *Från åttital till nittital. Om åttitalslitteraturen och Heidenstams debut och program* (Stockholm, 1953).

Lyons, Martyn. *Le Triomphe du Livre. Une histoire sociologique de la lecture dans la France du xixième siècle* (Paris, 1987).
Mählqvist, Stefan. *Böcker för svenska barn. En kvantitativ analys* (Stockholm, 1977).
Majewski, Karen. "Crossings and Double-Crossings: Polish-Language Immigrant Narratives of the Great Migration." In *Multilingual America: Transnationalism, Ethnicity, and the Languages of American Literature,* edited by Werner Sollors (New York, 1998).
Martellone, Anna Maria. "The Formation of an Italian-American Identity through Popular Theatre." In *Multilingual America: Transnationalism, Ethnicity, and the Languages of American Literature,* edited by Werner Sollors (New York, 1998).
Martinsson, Bengt-Göran. *Tradition och betydelse. Om selektion, legitimering och reproduktion av litterär betydelse i gymnasiets litteraturundervisning 1865–1968* (Linköping, 1989).
Marty, Martin E. "Religion: The Skeleton of Ethnicity in America." *Church History* 41 (March 1972).
Mattson, A. D. *Polity of the Augustana Synod* (Rock Island, 1941).
McKay, James, and Frank Lewins. "Ethnicity and the Ethnic Group: A Conceptual Analysis and Reformulation." *Ethnic and Racial Studies* 1 (October 1978).
Medelius, Hans, and Sten Rentzhog, eds. *90-tal. Visioner och vägval. Fataburen 1991. Nordiska Museets och Skansens Årsbok* (Stockholm, 1991).
Nelson, Helge. *The Swedes and the Swedish Settlements in North America,* 2 vols. (Lund, 1943).
Nordahl, Per. *Weaving the Ethnic Fabric: Social Networks among Swedish-American Radicals in Chicago 1890–1940* (Umeå, 1994).
Nordgren, J. Vincent. "Elementary Christian Education in the Augustana Synod." In *After Seventy-five Years, 1860–1935: A Jubilee Publication* (Rock Island, 1935).
Nordlinder, Eva. *Sekelskiftets svenska konstsaga och sagodiktaren Helena Nyblom* (Stockholm, 1991).
Nordstrom, Byron. "The Sixth Ward: A Minneapolis Swede Town in 1905." In *Perspectives on Swedish Immigration,* edited by Nils Hasselmo (Chicago, 1978).
Norman, Hans. *Från Bergslagen till Nordamerika. Studier i migrationsmönster, social rörlighet och demografisk struktur med utgångspunkt från Örebro län 1851–1915* (Uppsala, 1974).
———. "The New Sweden Colony and the Continued Existence of Swedish and Finnish Ethnicity." in *New Sweden in America,* edited by Carol E. Hofecker et al. (Newark, Del., 1995).
Norman, Hans, and Harald Runblom. "Research on Overseas Migration from the Nordic Countries: A Bibliographical Essay." In *Transatlantic Connections: Nordic Migration to the New World after 1800,* edited by Hans Norman and Harald Runblom (Oslo, 1988a).
———. *Transatlantic Connections: Nordic Migration to the New World after 1800* (Oslo, 1988b).
Nothstein, Ira O. "The Language Transition in the Augustana Synod." *Augustana Quarterly* 24 (July–October 1945).

Nyberg, Janet. "Swedish Language Newspapers in Minnesota." In *Perspectives on Swedish Immigration,* edited by Nils Hasselmo (Chicago, 1978).

Nystrom, Daniel. *A Ministry of Printing: History of the Publication House of Augustana Lutheran Church 1889–1962* (Rock Island, 1962).

Olneck, Martin, and Marvin Lazerson. "Education." In *Harvard Encyclopedia of American Ethnic Groups,* edited by Stephan Thernstrom (Cambridge, Mass., 1980).

Olson, Anita Ruth. "Swedish Chicago: The Extension and Transformation of an Urban Immigrant Community, 1880–1920." PhD diss., Northwestern University, 1990.

Olson, Ernst W. *Valda dikter/Selected Poems* (Uppsala, 1947).

Olson, Ernst W., Anders Schön, and Martin J. Engberg. *History of the Swedes of Illinois,* 2 vols. (Chicago, 1908).

Olson, Oscar N. "Cultural Life in the Synod." In *After Seventy-five Years, 1860–1935: A Jubilee Publication* (Rock Island, 1935).

——— . *The Augustana Lutheran Church in America 1860–1910: The Formative Period* (Rock Island, 1956).

Olsson, Karl A. *By One Spirit: A History of the Evangelical Covenant Church of America* (Chicago, 1962).

——— . "Paul Peter Waldenström and Augustana." In *The Swedish Immigrant Community in Transition,* edited by J. Iverne Dowie and Ernest M. Espelie (Rock Island, 1963).

Oredsson, Sverker. *Gustav Adolf, Sverige och Trettioåriga kriget. Historieskriving och kult* (Lund, 1992).

Ostergren, Robert. "Swedish Migration to North America in Transatlantic Perspective." In *Migration across Time and Nations: Population Mobility in Historical Contexts,* edited by Ira Glazier and Luigi de Rosa (New York, 1986).

——— . *A Community Transplanted: The Trans-Atlantic Experience of a Swedish Immigrant Settlement in the Upper Middle West, 1835–1915* (Uppsala, 1988).

Øverland, Orm. *The Western Home: A Literary History of Norwegian America* (Northfield, Minn., 1996).

——— . *Immigrant Minds, American Identities: Making the United States Home, 1870–1930* (Urbana, Ill., 2000).

——— , ed. *Not English Only: Redefining "American" in American Studies* (Amsterdam, 2001).

——— . "Becoming White in 1881: An Immigrant Acquires an American Identity." *Journal of American Ethnic History* 23, no. 4 (2004).

Park, Robert. *The Immigrant Press and Its Control* (New York, 1922).

Patterson, Orlando. "Context and Choice in Ethnic Allegiance: A Theoretical Framework and a Caribbean Case Study." In *Ethnicity: Theory and Experience,* edited by Nathan Glazer and Daniel Patrick Moynihan (Cambridge, Mass., 1975).

Person, Peter P. "A History of Higher Education among the Swedish Immigrants in America." EdD diss., Harvard University, 1941.

Peterson, Brent. *Popular Narratives and Ethnic Identity: Literature and Community in Die Abendschule* (Ithaca, N.Y., 1991).

Pettersson, Lars. *Frihet, jämlikhet, egendom och Bentham. Utvecklingslinjer i svensk folkundervisning mellan feodalism och kapitalism, 1809–1860* (Uppsala, 1992).
Pleijel, Hilding. "Bibeln i svenskt fromhetsliv." In *Våra äldsta folkböcker,* edited by Hilding Pleijel, Bror Olsson, and Sigfrid Svensson (Lund, 1967).
Rudolph, Frederick. *The American College and University: A History* (New York, 1962).
Runblom, Harald, and Hans Norman, eds. *From Sweden to America: A History of the Migration* (Uppsala and Minneapolis, 1976).
Runeby, Nils. *Den nya världen och den gamla. Amerikabild och emigrations uppfattning i Sverige, 1820–1860* (Uppsala, 1969).
Rydbeck, Kerstin. *Nykter läsning. Den svenska godtemplarrörelsen och litteraturen 1896–1925* (Uppsala, 1995).
Sanders, Hanne. "Om fanatiske sværmere og sande kristne. Den offentlige debat om den religiose vækkelse i Danmark og Sverige 1800–1850." *Historisk Tidskrift* 112, no. 2 (1992).
———. *Bondevækkelse og sekularisering. En protestantisk folkelig kultur i Danmark og Sverige 1820–1850* (Stockholm, 1995).
Saveth, Edward N. *American Historians and European Immigrants, 1875–1925* (New York, 1948).
Schersten, Albert Ferdinand. *The Relation of the Swedish-American Newspaper to the Assimilation of Swedish Immigrants* (Rock Island, 1933).
Schön, Anders. "Joh. A. Enander. Kort minnesruna för Ungdomsvännen." *Ungdomsvännen* 1910.
Sciences Historiques, Stockholm 21–28 Aout 1960, Rapports, V (Stockholm, 1960).
Scott, Larry E. *The Swedish Texans* (San Antonio, Tex., 1991).
Seller, Maxine. "The Education of Immigrants in the United States: An Introduction to the Literature." *Immigration History Newsletter* 13 (1981).
Smith, Anthony D. "Ethnic Myths and Ethnic Revivals." *European Journal of Sociology* 25 (1984a).
———. "National Identity and Myths of Ethnic Descent." *Research in Social Movements, Conflict and Change* 7 (1984b).
———. *National Identity* (Harmondsworth, 1991).
———. "Introduction: Ethnicity and Nationalism." *International Journal of Comparative Sociology* 33, nos. 1–2 (1992).
Smith, Timothy. "Immigrant Social Aspirations and American Education, 1880–1930." *American Quarterly* 21 (Fall 1969).
———. "Religion and Ethnicity in America." *American Historical Review* 83 (December 1978).
Söderström, Axel. *Minneapolis-minnen* (Minneapolis, 1899).
———. *Blixtar på tidnigshorisonten* (Warroad, Minn., 1910).
Söderström, Hugo. *Confession and Co-operation: The Policy of the Augustana Synod in Confessional Matters and the Synod's Relations with Other Churches up to the Beginning of the Twentieth Century* (Lund, 1973).
Sollors, Werner. "Literature and Ethnicity." In *Harvard Encyclopedia of American Ethnic Groups,* edited by Stephan Thernstrom (Cambridge, Mass., 1980).

———. *Beyond Ethnicity: Consent and Descent in American Culture* (New York, 1986).

———, ed. *The Invention of Ethnicity* (New York, 1989).

———, ed. *Multilingual America: Transnationalism, Ethnicity, and the Languages of American Literature* (New York, 1998).

Staionos, Kathryn Vance. "Ethnicity as Process: The Creation of an Afro-American Identity." *Ethnicity* 7 (1980).

Stephenson, George. *The Religious Aspects of Swedish Immigration: A Study of Immigrant Churches* (Minneapolis, 1932).

Stockenström, Göran. "Sociological Aspects of Swedish-American Literature." In *Perspectives on Swedish Immigration,* edited by Nils Hasselmo (Chicago, 1978).

Stolarik, M. Mark. "Immigration and Education: Some Ethnic and National Comparisons." In *Scandinavian Immigrants and Education in North America,* edited by Philip J. Anderson et al. (Chicago, 1995).

Svedjedal, Johan. "Bokmarknaden." In *Den svenska litteraturen. Bokmarknad, bibliografier, samlingsregister,* edited by Lars Lönnroth and Hans-Erik Johannesson (Stockholm, 1990).

———. *Bokens samhälle. Svenska bokförläggareföreningen och svensk bokmarknad 1887–1943,* vol. 1 (Stockholm, 1993).

———. "Kvinnorna i den svenska bokbranschen." In *Författare och förläggare och andra litteratursociologiska studier* (Hedemora, 1994).

Svensson, Birgitta. *Den omplanterade svenskheten. Kulturell självhävdelse och etnisk medvetenhet i den svensk-amerikanska kalendern Prärieblomman 1900–1913* (Göteborg, 1994).

Svensson, Sonja. *Läsning för folkets barn. Folkskolans Barntidning och dess förlag 1892–1914* (Stockholm, 1983).

Swan, G. N. "En återblick." *Year-Book of the Swedish Historical Society of America, Svenska Historiska Sällskapets i Amerika Årsbok 1914–1915* (Chicago, 1915).

Swanson, Mary Towley. *Elusive Images of Home: Stories of Swedish-American Art* (Stockholm, 1996).

Swedish-American Historical Quarterly 43 (July 1992).

Tarschys, Karin. "Svenska språket och litteraturen." *Studier över modersmålsundervisningen i högre skolor* (Stockholm, 1955).

Tedebrand, Lars-Göran. *Västernorrland och Nordamerika 1875–1913. Utvandring och återinvandring* (Uppsala, 1972).

Thander, Gunnar. "Valkyrian 1897–1909: A Study in Swedish-American Ethnicity." PhD diss., University of Minnesota, 1996.

Thernstrom, Stephan. *The Other Bostonians: Poverty and Progress in an American Metropolis 1880–1970* (Cambridge, Mass., 1973).

Thistlethwaite, Frank. "Migration from Europe Overseas in the Nineteenth Century." In *Comité International des Sciences Historiques. XIième Congrès Internationale des Sciences Historiques* (Stockholm, 1960).

Thomas, William, and Florian Znaniecki. *The Polish Peasant in Europe and Amer-*

ica, edited and abridged by Eli Zaretsky, orig. published 1918–20 (Urbana, Ill., 1985).

Tingsten, Herbert. *Gud och fosterlandet. Studier i hundra års skolpropaganda* (Stockholm, 1969).

Ulrich, Robert. *The Bennet Law of 1889: Education and Politics in Wisconsin* (New York, 1980).

Vecoli, Rudolph. "*Contadini* in Chicago: A Critique of *The Uprooted.*" *Journal of American History* 51 (December 1964).

von Schéele, K. G. H. *Hemlandstoner. En hälsning från modern Svea till dotterkyrkan i Amerika* (Stockholm, 1894).

Weiss, Bernard J., ed. *American Education and the European Immigrant* (Urbana, Ill., 1982).

Wendelius, Lars. *Kulturliv i ett svenskamerikanskt lokalsamhälle: Rockford, Illinois* (Uppsala, 1990).

Westerberg, Kermit. "Books and Reading in a Swedish-American Immigrant Community: A Case Study of the Lending Library of the Vega Litterära Förening (Vega Literary Society), St. Paul, from 1881 to 1948, with an Emphasis on Bookstock Characteristics, Patronage, and Circulation Statistics, and Popular Reading Tastes." Unpublished master's paper, University of Minnesota, School of Library Science, 1977.

———. "In Private and Public: The Dialogue of Libraries, Immigrants, and Society." In *Scandinavian Immigrants and Education in North America,* edited by Philip J. Anderson et al. (Chicago, 1995).

Widén, Albin. "Svenska böcker i USA." *Konung Oscar II:s Vandringsbibliotek Årsbok 1950* (Lund, 1950).

Williams, Anna. *Skribent i Svensk-Amerika. Jakob Bonggren. Journalist och poet* (Uppsala, 1991).

———. Review of *Den omplanterade svenskheten,* by Birgitta Svensson. *Samlaren* 116 (1995).

Yancey, William, Eugene P. Erickson, and Richard N. Juliani. "Emergent Ethnicity: A Review and Reformulation." *American Sociological Review* 41 (June 1976).

Yin, Xiao-huang. *Chinese American Literature since the 1850s* (Urbana, Ill., 2000).

Yinger, J. Milton. *Ethnicity: Source of Conflict? Source of Strength?* (Albany, N.Y., 1994).

Zelinsky, Wilbur. *Nation into State: The Shifting Symbolic Foundations of American Nationalism* (Chapel Hill, N.C., 1988).

Index

Åberg, J. O., 116, 117, 121
Adams, J. R. R., 118
Adams, Willi Paul, 177
Åhlén & Åkerlund, 112–14, 125
Åkerlund, Erik, 125
Americanization, 59–60, 66, 68, 83–84, 88, 103, 190
America Not Discovered by Columbus (Anderson), 186
American Revolution, 175–76, 198
American Swedish Historical Museum, 164
Amerikas siste svensk (Carlson), 167–68
Andeer, C. W., 35, 89, 134, 151, 199; writings of, 158, 160, 180–81, 197
Ander, O. Fritiof, 5, 53
Anderson, Benedict, 107–8
Anderson, Rasmus Bjørn, 185–86
Andra läseboken (Hammer and Wallgren), 146
Andra läseboken för skolan och hemmet (Magnusson), 140
Andreen, Gustav, 41–42, 58–59, 172, 187, 196; as first American-born president of Augustana College, 94, 104–5; on Founders Day, 182; Swedish language, view of, 65–66
Arden, G. Everett, 27, 28, 37
Attebery, Jennifer Eastman, 6
Augsburg Confession, 28
Augustana, 31, 35, 40, 55, 83, 110, 183; on careers, 100–101; circulation, 111; on commercial school, 57–58; cultural heroes discussed in, 178–80; on elocution contests, 80–81; language discussions in, 62, 64–67; on suitable reading material, 124–25; on Svenska Vitterhetssällskapet, 86–87; *Ur svenska sången* debate in, 128–29
Augustana Book Concern (ABC), 72, 77, 108, 113, 130–31, 191; board of directors, 153–54; board of publication, 119, 139; children and youth, publications for, 124, 133, 134–39, 159–60; history of, 119–30; imported books, 87, 120, 131; literary editor, 123–24, 130; nondenominational publications, 132–34; periodicals, 152–54; publication profile, 122–23, 132, 159; reflections on Swedish America, 155–56; schoolbooks, 133–34, 139–50, 159–60; selection of reading material, 126–30, 186; Swedish-American ethnic identity and, 156–59; Swedish-American history and, 154–55, 163; Swedish-American literature, 151–52; Swedish-American–oriented publications, 150–59; types of literature sold and published, 120–23. *See also Prärieblomman; Ungdomsvännen; Valkyrian*
Augustana College and Theological Seminary, 1, 19–20, 31; Americanization phase, 59–60, 68, 83–84, 88, 103; beginnings, 48–49; career patterns of graduates, 57, 99–102; celebrations of Gustavus Adolphus, 178–80; constitutions, 49–51, 55–56; contacts in Sweden, 41–42; daily religious services, 56, 62; Department of Swedish, 73, 103; departments, 49–50, 56, 64, 190; English language, role in, 59–60; fiftieth anniversary, 38, 40, 42, 66, 181, 183–85, 197; Founders Day, 80, 84, 181–83, 197; as Lutheran alternative, 66; phases in development of, 102–3; Reformation festivities, 79, 178, 179; religion, role of, 54–59; Rock Island location, 49, 82, 120; Swedish-American ethnic identity, role in development of, 46, 65–69, 85–86. *See also* curriculum, Augustana College and Theological Seminary; extracurricular activities; language, Swedish; student body

249

Augustana Ministerium, The, 91, 99
Augustana Observer, 67
Augustana sphere, 43–44, 171; occupations within, 100–101
Augustana Synod, 119, 170; Americanization phase, 59–60, 66, 68, 103, 190; American religious pluralism and, 29–30; antagonism toward secular societies, 37–39; colleges and academies, 46–47; combination of Swedish and American elements in, 83–84, 104, 181, 192; congregations within, 28–30; constitution of 1894, 30–31, 44; decentralizing tendencies in, 30–31; difficulty attracting later emigrants, 34–35, 43–44, 94; dual mission of, 184–85; ecclesiastical authority, view of, 29–30; education, role in, 46–48; educational institution, need for, 54–55; as ethnic institution, 3–4, 8–9, 44, 132, 191; in fiction, 1–2; fiftieth anniversary, 38, 40, 54, 154, 181, 183–85, 197; founding of, 19, 27–28; geographic profile, 34–36; growth of, 25–26, 30, 43; literature, view of, 124–25; membership in, 26, 30, 32, 32–33, 43–44; merger with Lutheran Church in America, 119; nonmembers, 32–33; phases of development, 132, 156, 190, 192; rooted in early phase of immigration, 9, 27, 43–44; schism with Mission Covenant Church, 31, 37, 68, 192; selection process within, 73, 195; seventy-fifth anniversary, 57, 59; Sweden, relationship with, 29, 39–43; Swedish America and, 36–39; visitors to, 40–42, 44, 54, 66, 79–80, 155, 179

"Babetistera" (Olsson), 89
Barnens andra bok för skolan och hemmet (Bersell), 140
Barth, Frederik, 15
Barton, H. Arnold, 4, 6, 36, 67, 155, 164
Bates, Barbara Snedeker, 138
Beck, Walter H., 57
Beijbom, Ulf, 6, 18, 38, 111–12, 164, 166
Bengtson, C. J., 130, 155
Bergendoff, Conrad, 5, 32–35, 63, 183
Berger, Vilhelm, 21, 106, 155, 156
Bergin, Alfred, 67, 156
Berovitch, Sacvan, 13

Bersell, Anders, 140–45
Beskow, Elizabeth (Runa), 135
Bethany College, 41, 46, 47, 50, 80
Björk, C. A., 58
Bjursten, Herman, 74, 76, 78, 114, 117
Blanche, August, 125
Blomgren, C. A., 178
Blommor vid vägen, 137
Bodnar, John, 162
Bohman, G. A., 119, 154
Bonggren, Jakob, 80, 107; *Sånger och sagor*, 126–27, 130, 134, 151, 160–61
Bonniers (publishing house), 112, 114, 121
Breton, Raymond, 8–9, 16–18, 162
Brink, Lars, 76, 77

Carlson, J. S., 71, 167–68
Carlsson, Erland, 27, 59, 119, 124, 190
Carlsson, Sten, 41, 97
Charles XII, 196
Charley Washington. Studentkomedi (Olson), 1–2, 46
Chicago, 9, 33, 38, 186
children's literature, 133, 134–39; American historical symbols in, 143–44; books, 134–37; literary serials and annuals, 137–38; schoolbooks, 20, 133–34, 139–50, 159–60
Church of Sweden, 3–4, 109; Augustana Synod, relationship with, 39–42, 44, 79–80; low-church revival movement, 29, 30, 36–37, 68
Civil War, 13, 22, 170, 193, 199; *Monitor* (built by Ericsson), 85, 148, 177–78, 198
Columbian Exposition (Chicago, 1893), 39, 167, 189
Columbus, Christopher, 164, 166–67
Constitution, U.S., 13, 48
"*Contadini* in Chicago: A Critique of *The Uprooted*" (Vecoli), 10
Conzen, Kathleen Neils, 16, 162
culture heroes, 176–81, 185
curriculum, Augustana College and Theological Seminary, 49–50; Christianity courses, 56, 60, 70, 103; classical, non-Swedish track, 52, 61, 64, 71; classical track, 51–52; commercial school, 57–58; core subjects, 52–53; development of, 50–54; languages, role in, 50–51; reforms,

54, 65, 75, 190; scientific track, 51–52, 58; student participation in Swedish language classes, 62–65; Swedish language, position in, 59–68; Swedish courses, 73–79, 103–4; modern literature course, 75–76; Old Norse literature and culture, 74, 75, 78; romanticism, idealism, and patriotism, focus on, 78, 87–88, 90, 104; survey courses, 75–76; textbooks used, 74–75, 76

Dahl, K. G. William, 68, 76, 89
Dahllöf bibliography, 113–14, 115, 120
Declaration of Independence, 173, 175–76, 186, 198
De svenska lutherska församlingarnas och svenskarnes historia i Amerika (Norelius), 4, 154

Eberhart, Adolf, 183
Edqvist, Märta, 147
education, 31; in Augustana Synod, 46–48; in Christian principles, 55–58; dual context, 53–54; ethnic traditions maintained, 45–46; *läroverk*, 53, 63, 76, 78; Mission Covenant Church, 58–59; parochial schools, 47–48; private schools, 45–46; public, 45, 47–48, 53, 56; religion and, 54–59; schools and academies, 45, 46–47; Sweden, 11, 53–54, 76, 78, 109; Swede Schools, 47–48. *See also* Augustana College and Theological Seminary; Bethany College; Gustavus Adolphus College; Upsala College
Elson, Ruth, 145
Enander, Johan, 17, 71–72, 119, 134, 144, 157; "A Dream" (En dröm) speech, 166, 174; historical society and, 187; lectures by, 81; New Sweden colony, interest in, 170, 171; *Prärieblommen* and, 152; as professor, 164, 179, 191; promotion of Viking history, 165–67, 198; role in formation of Swedish-American history, 163–64, 172–73; *Ur svenska sången*, 121–22, 127–31, 139, 191, 195
Engberg, Martin J., 4
Engberg-Holmberg Publishing Company, 108, 112–13, 115, 119–20
Engelbrektsson, Engelbrekt, 83
Englund, J. F., 88

Erickson, Scott E., 38
Ericsson, John, 85, 148, 177–78, 181, 198, 200
Esbjörn, C. M. E., 71, 73
Esbjörn, Lars Paul, 27–28, 30, 39, 48, 59, 119; views on need for educational institution, 54–55
Eterneller och vårblommor (Enander), 121, 139
ethnic categories, 7–8
ethnic identity, 7–10; continuum of, 8, 17–19; myths of descent and historical memories, 14–15, 162. *See also* Swedish-American ethnic identity
ethnic institutions, 8–9
ethnicity, 7; commonality, sense of, 162; cultural content of, 15–17; diverse expression of, 14, 24–25; range of responses to, 18, 188–89, 194; religion and, 9, 180, 184
"Ett fosterländskt minne" (Holmes), 175–76
Ett klöfverblad (Lenk), 124, 135
Evangeliska Fosterlandsstiftelsen, 29, 136
everyday ethnicity, 18, 188
extracurricular activities, 70; elocution contests, 80–81; lectures, 81; literary societies, 70, 86–90, 191, 194; Phrenokosmian Society, 81–85, 104, 151, 191; Svenska Vitterhetssällskapet, 86–90, 104, 151, 181, 191; Swedish-American cultural concerns in, 84–89; visitors from Sweden, 79–80

Fädernas gudasagor (Rydberg), 75
Fältskärns berättelser (Topelius), 114
Fänrik Ståls sägner (Runeberg), 74–78, 82, 191
Fersen, Axel von, 176
Fishman, Joshua, 14, 169
Fjellstedtska skolan, 102
Florin, Christina, 53
Förenta Staternas historia utarbetad för den svenska befolkningen i Amerika (Enander), 165–66
Församlingsskolans läsebok (Bersell), 140–45, 147, 148–50, 191
Forsander, Nils, 179
Första läseboken (Hammer and Wallgren), 146
Första läseboken för skolan och hemmet (Magnusson), 140

251

Fosterlandet, 127–29
Fosterländska minnen (Lindblad), 74, 78
Fosterlänska studentförbundet, 182
Founders Day, 80, 84, 181–83, 197
Från solsidan (Olsson), 152
Franzén, Frans Michael, 88, 127, 128
Fries, Nikolaus, 135, 136
Fritiofs saga (Tegnér), 74–78, 82, 87, 191
From Sweden to America: A History of the Migration (Norman and Runblom), 6, 21–22
Fryxell, Anders, 146
Fuchs, Lawrence, 13
Furuland, Lars, 11, 117, 141

Geijer, Erik Gustaf, 81, 82, 88, 121
generations, 19, 199; career patterns and, 99–100; first-generation immigrants, 2, 21–23, 93; geographic profile, 34–36, 95; second-generation Swedish Americans, 22–23, 35–36, 93; student body, composition of, 92–94, 94; third-generation Swedish Americans, 14, 93
Gerber, David A., 10, 17–18
German American Lutherans, 9, 17, 26, 45, 57, 107
Giftas (Strindberg), 114, 121
Gjerde, Jon, 10, 13–14
Glazer, Nathan, 13, 15–16
Gleason, Philip, 13
God Jul, 126, 157–58, 160
Greene, Victor, 16
Grimberg, Carl, 146
Gustavus Adolphus, 82, 178–81, 187, 199; celebrations of at Augustana College, 178–80; in children's primer, 143–44; as cultural hero, 187; monument proposal, 186
Gustavus Adolphus College, 46–47, 50, 71, 77, 80, 164
Gustavus Adolphus Day, 180
"Gustavus Adolphus. Why Honor Him?" (Anderson), 179

Hallström, Per, 87
Hammer, Bertil, 146
Hamrin, Margareta, 135
Handlin, Oscar, 9
Hasselmo, Nils, 6, 13–14, 18, 108, 113, 122

Hasselquist, Tuve Nilsson, 17, 27–28, 31, 51, 55, 57; Americanization, emphasis on, 59–60, 63, 103, 190; Augustana Book Concern and, 119; biography of, 154, 163; Founders Day visit to grave of, 182; *Hemlandet* and, 110, 119
Heidenstam, Verner von, 87, 121
Hemlandet, 31, 71, 110–11, 127; discussion of Swedish language in, 61–62; Enander and, 164, 165; on "Our Forefathers Day," 166; *Ur svenska sången* debate in, 130
Hemlandssånger (hymnbook), 123
Higham, Jon, 13, 16
history, Swedish-American, 4–5, 162–63, 185–86; American Revolution, 175–76, 198; culture heroes, 176–81, 185; Enander's role, 163–64; myths of foundation, 14–15, 162, 164–72; myths of ideological gifts, 172–76, 200; publications, 154–55
History of the Swedes of Illinois (Olson, Engberg, and Schön), 4
Hobsbawm, Eric, 11, 15, 188
Holmes, Ludvig, 80–81, 89, 129, 151, 156, 199; "Ett fosterländskt minne," 175–76; poem on Founders Day, 182
Holmgrain, O. V., 130, 153
homemaking myths, 10, 162, 164, 185, 187, 197
Hultkrans, C. A., 62
Hvenekilde, Anne, 150

I brytningstid (Andeer), 158
identity. *See* ethnic identity; Swedish-American ethnic identity
Imagined Communities (Anderson), 107–8
immigration, 2, 21–27, 156–57, 193; geographic profile, 23–24, 34–36; mid-nineteenth century, 2, 12; midwestern states as receiving area, 23–24; post-1900, 12, 22, 34–35; reasons for, 21–22; return migration, 23, 97; scholarship on, 4–6, 9; as topic for Phrenokosmian Society, 84–85. *See also* settlements
institutional completeness, 8–9, 27, 43
institutions, ethnic, 8–9
invented traditions, 11, 15, 188
Irrlichte. Eine Erzählung (Fries), 136–37
Italian Americans, 10, 167, 168, 200
I Västerled (Linder), 152, 156

Jansson, Torkel, 11
Jarvi, Raymond, 108
Johannesson, Eric, 117, 151, 186
Johansson, Ulla, 53
Johnson, Amandus, 164
Julklockorna, 137
Julrunan, 86, 89
Julstämning, 112, 125–26
Juvelskrinet, 137

Kantowicz, Edward, 9
Karsten, Peter, 145
Krantz, J. A., 184–85
Kussak, Åke, 135

Lagerlöf, Selma, 42, 77, 87
language, Swedish, 6, 68–69, 103–4; curriculum, role in, 59–68; discussions of, 61–62, 64–67; importance of, 190–91; literary competitions, 88; newspapers, 26–27, 109–11; student difficulty in understanding, 62–63; Swedish-American ethnic identity and, 65–66; teaching of, 70–73. *See also* curriculum, Swedish courses
läroverk (Swedish secondary schools), 53, 63, 76, 78
Läsebok för folkskolan (Furuland), 11, 109, 141–43
Läsebok till svenska litteraturhistorien (Ekerman), 75
leaders, 16–18, 17, 29, 35, 68, 188
Legreid, Ann, 33
Lekkamraten, 137
Levertin, Oscar, 87, 121
Lewins, Frank, 7–8, 27
Lindahl, Joshua, 127
Lindberg, C. E., 63, 66, 79
Linder, Oliver, 108, 134, 152, 156
Lindquist, Emory, 5
Linnaeus statue, 186, 187, 189, 199
literary societies, 70, 86–90, 191, 194
literature. *See* Augustana Book Concern; children's literature; curriculum, Swedish courses; publications; publishing houses
Löfström, Anders, 112, 113, 115
Lönnqvist, C. A., 88, 89, 151–52

Lundborg, Andrew, 112
Lutheranism, Swedish, 9
Lutheran publishing houses, 136–37

Magnusson, Hulda, 140
Malmström, Bernhard Elis, 74, 77, 87
Mårtensson, Mårten, 176
Martin, Arnold, 73, 113
Marty, Martin E., 9
Masterpieces from Swedish Literature (Augustana Book Concern), 77
Mattson, Hans, 169–70
Mauritzson, Jules, 1, 42, 72–73, 87, 138; and children's primer, 140, 145–49
McKay, James, 7–8, 27
medals, bestowed on Swedish Americans, 41, 79–80
Michigan, 34
Midland Lutheran College, 46
Midwest, 3, 23–24, 34–36
ministerial careers, 97, 99–101
Mission Covenant Book Concern, 123
Mission Covenant Church. *See* Swedish Evangelical Mission Covenant Church
Missionsförbundets Bokhandel, 114
Modin, Johan, 74–75, 76, 78
Monitor (ship), 85, 148, 177–78, 198
Montelius, Oscar, 180
monuments, 177, 186, 187, 189, 199
Morton, Johan, 175–76
Moynihan, Daniel Patrick, 15–16
myths, homemaking, 10, 162, 164, 185, 187, 197
myths of foundation, 14–15, 162, 164–72; ideological gifts, 172–76, 200

Nahirny, Vladimir, 14, 169
nationalism, 11–14, 19, 28–29, 46; children's literature and, 141–43; print culture and, 107–8; Sweden, 11–12, 68, 192–93; United States, 12–14, 200–201
Nelander, Edward, 55
Nelson, Helge, 23
newspapers, 26–27, 31, 109–11; fiction series in, 114–15, 118
New Sweden colony, 54, 164, 172, 174, 179, 189, 197–98; 250th anniversary, 39, 169–70; as topic in publications, 147–48, 170–71

253

Index

Nordmännen i Amerika (Enander), 167
Noreen, Adolf, 41, 42, 72
Norelius, Eric, 4, 27, 40, 63, 171; Americanization, emphasis on, 59, 63, 190; biography of Hasselquist, 154, 163; at fiftieth anniversary, 184; Founders Day speech, 182; lectures, 79; on role of Augustana Synod, 38–39, 132
Norman, Hans, 6, 21–22, 23
Norwegian Americans, 28–29, 38, 150, 185–86
Nyberg, Janet, 38
Nytt bibliotek för barn och ungdom, 137
Nyvall, David, 38, 59, 157–58, 160

Olson, Anita Ruth, 33
Olson, E. W., 1–2, 4, 46, 80, 89–90, 108; on Declaration of Independence, 175; as editor of *God Jul,* 126; preface to Person's book, 157; *Ungdomsvännen* and, 153; Vikings, interest in, 198
Olson, Oscar N., 57
Olsson, Anna, 89, 134, 152
Olsson, Olof, 57, 62, 83, 145, 152, 158, 182
organizations, Swedish-American, 25–27, 33, 189–90
Ostergren, Robert, 23, 33
Österholm's (publishing house), 116
Our Forefathers Day, 166. *See also* Founders Day
Øverland, Orm, 10, 107, 162, 164, 172, 197
Översikt över svenska språkets och litteraturens historia (Bjursten), 74, 76, 78

Park, Robert, 110
Pehrsson, Per, 43, 184
periodicals, 17, 109–11. *See also* Augustana; Hemlandet; Präriblomman; Ungdomsvännen
Person, Johan, 12, 134, 152, 155–57, 196–97
Peterson, Brent, 107
Peterson, C. F., 4, 12, 67
Phrenokosmian Society, 81–85, 104, 151, 191
Polish Peasant in Europe and America (Thomas and Znaniecki), 8
Präriblomman, 17, 31, 110, 134, 150, 156, 191, 197; Ericsson discussed in, 177–78; New Sweden colony as topic in, 170–71; Swedish-American themes in, 152–54; Tegnér in, 77
Printz, Anders, 147–48
Printz, Johan, 171
publications, 17, 20; audience for, 108–9, 159; books, 111–12; Christmas, 86, 89, 137–39, 157–58, 160; fiction, 116–17; fiction series, 114–15, 118, 137–38; imported books, 87, 108, 120, 131; newspapers and periodicals, 26–27, 109–11; non-English, 106–7, 110; sources for, 113–15; Swedish-American ethnic identity and, 196–97; types of literature available, 115–19. *See also* Augustana Book Concern; children's literature
publishing houses, Lutheran, 136–37
publishing houses, Swedish-American, 26, 31, 108, 112–15; denominational publications, 114, 118, 123, 132; "trash literature," 125, 195. *See also* Augustana Book Concern

Reformation, 40, 108–9
religion: American pluralism, 29–30; denominations, 25–26; ethnicity and, 9, 180, 184; role of in Augustana College, 54–59
Religious Aspects of Swedish Immigration, The (Stephenson), 5
Roos, Mathilda, 121, 135
Royal Commission of Inquiries (Emigrationsutredningen), 5
Rüdiger, Minna, 135, 136
Runan (The Rune), 86–89, 104
Runblom, Harald, 6, 21–22, 29
Runeberg, Johan Ludvig, 74–78, 81, 121, 196, 199; discussed in student societies, 82, 87, 88
Rydberg, Viktor, 77, 87, 121

Sagor (Strindberg), 121
Sånger och sagor (Bonggren), 126–27, 130, 134, 151, 160–61
Scandinavian Fraternity of America, 26
Schéele, Knut Henning Gezelius von, 42–43, 103, 128, 184; visits to America, 40–41, 44, 66, 79–80, 179
scholarship, 4–10, 19; historical literatures, 4–5; quantitative studies, 5–6; social history, 5, 10, 95
Schön, Anders, 4, 152, 170–71, 172, 174, 187

schoolbooks, 20, 133–34, 139–50, 159–60
schools. *See* Augustana College and Theological Seminary; education
Schück, Henrik, 42–43, 54, 72, 183–84
Schwarz, Marie Sophie, 117, 125
secular societies, 36, 37–39
settlements, 3, 23–24, 49, 166; geographical patterns, 23–24, 94–95. *See also* New Sweden colony
slavery, Swedish-American opposition to, 170, 173, 178
Smith, Anthony D., 8, 14–15
Smith, Timothy, 46
Snoilsky, Carl, 121
socialism, 35, 37
Society for the Advancement of Scandinavian Studies, 72
Söderström, Axel, 111
Söderström, Hugo, 27, 28, 37
Sollors, Werner, 15
Springer, Carl, 147–48
Stedingk, Curt von, 176
Stephenson, George, 5, 27, 30, 62
Stiernhielm, Georg, 87, 143, 144
Stockenström, Göran, 108
Stolarik, M. Mark, 45
Strindberg, August, 77, 87, 114, 117, 121, 125, 146, 195
student body, 90–102, 193; career patterns, 57, 99–102; generational and ethnic composition, 92–94, 94; geographical recruitment patterns, 94–95; non-Swedish students, 93, 96; registration forms, 91–92; social background of, 95–98, 96, 98. *See also* students
students: difficulty understanding Swedish, 62–63; greetings to Sweden, 182; participation in Swedish language classes, 62–65, 191; Swedish patriotism of, 66–67. *See also* literary societies; student body
Sue, Eugène, 117–18
Sundbärg, Gustav, 5
Sundbeck, Carl, 80, 155, 156, 157, 182
Sundén, D. A., 74–75, 76, 78
"Svea" (Tegnér), 75, 78, 82
Svedjedal, Johan, 112
Svenska Amerikanaren, 110, 111, 126, 127, 130
Svenska Familjejournalen, 117

Svenska folkets tidning, 114–15
Svenska Kuriren, 127–30
Svenska Lutherska Tryckföreningen, 119
Svensk-amerikaerna. Deras andliga och materiella strävanden (Sundbeck), 155, 156, 157
Svensk-Amerikanska Historiska Sällskapet, 171–72, 187
Svensk-amerikanska meditationer (Berger), 155, 156
Svensk-amerikanska studier (Person), 155, 156–57, 196–97
Svenska Missionsförbundet, 25, 29, 37, 58–59, 135
Svenska Socialisten, 113–14
Svenska språkets och litteraturens historia (Claesson), 74, 76
Svenska Tribunen, 111
Svenska Vitterhetssällskapet, 86–90, 104, 151, 181, 191
Svensk läsebok för elementärläroverken (Sundén and Modin), 74–75, 76, 78
Svensk litteraturhistoria (Warburg), 75–76
Svensson, Birgitta, 6, 77, 152, 154
Sverige i Amerika. Kulturhistoriska och biografiska teckningar (Peterson), 4, 67
Sveriges historia för folkskolan (Grimberg), 75, 146
Swan, G. N., 81, 155, 180
Swärd, A. A., 37, 89
Sweden: Augustana Synod, relationship with, 39–43; delegations to fiftieth anniversary, 183–84; education, 11, 53–54, 76, 78, 109; fund-raising for college in, 41–42; Gotland, 40–41; literacy rate, 108–9; nationalism, 11–12, 68, 192–93; publishing houses, 112, 136; reading habits in, 117–18; schools, 11, 76, 78, 109
"Sweden's Role in World History" (Enander), 172–73
Swedes and the Swedish Settlements in North America, The (Nelson), 23
Swede Schools, 47–48
Swedes on the Delaware series (Anders), 170–71
Swedish Academy, 86
"Swedish-American, The" (Andeer), 158
Swedish American, as self-description, 84, 89–90

255

Swedish-American community, 24–25, 192; cultural differences and commonalities, 37–39, 189; institutional completeness of, 27, 43; organizations, 25–27, 33, 189–90; politically radical groups, 6, 36; slavery, opposition to, 170, 173, 178

Swedish-American ethnic identity, 3, 188–89; ABC publications and, 132–33, 138–39, 149–50; analysis of, 194–99; Augustana College, role in development of, 46, 65–69, 85–86; as constructed, 18, 188, 195, 200–201; creation of, 190–94; duality of, 6–7, 19, 192; extracurricular activities and, 87–88; phases in development of, 9, 102–3; reasons for development of, 199–201; Swedish-American publications and, 196–97

Swedish-American Republican League, 177

Swedish cultural symbols, 66–67, 144, 195–96

Swedish Evangelical Mission Covenant Church, 25–26, 36–37, 114, 157; education and, 58–59; schism with Augustana Synod, 31, 37, 68, 192

Swedish Pioneer Historical Society, 5

Swensson, Carl A., 64, 105, 170

Synod of Northern Illinois, 28, 48, 182

Tarschys, Karin, 76, 78

Tegnér, Esaias, 121, 143, 196, 199; discussed in student societies, 82, 87, 88; *Fritiofs saga*, 74–78, 82, 87, 191

Tegnér-förbundet, 86, 88

Texas Posten, 110, 111

Thander, Gunnar, 161, 187

Thirty Years' War, 179, 199

Thistlethwaite, Frank, 5

Thomas, William, 8

Thomasson, Pehr, 114, 116, 117, 121

Topelius, Zacharias, 87, 114, 121

Transatlantic Connections: Nordic Migration to the New World after 1800 (Norman and Runblom), 21–22

Tredje läseboken för skolan och hemmet (Mauritzson), 140, 141, 145–50, 191, 197

Udden, J. A., 58, 66, 79

Ungdomsvännen, 17, 31, 62, 110, 120, 134, 150, 153–54, 156, 191, 197, 199; articles on Swedish-American culture, 157, 158–59; Ericsson discussed in, 177–78; New Sweden colony as topic in, 170–71

United States: as ideological construct, 12–13, 200–201; national identity, 12–14, 200–201; Swedish contributions to, 172–76, 200

Uppsala project, 5–6

Uppsala University (Sweden), 41, 42, 54, 80, 95

Uprooted, The (Handlin), 9

Upsala College (East Orange, New Jersey), 46, 47, 72

Ur svenska sången (Enander), 121–22, 127–31, 139, 191, 195

Valkyrian, 161, 187

Vårt språk (Berger), 155

Vasa, Gustav (King), 1, 82, 143–44

Vecoli, Rudolph, 10

Vid fyrelden (Fries), 137

Vid Jesu krubba, 138

Vid Juletid. Vinterblommer samlade för de små, 137–39

Vikings, 165–66, 186, 198; contemporary context, 167–68; independence and self-governance, 173–75; influence on Columbus, 166–67; rune stone controversy, 168

Vitterhetens vänner, 152

von Heidenstam, Verner, 42, 77

Waldenström, Paul Peter, 37, 58–59

Wallgren, Anders, 146

Wallin, Johan Olof, 82, 87, 121, 128, 182

Warburg, Karl, 75–76

Wenaas, August, 28

Wendelius, Lars, 38, 108, 111–12

Westerberg, Kermit, 117

Western Home, The (Øverland), 107

Williams, Anna, 6, 17, 38, 77, 107, 120, 126, 130, 151, 160

World War I, 19, 22, 104

Youngert, S. G., 89, 153

youth organizations, 127, 133, 153–54, 180–81

Zelinsky, Wilbur, 12–13

Zetterstrand, Ernst A., 72–73, 138, 177

Znaniecki, Florian, 8

Index

Dag Blanck is an associate professor of history at Uppsala University in Sweden and director of the Swenson Swedish Immigration Research Center at Augustana College, a national archive and research institute for the study of Swedish immigration to North America. His research has focused on the history of Swedish migration to the United States and on transnational cultural processes between Sweden and the United States. His publications include "Swedish-American Life in Chicago: Social and Cultural Aspects of an Immigrant People 1850–1930" (coedited with Philip J. Anderson) and "Swedes in the Twin Cities: Immigrant Life and Minnesota's Urban Frontier" (coedited with Philip J. Anderson).